Cambridge studies in sociology 5

FAMILY STRUCTURE IN NINETEENTH CENTURY LANCASHIRE

Cambridge studies in sociology

1. *The affluent worker: industrial attitudes and behaviour*
by John H. Goldthorpe, David Lockwood, Frank Bechhofer and Jennifer Platt
2. *The affluent worker: political attitudes and behaviour*
by John H. Goldthorpe, David Lockwood, Frank Bechhofer and Jennifer Platt
3. *The affluent worker in the class structure*
by John H. Goldthorpe, David Lockwood, Frank Bechhofer and Jennifer Platt
4. *Men in mid-career: a study of British managers and technical specialists*
by Cyril Sofer
5. *Family structure in nineteenth century Lancashire*
by Michael Anderson

Family structure in nineteenth century Lancashire

MICHAEL ANDERSON
Lecturer in Sociology, University of Edinburgh

CAMBRIDGE
at the University Press 1971

Published by the Syndics of the Cambridge University Press
Bentley House, 200 Euston Road, London NW1 2DB
American Branch: 32 East 57th Street, New York, N.Y. 10022

Library of Congress Catalogue Card Number: 79-164448

ISBN: 0 521 08237 4

Printed in Great Britain by
William Clowes & Sons Limited, London, Colchester and Beccles

Contents

Figures

Maps

Preface

This book is a sociological study of the impact of urban-industrial life on the kinship system of the working classes of nineteenth century Lancashire. As it is primarily a sociological study much of its argument is oriented towards theoretical and substantive matter relevant to theory of a sociological kind. However, such a book (and particularly its mass of ethnographic material) is also, I hope, of interest to many social historians. This has posed problems in the writing and particularly in the ordering and presenting of the interpretations, for different people will want to take different things from it, and will need detailed information on different things if they are to get the most out of the book. I have, in consequence, divided the work into four Parts. The first and third of these, which are largely self-contained, pose the problem and contain most of the data and historical analysis. Part 2 has two chapters, the first of which describes in some detail the underlying theoretical perspectives I have employed, while the second describes the data sources and some of the research methods I have used. Some readers may find it suits them better on first reading to skim through Chapter 2 for the main ideas, only coming back to it where they find they require detailed justification for arguments of later chapters. In particular, many may find that the last section of Chapter 2 is best left until later. Specialist readers, by contrast, will find that the background of and justification for many statements in Chapter 2 have been relegated to the notes in order to leave the text as clear as possible for the non-sociologist. Some may even wish to read the theoretical section in proposition form before proceeding to the data. This will be found on pp. 172–5. The last chapter of the book, which forms Part 4, looks at the wider theoretical significance of the findings for the sociology of the family by setting them, and my interpretations of them, in a wider historical and cross-cultural perspective.

This study breaks new ground in a number of areas. The most fruitful sources and the best methods of analysing data have often had to be found by trial and error, and if I were beginning again now I should do some things in slightly different ways. In many ways this should really be seen as an exploratory study. Future research will undoubtedly reveal faults in its interpretations, some of which are highly speculative given the data available. It will also produce new and better techniques and other valuable data sources which I have not tapped. Indeed I very much hope that this will be the case.

Because of the cross-disciplinary nature of this research I have been even more dependent than are most researchers on the help and criticisms of others.

If I do not name them individually it is only because they are so many, not because I have forgotten or am not grateful to them. I must, however, acknowledge the help of David Thompson of Fitzwilliam College, Cambridge, without whose comments over dinner one night this research would never have begun. I am also grateful for his many subsequent attempts to keep me on the historical straight and narrow. I must also thank Professors David Lockwood and T. H. Marshall for their patient and cogent criticisms as my research supervisors during my period as a postgraduate student in Cambridge, and also Dr Tony Wrigley and Professor J. A. Banks for the many substantive and stylistic criticisms which they made during my oral examination on an earlier version of this study for the Ph.D. degree; their comments have made the resulting book far better than it would otherwise have been. I am indebted also to Mrs Margaret Liston who has so patiently unravelled two highly disorganised drafts of this work and turned them into typescript; she has spotted many mistakes that would otherwise have gone unnoticed. Finally, I owe a great debt to Rosemary, my wife, not only for her superabundance of the patience that is demanded of the spouse of any author but also for her help in checking and preparing the index. Since all those who have helped me will find that I have by no means always taken their advice, I of course retain total responsibility for the many errors and imperfections that I am sure remain.

March, 1971 M.A.

Abbreviations and symbols used in this work

NOTE: abbreviations of journal titles follow the conventions of the *International bibliography of social sciences*, except where listed below.

App	Appendix
div	Division
esp	especially
LCS	Life-cycle stage
LDM	*Reports addressed to the Committee of the Liverpool Domestic Missionary Society, by their ministers to the poor*
LHoTA	*The Liverpool Health of Towns Advocate*
LSP	*Lords Sessional Papers*
MC	*The Morning Chronicle*
MCS	*Supplements to The Morning Chronicle*
MSS	Manchester Statistical Society
Nar	Narratives
PHoC	*Chaplain's reports on the Preston House of Correction*
Pt	Part
PP	*Parliamentary Papers*
PRO	Public Record Office
SEG	Socio-economic group
Ses	Session
Soc. for Poor	*Reports of the Society for Bettering the Condition and Increasing the Comforts of the Poor*
R.D.	Registration District
vol	volume
*	Reference refers to single case only
**	Reference refers to limited number of cases only
..	In tables; not applicable
–	In tables; no cases in cell
0	In tables; at least one case in cell, but rounded percentage less than 0.5
( )	In tables; e.g. (3); percentage based on a total (100%) of less than 10.

Part One. Introduction

1. The origins of the study

This study was conceived early in 1964. During a discussion over dinner about the relationship between industrialisation and family structure a chance remark made me suddenly aware of a paradox. All the sociological literature that I had read implied that industrialisation typically and at least to some extent disrupted pre-existing wider kinship systems. The historical writings to which this remark drew my attention stressed that pre-industrial family patterns in Britain, at least among the poorer sections of the population, were predominantly of a nuclear kind. By contrast, the writers on family patterns in modern 'traditional' working class communities were adamant that kinship relationships in such communities were well developed. It thus, superficially at least, appeared that modernisation in Britain had increased not decreased kinship cohesion. Why, I asked myself, should this have been so?

As soon as I started a more detailed investigation, the issues, predictably, became less clear cut. True, most theorists[1] did argue that the more extended types of family systems were incompatible with a modern industrial society, though the theoretical rationales by which they justified this position differed widely. It was also the case that there was a mass of literature on societies currently undergoing the take-off process into economic development most of which tended to support this position and to suggest that the process of industrialisation did tend in many societies to be accompanied by a move to a more nucleated type of family system.[2] But there was also some suggestion that those undergoing industrialisation sometimes used their kinship ties as a basis for the solution of the new problems which arose during adjustment, that indeed, some degree of functioning kinship relationship was not merely compatible with, but desirable for, a smooth transition to urban-industrial life.[3] Such notions were not easily integrated into the existing theoretical pronouncements. Nor, really, was the fact that the nuclear system was not uniquely a product of industrialisation, but was found in many pre-industrial societies all over the world.[4] Thus, the underlying rationales of the existing body of theory were already open to question. If my hunch about developments in Britain was right this would simply strengthen the need for a reconsideration of the whole problem, and the new insights which might be gained from studying it in a different context might well be a great help in the process.

When I turned my attention to the mass of empirical studies of kinship in present day Western societies,[5] I found, as I had expected, that most of the population did apparently maintain some relationships with kin, that some services were exchanged, that many people saw these relationships as very important to them, and that, at certain periods in the life-cycle in particular, many people lived in households whose members were wider than a single nuclear family. Some writers went on to suggest that kinship relationships in today's 'mobile' society were themselves in some sense less 'close' than they had often been in an earlier 'cohesive' society.[6] It was obvious, then, that kin had a definite role to play. However, it could, I thought, be legitimately argued that some of these writers had overstated the importance of kinship relationships. For, by contrast with many non-Western societies, relationships with other than first degree kin are very insignificant, except in certain rather limited sectors of the population. Relationships with siblings, once one is adult, are subject to a considerable degree of choice; interaction is rather on the basis of liking than of prescription.[7] Even relationships which adults maintain with parents usually affect their life chances far less than do their relationships within the nuclear family on the one hand, and relationships with other social organisations or primary groups (schools, employers, or social welfare agencies, and often even friends and neighbours) on the other.[8] Yet people continue to see kinship relationships as useful and important for them, and it does indeed seem likely that those who lack functioning ongoing kinship relationships not only believe they are, but often actually are, at some disadvantage in terms of assistance or emotional support.[9]

There was, then, a mass of empirical studies of kinship relationships in modern societies, and they did seem to show that kin did perform some important functions for most sectors of the population. By contrast, there were almost no studies of kinship relationships in pre-industrial England, and what there were suggested that kin were of comparatively little import to most of the population. The work of Laslett and associates[10] suggested that the predominant residential group in pre-industrial England was the nuclear family; some households had, in addition, an odd co-residing niece or nephew or other kinsman, often an orphan. Few households contained two parents and a married child and that child's spouse. Subsequent research has shown that only some 10% of households in England of the sixteenth to the early nineteenth centuries contained kin outside the current nuclear family and that very few of these kin had ever been married.[11] In 1966, for England and Wales as a whole, the proportion of households with kin was also 10%. But, by contrast with the pre-industrial situation, a majority of these households with kin contained three or more married or widowed kinsmen.[12] If only 'traditional' working class areas were considered then the overall proportion of households with kin would undoubtedly be higher.

Census type data can, of course, be misleading. They can almost totally conceal such phenomena as short period co-residence after marriage.[13] Also, if death rates and gross reproduction rates are high, there may be in any community many young families and few old people to reside with them, at least by comparison with the present day. Both these factors will tend to reduce the proportion of households containing additional married kin, even though for those of the population who are alive at the relevant period of the life-cycle, co-residence may be very important at a crucial time of their lives. Even making allowances for these factors, however, parent/married child co-residence was rare in pre-industrial England.

Evidence on the other functions which kinship might have performed in the past, and on the strength of affective ties is very scanty even today. In as far as farms and businesses were inherited and relatives worked together in them, some kind of bonds undoubtedly developed, and they may well often have been quite strong, though still of very limited extent.[14] But for both seventeenth century Clayworth,[15] and for various areas of rural England in the nineteenth century[16] there is also evidence of a calculative, even to our eyes callous, attitude to kin – Joan Bacon put by her son on to public charity, children bargaining with the Poor Law authorities for payment for looking after their sick or elderly relatives. How widespread this kind of behaviour was we do not yet, and may well never, know. That it would have been almost unthinkable in Bethnal Green in the early 1950s is certain.

What, then, did 'modernisation' do to family structure in Britain? The answer to this question can only be found by an investigation of family structure at some point during the industrialisation period. For various reasons which are further discussed in Chapter 3, the early and mid-nineteenth century is a good period on which to begin such a study.

Yet, when this research began, hardly any work had been done on any aspect of family life during the period of industrialisation. There are a few contemporary nineteenth century studies, but, with the notable exception of the work of LePlay,[17] they are either the impressionistic work of middle class persons, to some extent unfamiliar with the realities and demands of working class life,[18] or they are attempts at picturesque description, for a middle class audience, of extreme (and undoubtedly to a considerable extent atypical)[19] lower class behaviour. Both tend to emphasise the more remarkable features of family life (and perhaps those more calculated to shock Victorian sensibilities), without any attempt to assess quantitatively either their frequency, or their distribution over the population as a whole.[20]

Recent works were equally few in number. A certain amount was known about changes in the economic functions of the urban family, from the work of Collier[21] and Smelser.[22] Margaret Hewitt[23] had discussed the effect that a factory-working mother could have on the family as a domestic group. Ivy Pinchbeck[24] had reviewed more generally the roles of wives and mothers in the period of industrialisation. Redford's pioneering study of migration[25] posed interesting questions of great significance for family analysis, but these had never been followed up in the way that they deserve. Williams[26] had used the enumerators' books from the 1841 and 1851 censuses to come to some interesting conclusions about residence patterns in a West Country parish. And that was more or less all that had been done.

In the last few years a few studies more relevant to the problem have appeared or have been begun. Armstrong and Smith, Dyos, and Drake and Pearce, among others, have investigated the broad social structure of a number of nineteenth century towns using enumerators' books and other data.[27] Crozier has concluded an important investigation of middle class family patterns in Highgate, North London.[28] Some limited data on the population of this area as a whole has also been published.[29] But the only published study which to my knowledge has specifically considered family and kinship structure in nineteenth century industrial towns is Foster's work on Oldham, Northampton, and South Shields, and even he, because this topic was largely incidental to his main purpose, has confined himself to a few tables and some stimulating discussion.[30]

Thus, after my initial survey of what was known, my original research question seemed even more worthy of investigation. Moreover, a few weeks' work suggested that data could be obtained that would throw at least some light on the issues involved. The remainder of this book can be seen at one level as a first attempt to throw some light on the original question 'What did industrialisation do to kinship in Britain?' But it is also, I hope, something more. For as I proceeded with my study I became increasingly unhappy about the basis of the larger part of the body of sociological theory which deals with kinship and social change. Much of the data I generated could not, it seemed, be handled by the traditional approaches. I became more and more interested in the new insights which could be obtained from recasting my conceptual frameworks within an actor cum exchange theory formulation. In Chapter 2 I have attempted to formalise some of these ideas. Although I believe that they have much wider relevance to the general problem of the impact of social change on family structure, I have only developed them here in as far as they seem to me to help in illuminating and interpreting the data of this study. In Chapter 3 I go on to describe how the original vague ideas discussed above were subjected to investigation.

Part Two. Theory and method

2. Heuristic perspectives

In this chapter my aim is to summarise briefly the main theoretical ideas which underlie my interpretations of family structure in nineteenth century Lancashire. I first outline what I see as the main parameters of variation that I am trying to explain. Then I describe the analytical perspectives that I have used to tackle the problem. Readers who find this chapter rather heavy going at this point in the book may prefer to leave a detailed reading of it until they have seen the theory in action in Chapter 7. However, I hope that a grasp of the main principles now will help most readers to see how the whole work hangs together and why I have tackled the problem in the way that I have.

Between any two kinsmen, a biological relationship of blood or coitus always exists directly, indirectly, or by adoption. However, not all these biological relationships provide a basis for social relationships, for a social relationship only exists when one actor, through the influence of another, adopts behaviour or attitudes which are different from what they would have been had this influence not occurred. Thus, one way, ideally at least, of establishing the existence of, and also the extent and effects of a social relationship between, any two classes of individuals, is to make a systematic comparison between the resources, attitudes, and behaviour of those who do interact in any particular way, and those who do not. This in turn leads me to try to use these variations in effects as a basis for establishing a set of underlying parameters.

The underlying parameter which seems to me to be most significant in terms of general sociological theory, which I have adopted here, and which seems to me to underlie implicitly much other writing on this topic, is power, not in the sense of control over the behaviour of others, but in the more general and prior sense of ability to control one's own life chances and increase one's attainment of one's goals. In other words the underlying parameter I conceptualise as the importance or significance to an actor of kinship in helping him to attain his goals.

Significance can, analytically, be considered of two kinds. Firstly, one can study the effects as the actors themselves see them, and their definitions of the deprivations that the termination of the relationship would involve. This line of attack through the actor's own definition of his situation is of course essential if we are to begin to make a total interpretation of a kinship situation, particularly in a time of rapid social change.[1] But, I believe it is inadequate alone for any useful comparative sociology at least at the present time.[2] The second approach is to assess effects in terms of some concept imposed by the sociologist, but this raises serious problems regarding the criteria by which effects are to be judged, even if one argues, as I think one must and as I shall below, that it is effects in terms of the actor's own goals which must be considered.[3]

A further problem arises from the fact that, in some senses at least, there is an important feedback relationship between this second or 'structural' level, and the first or 'phenomenal' level. For, in as far as the way one actor sees a relationship is known to or suspected by the other partner to it, this may itself affect the long-run structural significance of the relationship to this other person. I shall elaborate this point below. But the crux of the issue is that the extent to which someone is prepared to maintain a relationship which is costly to him in the short run, but potentially highly rewarding in the long, will often, and perhaps typically, depend on whether he sees the other party as trustworthy, as committed to it 'morally' rather than just for the short-run instrumental advantage (or in popular jargon, 'in it only for what he can get').

Nevertheless, for comparative purposes some fairly general concept is necessary. Thus, while I have produced some data on most forms of social activity for which they are available, I have concentrated particularly on those variations that seem to have been most influenced by the presence or absence of any particular kinsman, or which, while in the Lancashire context such influence was minimal, have been shown by other studies elsewhere to have been influenced by kinship considerations.

More specifically, I have ordered the data around two sets of parameters. Firstly, in the structural element of my analysis, I have tried to assess the extent to which the absence of any given kinsman[4] adversely affected or would have affected the actor's life chances or satisfactions at any period of his life. The effects are assessed as far as possible in terms of the goals, both material and non-material, which the actor set himself.[5] The analysis relates particularly to the longer run, ideally to the actor's average life span.

Secondly, in the phenomenal element of my analysis, I have also tried to show something of the actor's own perceptions of the nature and significance of his kinship relationships. In particular, I have been interested in how variations in these definitions (due, for example, to different socialisation or to different cultural origins) affected behaviour with consequences at the structural level. I have also asked how variations in the 'quality' of commitment to relationships (in terms of a continuum from highly normative commitment to highly calculative commitment) affected structural level behaviour. The theoretical elements underlying these uses of the phenomenal data are outlined in the next sections.

A structural level actor-based perspective

I now turn attention to the principle issue of this chapter, the need briefly to describe the heuristic framework which I have used to generate my approach to the data and to order my interpretations, and in terms of which at a higher level I shall treat my interpretations as validated.

I saw the need to develop a somewhat new and more formalised heuristic framework for this study for a number of reasons. While recognising their importance for a total understanding, I wanted to get beyond interpretations limited to the phenomenal level, solutions which explained change in terms of normative change and states in terms of normative consensus. Such interpretations seemed to me to beg important questions, for I should then want to know what were the conditions which maintained the normative consensus in one situation and allowed change in others without crippling sanctions being imposed on the innovators. This requirement pointed me to the need for an analysis of the underlying structural conditions of any situation.[6]

Dissatisfaction with some other current perspectives also influenced my thought. Much writing on the impact of industrialisation on family structure has had strong convergence overtones.[7] It has treated industrialisation as an almost irresistible force and has failed to do justice to the empirical diversity and complexity of reactions to similar pressures for social change. The main reason for this, it seems to me, has been that it has ignored almost completely the fact that other power and influence centres exist, and among these one must include not only those which are formally organised for the mobilisation of power but also those, like the family, which, supported by tradition, its control of socialisation, and often considerable economic influence as well, can also, as long as its power is maintained, inhibit and channel social change in some directions rather than others.[8] Thus industrialisation will not have identical effect on all family systems, even if it is approximately similar in form. The ability of different family systems to maintain commitment of their members is variable and must enter into the analysis.[9] So, an analytical perceptive must be used which can tap the tensions between these potentially conflicting power centres of family and industry as the conflict develops.

However, the very flexibility that this analysis suggests will exist in responses to industrial development, raises a further issue for investigation for it leads one to expect that some groups of individuals within the same society will be more willing than are others to accept any given set of blandishments from the industrial system. Those who accept will presumably be those who are least committed or drawn to the pre-existing situation, and who are, therefore, most willing or able to accept change in the pre-existing normative patterns. Moreover, it will not usually be the case that all members of whole families will welcome these new developments with equal enthusiasm. Rather some will be more attracted by the opportunities for change than others, and it will be the actions of these individuals that will be instrumental in effecting the changes that occur. Thus an approach is required which can tap these processes of conflict, power and compromise, and this means one which can look at these processes from the standpoint of the individual actor.[10]

It seemed to me, then, that some kind of egocentric or actor-based approach was the most appropriate for the problem at hand.[11] But the data I was collecting also suggested to me at an early stage that this kind of perspective was required. Fortunately, these early data further suggested to me the lines along which the perspective that I finally adopted should be developed. For the data implied that, at the phenomenal level, both in urban Lancashire and in rural Ireland, some children were interacting with their parents in a manner which can only be described as one of short-run calculative instrumentality. Social relationships of any significance were only being maintained, by considerable sections of the population, in situations where both parties were obtaining some fairly immediate advantage from them; in other words, where exchanges were reciprocal and almost immediate. I was thus called upon to consider the conditions under which such an orientation, so foreign to the thinking of many earlier writers, might arise. In order to do this I had to pose explicitly the analytical question 'Why should an actor want to maintain relationships with kin rather than with the myriads of other individuals with whom he could make contact?' In my explorations of possible solutions to this phenomenal level problem (which, put a different way, can be seen as a problem of choice between possible network members) I began to see that there might be certain advantages in extending both the question and some of the solutions to the structural level as well. In the rest of this section I briefly outline some of the main features of the perspective I consequently came to adopt as the basis of this research, a perspective that has its origins in exchange, network, and to some extent social action theory.[12]

Briefly I start from a heuristic assumption that cross-cultural or cross-time differences in kinship structure can be seen as having one or both of two kinds of explanation. Either they may result from differences in goals or in the hierarchy of goals, or they may result from differences in the constraints and opportunities with which an actor is faced.[13] In this study I shall largely concentrate on the latter since I believe that goals and goal hierarchies can be treated as if they were relatively homogeneous within the populations under study, so that most variation came from differences in structural constraints (or phenomenally in the actors' definitions of their situation), and the approach I outline below is thus oriented to dealing with this kind of variation.[14]

My analysis is based on the following heuristic premises and intuitive derivations from these premises:[15]

1. All actors have a number of goals, the attainment of which would maximise their satisfactions or psychic rewards.

2. All actors in any society are faced with a social, physical, and technical environment which presents them with problems which must be solved if any given goal is to be attained.

3. Any society has only a limited number of known ways of solving these problems.

4. These techniques typically mean that actors are unable without assistance to solve these problems and maximise rewards.

5. A number of alternative sources of assistance exist in any society and are theoretically available to the actor to assist him in the solution of any problem.[16]

6. Choices between these alternative sources of assistance (choices which in turn determine their patterns of relationships) are made in such a way that the actor in the long run maximises his goal attainment within the limits imposed by his resources, by known techniques and alternatives, and by the willingness of others (who are also pursuing goals through social action) to meet his needs.

It is in the understanding of the factors determining choices and determining the willingness of *alter*s to meet *ego*'s needs that exchange formulations seem to me to be of assistance.[17] Three parameters seem to warrant formal attention; these are:

A. How much psychic profit does this exchange offer me now compared with that; i.e. by how much does what I get out exceed what I put in, and could I get more elsewhere, or have to put in less?

B. When do I get the reciprocation; i.e. is the return immediate or only in the long run?

C. How certain am I that I will receive the reciprocation in any relationship I enter expecting rewards in exchange?

Exchange theory has tended to stress the first of these, but in this study the second and third will be of key importance. Indeed, it is the insights which can be obtained from the second and third which I believe provide some of the most interesting interpretations offered in this book.

I shall now consider each of these three elements at greater length.

A. Psychic profit

An exchange theory formulation would assume that an actor, faced with a problem and a number of alternative sources of solution to that problem, would, in the absence of uncertainty or time considerations, and of cultural or internalised pressures towards any one relationship, seek to enter a relationship for the solution of the problem with whichever actor or collectivity gave him maximum returns (satisfactions) in return for minimum outgoings (dissatisfactions).[18] If at some future time he saw a better bargain obtainable in another relationship, then the actor would seek to improve the terms of the present bargain, and if he failed, would seek instead to enter into a relationship with whichever actor or collectivity offered better terms. The actor thus regulates his outgoings according to his returns, and chooses between conflicting demands upon him in terms of these costs and returns.[19] These costs and returns consist of rewards from activities and sentiments provided by alters on the one hand, and costs from resources used up by ego in performing reciprocal services and from activities and sentiments withdrawn by alters who disapprove of ego's relational choices, on the other.

It is of course true that bargaining on each individual activity does not take place in a vacuum. Firstly, bargains do, in fact, take place over whole *sets* of needs rather than over individual needs. To give shelter to an aged relative almost necessarily involves also feeding him and caring for him when he is sick.

Secondly, as Blau has noted, circumstances may arise where actor A offers some reward which is unobtainable by B from any alternative source. In as far as this reward is deemed by B as essential to him, B is under the power of A. This situation may also arise indirectly via B's dependence on the members of a close-knit network or other collectivity as a whole. For example, if, as was the case in a number of pre-industrial societies, an actor who leaves the family loses all his economic, legal and political rights, the ability of the individual to break his bonds with his family is highly circumscribed. As long as these circumstances prevail, an actor's choices of relational patterns are limited by the preferred relational patterns of collectivities outside the family which will only deal with individuals as *part of* a family.[20]

But there is also another much more important sense in which bargaining does not usually take place in a vacuum. So far values have been largely ignored in this analysis. But, as Durkheim was one of the first to point out, exchange relationships take place against a background of shared values which lay down the rules to be followed by each party to the relationship.[21] This body of shared values performs the function of convincing both parties to the relationship that reciprocation will occur to the extent, in the manner, and at the time expected by each.[22] Without some such basis of certainty no relationships would develop, or only over matters of the most trivial interest to the parties.[23] Now Durkheim appears to have seen this body of values as something which was in the main apart from the relationship itself, but Blau has noted in his discussion of the process of attraction how a body of shared values to some extent unique to the relationship can be built up through processes of exchange.[24] Briefly, Blau suggests that new relationships are essentially tentative in nature with both parties limiting their commitments until they are sure that alter will reciprocate in the manner, at the time, and to the extent that they would expect.[25] In other words they are seeking to ascertain whether alter defines the rights and obligations of any given relationship in which both are involved, in the same way as they do themselves. Over time they become more certain, as a result of favourable past experiences, that they can predict, and approve of, alter's performance in reciprocation. A set of shared values has built up as to what constitutes 'correct' performance of roles. Some of these shared values were already held by each as a result of performance of other relationships, or from socialisation, and merely required articulation, but some values are unique to the relationship and have been mutually evolved by the partners to it.[26]

Thus, values governing a relationship and the certainty that alter will reciprocate appear to be derived from two sources. In part they derive from a pre-existing more generalised or less specific common set of values to which each actor initiating a relationship appeals in his attempts to increase his satisfactions by increasing the predictability of his relationships.[27] In part they are evolved through the exchange relationship itself, which may both lead actors to agree to alter the societal values, and which will also, almost inevitably, lead to the development of some rules which are more specific or even unique to this relationship. Both sets of values are, however, similar in kind, and both serve the same purpose of increasing predictability.

However, this analysis is based on the further heuristic premise that norms are only in the long run viable if they really do support what would anyway be the optimal bargains that both parties to a relationship, given their goals, could obtain in the current situation. If the environment offers better bargains to one or both of them then it is assumed that in the long run the old values will break down as new optimal behaviour patterns are adopted by them.[28] Subsequently new values are seen as emerging to support the new optimal relationships. This process of change is perhaps best understood by reference to Figure 1. Stable

		Relationship between present situation and that which would result from conscious calculation of all advantages and disadvantages known within the population	
		Totally congruent	Totally incongruent
Actions justified	Totally by reference to constraints	D (Instrumental equilibrium)	(Unstable disequilibrium) C
	Totally by other means	(Normative equilibrium) A	(Normatively maintained disequilibrium) B

FIGURE 1. A structural model of change

populations where optimal patterns have evolved over long time periods are seen as tending to gravitate towards position A. Changes in environmental constraints or opportunities are seen as leading to pressures towards B and then to a tendency to move vertically towards C until behaviour patterns within the organisation begin to change. This involves pressures leftwards towards AD, whence they again begin to drift towards position A as new normative patterns are established. The precise processes which are seen here as involved in the establishment of new normative patterns are discussed below.

B and C. Timing and certainty of reciprocation

So far I have assumed that bargains as struck, and therefore social relationships as they emerge are determined only by costs and benefits arising through simple exchange. However, economic theory has long recognised that, in the case of commercial bargains, certain qualifying factors enter in, except in an ideal situation of instant reciprocation and perfect knowledge of outcomes. Any deviation from either of these conditions leads to changes in the rate of reward. Any move away from instant reciprocation gives to the partner who has to await reward a surplus, what economists call rent; any move away from perfect knowledge of outcomes gives to the person who takes the risk a surplus, what economists call profit.

It is perhaps not surprising, then, that the inclusion of analogous concepts in an exchange theory formulation seems to make possible some interesting additional interpretations and hypotheses. Put very briefly in summary form they lead me to suggest, *ceteris paribus*:

1. The more that reciprocation is to be delayed, the more will an actor making an investment tend to consider the options open to him carefully, unless there are many exact precedents in which the outcome has been successful.

2. The larger the commitment that an actor has to make now, the sooner he will require reciprocation.

3. The more uncertain is the future, the greater the tendency to calculate options and outcomes and the greater the pressure for rapid reciprocation.

4. In general, a fall in resources increases the need for assistance from others. Exchange is particularly advantageous in the long run when periods of low income for some alternate predictably with periods of high income for others. In fact, in certain situations which I shall discuss formally in Chapter 12, the most logical procedure is for anyone who has surplus resources at a point in time to help someone in need, trusting that when he, in turn, falls into need someone else, not necessarily the person he helped, will come to his rescue; in other words, what one may call indirect, generalised or third party exchange is encouraged. However, beyond a certain point, the greater one's current poverty, the greater is the pressure to reduce commitment to all relationships and, in particular, to restrict oneself to relationships offering fairly immediate returns. This, of course, militates against generalised exchange nets.

5. The weaker are norms or trust, the greater is the tendency to calculate options and outcomes and the greater the pressure for rapid reciprocation. Under these situations generalised exchange nets tend to collapse because for them to be viable absolute trust that others in the community will conform to expectations is required.

6. The ideal basis for calculation of advantages would be average life expectation for an average person in one's present status, subject to an insurance policy against a lengthy and improverished old age.

7. Where any of the conditions summarised under points 1–5 above occur generally in the population the value system of the whole population will come to reflect a calculative orientation and/or an emphasis on short-run reciprocation as the case may be.

8. The more calculative are orientations to relationships in a community, the more variable will patterns of social behaviour be.

The rest of this chapter elaborates the logic underlying the points just made. Some readers may, however, wish by now to get on to the data. If so, they are advised to turn on to Chapter 3 (page 17), returning to the rest of this chapter if, after they have read Chapters 7 or 8 or 11 or 12, they wish to understand further the justifications for the theoretical interpretations offered there. A summary of the whole of this chapter in more rigorous propositional form is presented in Chapter 12. Readers who like to have their formal theory completely tied up before starting on the data may like to read through these propositions before proceeding to Chapter 3. Such readers should turn to page 172.

Timing and uncertainty elaborated

Dealing first with the consequences of delay in reciprocation, it is reasonable to suggest that the surplus required in compensation will become larger the larger is the time delay, the larger is the amount one has temporarily foregone as a proportion of one's total stock of assets,[29] and the greater the alternative demands on those funds during this time period. If a man is asked to lend twopence for five minutes in the middle of the night he will not usually require much surplus in return. If he is asked to lend four-fifths of his income for ten years when his family is at its most expensive, he is likely to ask for a very considerable bonus in return even if he is absolutely sure that there is no risk involved.[30]

Thus it appears logical to assume that, even in a situation of certainty, the larger the proportion of total resources involved, the longer the time period, and the more the alternative uses of the item foregone, the more costly is this foregoing and, in consequence, the more likely is a man to wonder whether a particular option is really the best one and the more likely he is to look elsewhere for an alternative. The corollary of this is also interesting. If one is asked to give up for a short period something not very costly and with no important alternative uses, then one normally does so almost without thinking. If one is asked to give up something very valuable (high share of resources, many alternative uses), then one normally wants it back quickly, because one cannot usually do without it for very long. Or one wants back something else equally valuable, again quickly. In other words one desires relatively immediate reciprocation. And one will think rather carefully about it.

The increased surplus required to compensate for uncertainty has rather similar consequences. This part of the analysis is best considered in two parts.

Firstly, consider the situation where, even if a man is sure that alter will reciprocate to the best of his ability, he is unsure about his ability to do so, or about the utility to himself of what alter ultimately would produce at the time when reciprocation came to be made. In this situation one might assume that the size of the surplus that will be required in compensation will vary with the perceived degree of uncertainty about alter's ability to reciprocate, with one's estimate of one's own needs, and with the proportion of one's resources involved and with alternative uses of them. Thus, if ego is asked to lend all his money to someone he knows is honest but who stands only a very remote chance of paying it back, and if there is a good chance that ego will be dead by this time anyway, then ego will expect a large surplus to compensate him for the risk. If such a bargain was offered as the price of maintaining a relationship which offered otherwise only slightly superior terms then he would probably terminate the relationship if this condition could not be cut out. Analogous arguments can be applied to other scarce resources.

The expected time span before reciprocation also has a special role to play here, though it is quite distinct analytically from the rent surplus discussed above. If reciprocation is to be instantaneous, if alter is known to be willing to reciprocate to the best of his ability and if all facts about his access to resources and about other demands upon him can be ascertained, then no risk is involved. The longer the gap between service and reciprocation, however, the greater is the uncertainty both about alter's ability and about one's own needs. And, the greater the risk in terms of uncertainty about alter's ability and one's own future needs, the greater, one may suggest, will be the tendency either to demand a large surplus in the future, or to demand instant reciprocation in the form of some other desired resource. The greater also, it would logically seem, will the tendency be to investigate carefully one's own and alter's present and future situation, to calculate the outcomes.[31]

Another corollary of this analysis is also of interest. In situations of great uncertainty rapid returns are required. But what would the optimal patterns be even if one was wholly certain about alter's ability to reciprocate at some time in the future, though this time were distant? The problem is that one is not merely uncertain about alter's future, but one is also uncertain about one's own future, notably about one's own life span. And there is no point in entering bargains and thus using up scarce resources which would be useful now, if when the time for reciprocation arrives one is no longer able to take advantage of the reciprocated resource. Logically, it would seem that the individual's psychic profit would be maximised if he made bargains the returns of which were maximised if he survived to the point of average life expectation at the time he entered the bargain. He would, logically, similarly maximise his satisfactions if he assumed that he would have as resources in the future the average for someone of his status now. But he would also surely if possible seek to insure himself in some way so that if he lived for much longer or fell into some disaster, he would still be able to maintain some satisfactory minimum standard of living. In other words, it would seem that his optimal patterns would be to balance his outgoings and returns so that returns were maximised over an average life span, but also to take out an insurance policy against a lengthy and impoverished old age.

However, certain aspects of their present structural situations may force actors to follow courses of action advantageous only in the short run, even though long-run alternatives are known to be advantageous. In particular this is so when the short run suffering to one's own life chances involved in maintaining or entering a relationship advantageous in the long run, outweighs any long-run advantage. It may, indeed, even make it impossible to get to the long run at all, because the first obligation consumed resources necessary to reach the long run in a state where one is able to benefit from the long-run rewards.

This analysis has so far been carried out as if at the individual phenomenal level, the level at which economists originally developed these ideas. However, there is, of course, also a counterpart at the structural level and, indeed, it is because they have these counterparts at the structural level that many macro-economic theories of saving, profit, cost, and so on, work at all. Thus, for example, in situations of extreme poverty where rent on the marginal pound is high one would expect that the dominant value in the community would be to concentrate on bargains which involved a rapid reciprocation, in preference to bargains where the reciprocation was delayed. Similarly, in situations of high uncertainty, one would expect, in line with the earlier analysis, that the dominant value pattern would involve an emphasis on short-run returns plus calculation of expected returns on the basis of all currently known data on the future. I explore this topic in slightly more detail in Chapter 12.

I now want to turn attention to the other source of uncertainty, that which arises through doubts over alter's willingness to reciprocate even if he has the resources to do so. Extreme uncertainty on these grounds has obvious similar consequences at both the phenomenal and structural levels to uncertainty of the kind already discussed, viz: it leads to a need to increase profit and thus to a tendency to reduce the time span of reciprocation and to increase calculativeness. However, it also appears likely to have two further important behavioural consequences. Firstly, this calculativeness in turn leads to increased variability in behaviour within a population. Secondly, the arrival of calculative orientations in a community will logically lead to the termination of generalised exchange; for this to be viable absolute trust that others in the community will conform to expectations, is required.

I suggest that there are at least four structural parameters variations along which will raise or lower certainty (or trust) of this second kind, or, more precisely, since a totally normless society is not conceivable, variations along which will vary the specificity of norms, or, conversely, the range over which calculativeness and uncertainty occur:

(*a*) The more homogeneous the society, the more specific norms can be.

Conversely, the more diverse are the present and the past situations of actors, the less easy it appears logically to be to apply absolute and general principles to their behaviour, because each individual has a different pattern of role relationships. There are no *exact* precedents in this situation, norms can seldom be mandatory ('You must support your father when he is old'). Rather they either allow qualifications such as 'unless you are too poor, have too many children of your own, and provided he does not make himself intolerably unpleasant or inconvenient now', or they are vague ('If you can possibly manage it you should help your father when he is old as well as you can'). These qualifications and this vagueness, however, introduce some scope for interpretation, for calculation, for some actors defining a given demand as more, and others as less pressing, even when all other things are equal. Under these situations, in particular, third parties are much less able to impose sanctions; thus uncertainty about reciprocation increases.

(*b*) The more connected is an actor's social network (i.e. the more the people he knows know each other and can communicate with each other independently of him), the more specific norms can be. For, it is logical to suppose that sanctioning power depends on information being passed round all alternative sources of assistance so that deprivation by one source cannot simply be substituted by turning to another. Adequate sanctioning power often also depends on piecing together scraps of information about an individual from various sources so that his total set of role demands and role performances can be appreciated and assessed.[32]

(*c*) Taken together, the first two factors are relevant for a third, viz: that an increase in scale even in a relatively homogeneous community allows the existence of viable variant subcultures, especially in a situation where networks are not close knit, because anonymity and segmented relationships become more possible.

(*d*) Finally, social change, particularly if it is seen to involve decline in commitments to certain values and to be upsetting the traditional balances of authority and power in a community, is itself likely further to reinforce uncertainty by raising fears that people may consider old values no longer appropriate as guides to action. Once some people start to reject old values this fear will be reinforced still further, particularly, perhaps, where frequent opportunities do not exist for interacting with relevant alters in ways which allow testing of beliefs and expectations.

3. The design of the research

The choice of locale, period, and population

The full detail of the theoretical analysis presented in the last chapter was only worked out after most of the data had been collected. But several earlier drafts containing most of the same ideas in a less formalised presentation were written between 1965 and 1968 during the data collection process. These earliers drafts, as I noted in Chapter 1, were partly stimulated by a need to order the problematic descriptive data which I was finding for Lancashire and later for rural Ireland. All the census data have been worked under the influence of these ideas, and some of the key data sources have been re-examined in order to check that no large body of contradictory data had been missed in the original data collection. In addition, it was only after the theoretical discussion had been developed to a fairly advanced stage that the full significance of much of the unordered descriptive data collected became apparent. Nevertheless it must be admitted that the interpretations of the total cultural context of kinship behaviour in nineteenth century Lancashire and in rural Ireland do contain more than an element of *ex post facto* reasoning. The comparative analysis, both synchronic and diachronic, which is presented in Chapter 12 is a very preliminary attempt to support these interpretations in a different way by putting the nineteenth century data in its historical and cross-cultural context.

The choice of Lancashire as the locale for this study and of the mid-nineteenth century as its period was not, then, wholly determined by the desire to provide some kind of test case for the utility of a set of propositions, though it does turn out in fact to have been a particularly interesting case to have chosen. I had hoped in the beginning to take as my test case of the original vague theoretical notions, a study of the family structure of the industrial workforce of one area for the whole of the industrialising period from the mid-eighteenth century onwards, concentrating particularly on the early years when the new labour force was gradually adapting to the impact of factory and wage labour employment. It soon became obvious, however, that descriptive data for the early period were very sparse, while adequate data on residence patterns did not exist before 1851. It also became clear that there were certain theoretical advantages in studying the industrial workforce in the mid-nineteenth century, for it was only then that cottage elements became unimportant, only then that the characteristic occupational constraints of industrial employment – differentiation of workplace from home, concentration of work into large units, money wages, regular hours of employment, and absence of ownership by the workforce of the means of production – really began to operate on a substantial proportion of the population even of the industrial areas of Britain.

Thus there were both pragmatic and theoretical reasons for my decision to concentrate particular attention on the period 1830 to 1865. I have not, however, restricted myself rigidly to data on conditions between these two dates. Where interesting supporting material exists only for dates outside this period I have used it as long as there is no apparent reason to suggest that it is not applicable to the mid-century situation.[1]

There were also both pragmatic and theoretical reasons underlying my decision to choose Lancashire as the locale for this research. All through the industrial revolution Lancashire typified or led industrialising Britain. In 1851, the Lancashire textile areas contained about a quarter of the adult male industrial employees of Great Britain[2] but under 3% of its agricultural population, in an area about 70 miles from north to south and between 10 and 50 miles from east to west. Many more people depended directly or indirectly on factory-based industry for their livelihood, and a majority were employed in it at some period of their lives.[3] And, predictably, with this rapid growth of industrial employment had come all the characteristic social problems of early industrialisation – cyclical unemployment, rapid growth of towns and vast inmigrant populations, large families struggling on low wages, and a whole range of the other critical life situations which confront those adapting to urban industrial life. But the formalised means that have since been developed for reducing the impact of these problems were as yet absent or only feebly developed.

In Lancashire, then, if anywhere, the disruptive effects of industrialisation on kinship relationships should have been found in large measure. It was, in this sense, something of a theoretical test case. But Lancashire, precisely because it had experienced this booming industrialisation and its concomitant social problems, was also one of the areas for which data were most abundant. Furthermore, Smelser, though engaged on a rather different problem, had already worked over many of the data sources likely to be relevant, and had also explored and summarised in his book[4] much of the necessary background material. This was, then, a further factor which weighed in favour of the Lancashire cotton districts as the locale to be studied.

Within this area and time I have concentrated attention above all on 'the class of labourers and small shopkeepers', as the group whose kinship relationships were most likely to have been disrupted by the impact of urban-industrial life. The justification for treating this particular aggregate as a meaningful totality and for including small masters and small shopkeepers with the operatives are again partly pragmatically and partly theoretically justifiable, viz.:

1. Residence and interaction within the same local communities.[5]

2. Rather similar occupational histories[6] and patterns of education for their children.[7]

3. The fact that the 'interests of the shopkeepers are so closely connected with those of the labouring class',[8] so that in a depression they suffered as, or almost as, severely as the employees around them, and often lost all their capital.[9]

4. The great practical difficulty of differentiating adequately in census analysis between small masters and journeymen artisans.[10]

As far as population is concerned, this study is mainly concerned with family life in the towns. As a rough working procedure I have ruled out most data on communities with populations of under 10,000. Most of the data, indeed, refer to conditions in towns that are considerably larger than this. Where the impact of industrial life is the particular subject of consideration I have not used data on the predominantly commercial centre of Liverpool.

Available data, collection, and analysis

I have discussed in some detail elsewhere[11] the kinds of data which can be used for a study of this kind, and some of the principal problems that their use involves.

The prime source of quantitative material is the census enumerators' books for 1841, 1851, and 1861.[12] These give the address of every household,[13] and, for each member of the household, the name, relationship to household head, age, sex, occupation, and birthplace. Their reliability is usually considered to be high. Other listings of various kinds have also been used and details are given where they are referred to in the text.

For the census data, one town, Preston, was chosen for particular study. The town was in most relevant ways typical of the larger towns of the area.[14] (All the towns were in most ways anyway fairly similar.[15]) All the enumerators' books for the town were in reasonable condition. It was one of the towns for which distributions of the population by birthplace and occupation were given in the published census tables so that the representativeness of the sample could be checked and its findings on these points supplemented in more detail.

A one in ten sample was taken of all occupied private residences[16] in the Municipal and Parliamentary Borough of Preston. Data were coded and punched on to 80-column cards for mechanical tabulation.

The age, sex and birthplace distributions of the sample were checked against the published tables for the population. In all cases the distributions were well within a 5% tolerance limit.

Two comparison samples were also obtained from surrounding villages. Since they were to be used for comparison with the migrants, these samples were taken, after much consideration of alternative universes, on the basis of the distribution, in the Preston sample, of the identifiable birthplaces of all heads of households and their wives born within 30 miles of Preston, in villages with an 1851 population of under 5,000. The only exception was that villages in which only one migrant had been born were excluded, so that sampling fractions would not become impossibly huge. The number of houses in these samples from any village was thus approximately proportional to the number of migrants in the urban sample born in that village, and the sampling fractions for each village varied accordingly.

Of these samples, the one most used below was taken from 'agricultural villages' as defined in Chapter 4. Henceforth this will be called 'the agricultural village sample'. A sample was also taken from all other villages in the universe. There were 781 houses in the 'agricultural village sample' and 913 in the 'other villages' sample. The houses to be sampled were selected by the use of a table of random numbers.

These samples only give a picture of family structure at a point in time. They also, because they are based on a fraction of the population selected at random, show nothing about the relationships, familial and otherwise, between the inhabitants of different houses in the same street or area. I thus decided to study residence patterns in one area of the town on an intensive basis. This is referred to as 'the intensive study'.

One enumerator's district considered after careful inspection and trial surveys elsewhere to be not untypical of working class sectors of the town was selected. The names of the occupants of all the houses in that district at the censuses of 1841, 1851, and 1861 were recorded. Attempts were then made to build up family histories of as many of these individuals as possible, by searching for them in the base enumeration district and in all contiguous enumeration districts.[17] Because of the very considerable amount of residential mobility in these towns by no means all persons were traced in earlier or subsequent censuses,[18] but the results obtained are still of great interest.

For certain other purposes details were recorded for all the 1,700 houses in the area surveyed. These 1,700 houses represented about 15% of the houses in the town. It would have been interesting to search the whole town, but the process involved is extremely arduous and time-consuming, and, significantly, is subject to rapidly decreasing returns in terms of families traced.

These quantitative data are supported by a mass of descriptive material abstracted from contemporary sources of all kinds. A full list is given on pages 181–94 below, and the way the data were handled in an attempt to minimise the degree of *post hoc* rationalisation is briefly described in an Appendix (page 180).

Although it is obviously often impossible to be certain of the accuracy of any given statement used as a source for this work, there is seldom any reason to suspect deliberate bias on the part of the authors cited, because the data used here were usually incidental to their main concern. Some of the data refer to isolated cases found in the literature. Since these may not always have been typical, they should be considered as less reliable. Sources referring to individual cases only are asterisked in the footnotes. The overall balance of evidence, rather than any isolated example, is anyway of key importance here.

Some use is also made of material from novels. Several limitations were, however, applied to such data. All material used must have been entirely incidental to the plot of the novel. The work must have been by a writer familiar with working class life and, if possible, the work must have been one known to be read by working class contemporaries.[19]

Plan of the remainder of the book

This, then, concludes the second part of this book. In Part 3 the available data on the family in nineteenth century Lancashire are discussed in detail. Chapter 4 describes something of the social and economic setting in which family life was lived, concentrating particularly on the constraints and problems that the mass of the populace had to cope with in their daily lives, on the opportunities that were offered them by their environment, and on the resources that were available to them to attain their goals. Chapter 5 presents some preliminary outline data on the strength, quality and extent of family and kinship ties in the cotton towns, while Chapter 6 briefly fills in the background on the relationships between parents and their adolescent and pre-adolescent children. In Chapter 7 a slight digression is made in an attempt to show the extent of the impact of urban industrial life on the migrants to the towns, by turning attention back to family life in the areas of rural Lancashire and rural Ireland whence large elements of the migrant population had come. Chapters 8 to 11 are primarily analytical, attempting to provide some interpretation of the patterns of urban family life in the context of the general theoretical formulation and of the propositions outlined in Chapter 2. Chapter 8 looks primarily at the phenomenal level, at normative sanctions, at socialisation and at ideologies. Chapter 9 looks at the central issue of the impact of industrial employment on family life. Chapter 10, which is in many ways the other key chapter of the book, looks at the impact on the urban proletariat of the continual social and personal crises of all kinds which struck them so often in a situation where formalised sources of assistance were little developed. Part 3 is concluded in Chapter 11 where the impact of uncertainty, population turnover and poverty are examined. Finally, Part 4 considers some of the wider implications of the findings by setting them, and the propositions which underlie them, in an historical and cross-cultural setting.

Part Three. The family in nineteenth century Lancashire

4. The social and economic background

In this chapter I try to provide the reader with basic background material on the kinds of problems that the Lancashire working class of the last century had to face in their daily lives, the community and economic environment in which they had to face them, and the resources they could call upon in their attempts to do so. I consider first the employment situation in the cotton towns. Then I focus attention successively on family incomes, saving and poverty, on urban population growth and the consequent effects on housing standards, mortality and sickness, on migration, and finally, on population turnover within the urban communities.

The employment situation

By the 1830s the old handicraft system where whole families worked together in their scattered farms and villages, as well as in the towns, to turn cotton into thread and then into cloth, was already on the verge of extinction. Cotton spinning had long been concentrated in factories, latterly mainly in factories in towns on or near the coalfields. Weaving by power was also spreading rapidly in the 1830s, and in the next decades the hand-loom weavers, once the most prosperous of all Lancashire working men, were steadily falling into destitution. In the rural areas many hung on to their trade, relying increasingly on the tiny farms which had previously provided only supplementary income. Many depended heavily on poor relief, but as late as 1861 substantial numbers still practised their craft in such centres as Wigan and Manchester, and in Preston.[1]

While hand-loom weaving of cotton declined over the period covered by this study, few major innovatory changes occurred in the factory branch of the industry. Rather, this was a period of consolidation, with a secular, if not steady, increase in the number and size of factories, in the efficiency of machinery, and in the numbers of employees.[2]

In 1851 almost 17% of men aged 20 and over in Lancashire were engaged in cotton manufacture.[3] The industry also employed very large numbers of women and girls, and many branches employed them to the almost total exclusion of men. By 1851 some 15% of the county's adult women, and nearly 38% of those in employment, were employed in cotton. However, employment in cotton had at some time, particularly during adolescence, been the lot of a much larger section of the population, and intimately affected the lives of many more. Thus, simple aggregate figures at a point in time greatly underestimate the true significance of the cotton industry in the lives of the inhabitants of these communities.

In the early days of the industry, much of the labour force had been small children, but now, notably because of the legislation which made it illegal to employ children under 8 at all, and children under 13 full-time,[4] very young children were seldom employed. Only 5% of the Lancashire cotton labour force in 1850 was under the age of 13.[5] In consequence, even the children of families near the poverty line could seldom by the middle of the century obtain employment in cotton much before they were 13, though there were some openings in other trades.

Wages in the cotton industry were high relative to wages in other occupations.[6] Children could earn 3*s.* to 6*s.* per week, young men and women under 18 5*s.* to 13*s.*, women 9*s.* to 16*s.* (with most probably taking home 10*s.* to 12*s.*). Men of 18 and over were only 31% of the labour force in 1850.[7] Some, the mule spinners, warpers, dressers, sizers, overlookers, and engineers, had net earnings of over – in some cases substantially over – 20*s.* per week. Others, however, probably half of the men in the industry, were employed in more lowly paid occupations, particularly as factory labourers and power-loom weavers.[8] Few of this group earned more than 15*s.* per week.

Cotton, however, though the main industry of Lancashire, was not the only one. A further 5% of men and 6% of employed women were employed in the various processing industries (especially printing and dyeing) and in worsted, fustian, wool (mainly in Rochdale), and silk, though this last, in particular, was still dominated by domestic manufacture. In addition, Lancashire had small but important engineering, metals and textile machinery industries,[9] which employed a further 3% of the adult male population.

From the point of view of the employee, textile factory work had many advantages. Hours of work (after 1850, 10½ on 5½ days a week[10]) were little longer than those in many other occupations,[11] and, in good times, employment from day to day and week to week was more or less guaranteed to most of those with the necessary skill and experience. Periodically, however, the cotton industry suffered severe depressions which gradually affected almost the whole of the rest of the population, as demand for investment and consumer goods fell off. There had been several severe depressions before 1830. Thereafter, major slumps, with one-third or more of the population unemployed, and many more on reduced wages, occurred in the mid-1830s, again in 1839–43, the late 1840s, and mid-1850s. Finally, the incipient depression of 1861 was turned into the disastrous distress of the Cotton Famine by the cessation of cotton supplies from America in the following year.[12] The implications of these periodic depressions for family structure are discussed in Chapter 10. The intervening years, however, were mainly periods of high wages and high employment; this was particularly true of the census year 1851, which one Preston commentator described as in the middle of 'a period of great and continued prosperity'.[13]

Factory work, then, was the basis of Lancashire's prosperity, even though at any one time it actually provided employment for a minority of the labour force. Some 7% of the labour force were labourers of various kinds. Most of this group would only have obtained casual irregular employment,[14] earning at maximum some 15*s*. per week, though a few were artisans' assistants, who might in the summer make up to 18*s*., or navvies who could make even more, though under atrocious living and working conditions.

With the exception of a small professional and clerical sector, the remainder of the population, about half in all, were engaged in trading or artisan occupations. A few were very prosperous, but these were far outnumbered by those whose principal affinities were with the working class. About a third of the population were artisans. Some of these were master artisans, employing anything from one to over a hundred journeymen. Some had little shops of their own where they sold their products or took in work for repair. Many others worked for a master or took in work on a subcontract basis.[15] The skilled good workmen could count on regular work for most of the year, earning in good times 20*s*. to 30*s*. or more per week, but many were much less regularly employed.[16]

The rest of this group were the tradesmen and shopkeepers of all kinds. Some high class specialists, in the town centres, had customers of the higher social groups and were reasonably affluent. More typical, however, and more of concern in this study, were the little provision shops, pawnbrokers, beershops, and public houses scattered here and there in the working class districts of the towns. From these little shops the family scraped a living little better, at best, than that of the families round about.[17] Below even this group, came the mass of itinerant salesmen of all types and of both sexes, many of whom were almost totally destitute.

For those women who did not work in factories,[18] the largest single occupation was domestic service. Most of these servants lived with their masters and mistresses. The same was true of a proportion of the milliners, dressmakers, and seamstresses,[19] but for many these trades were simply a way of eking out the family income with a few extra shillings from work done in the home whenever the occasion arose. Another important group, perhaps the poorest of all, and frequently widows, were the charwomen and washerwomen who made up some 7% of the female working population.

I turn now to a brief outline of the occupational structure of the borough of Preston. This town will provide most of the statistical material in later sections.

The total population in 1851 was 69,542 and the total number in the sample 6,943. Before industrial development had begun, Preston had been an important market town and a not inconsiderable port, but the cotton trade had gradually come to dominate the town. This made its population particularly susceptible to distress during periods of depression, since there was so little alternative employment to which men could turn and from the earnings of which some members of families could ease the burden on others.[20] The census authorities found 32% of the men of 20 and over and 28% of women in this age group (53% of all women in employment) engaged in cotton manufacturing.[21] In general the town's occupational structure was very similar to that of the urban areas of the county as a whole.[22]

For detailed analysis of the sample data it was obviously necessary to try to aggregate these different occupations into more or less meaningful and mutally exclusive groups. There is no agreed basis for doing this on nineteenth century census data.[23] I therefore began by positing three parameters which seemed likely on theoretical grounds to have affected family structure, viz: size of income, regularity of employment, and 'employment status'.[24]

On the basis of these criteria the employed male population was aggregated into eight groups. There were, however, a number of occupations the precise nature of which could not adequately be deduced from the enumerators' books. So as to keep the occupational groups reasonably precise all doubtful cases were assigned to a separate group,[25] as were all non-employed persons.

Table 1 shows how the population was broken down, and the proportions of the total and of the adult populations which fell into each of the resultant socio-economic groups (SEGs). Figure 2 breaks down this SEG data by age, and shows that at a point in time the age distribution of the members of the different employed SEGs varied widely.[26]

The pattern revealed in Figure 2 reflects above all two forces both powerfully at work in the community and both with considerable implications for family structure.[27] Firstly, over the life-cycle, men left or were forced to leave the cotton industry and go into other employments, notably into labouring and various forms of trading, where many earned far less than they had in cotton. This point will be taken up again below. Secondly, many of the men who inmigrated into Preston as adults (and, as will be shown shortly, inmigrants made up a substantial proportion of the population) were unable to obtain well-paid employment in the factories and futher swelled the ranks of the labourers. Data bearing on this point are presented in Chapter 10.

As will become clear in Chapters 8 to 11 these life-cycle changes in patterns of employment have considerable implications for family structure. Contemporaries frequently alluded to the problem of the factory worker forced to find alternative employment as he grew older, but most of the polemic on both sides is exaggerated, and some can only be described as hysterical.[28]

It would be interesting to explore this topic further, but this would be beyond the scope of the present research. As part of the intensive study of the enumerators's books of one area of the town, however, some very incomplete data were obtained on the job histories of a number of men and these throw some light on

TABLE 1 *SEG distribution of the Preston sample population, 1851: males*

	SEG	Income (full work)[a]	Regularity of income[b]	Employment status[c]	All aged 10 and over %	All aged 20 and over %
I	Professional and managerial[d]	vh/h	r	E/SE	2[e]	2
II	Clerical	m/l	r	Ed	3[e]	4
III	Trade	most m	rd	E/SE	8	11
IV	Higher factory	m	rd	Ed	10	13[f]
V	Artisan	m	sir	Ed/SE(E)	18	20
VI	Lower factory	l	rd	Ed	21	13[f]
VII	Labourer etc.[g]	l/vl	ir	Ed/(SE)	14	18
VIII	Hand-loom weaver	vl	ir	SE(Ed)	4	5
IX	Unclassified	mixed	mixed	mixed	8	10
X	Not employed	..	..	..	12[h]	4
All		..	..	..	100 (*N* = 2,346)	100 (*N* = 1,607)

[a] vh = very high; h = high; m = medium; l = low; vl = very low. Medium is above about 20*s.* per week; low 10*s.* to 20*s.*; very low under 10*s.* according to the sources noted in note 6 (see p. 200 below).
[b] r = regular; rd = regular except in depressions; sir = somewhat irregular; ir = irregular.
[c] E = employer; SE = self-employed; Ed = employed. Symbols in brackets indicate that this is a small minority only. SE includes those employing family members only.
[d] Including all tradesmen with more than one domestic servant.
[e] A considerable amount of comparative research is now under way using the enumerators' books; space forbids giving all tabulations both for the working class and for the whole sample. I have therefore included the whole sample in the tabulations of aggregate data (even though conclusions and hypotheses only apply to the working class) so that comparison can be made with other studies. This seems justified in view of the small size of these middle class groups.
[f] In all, 26% of the male population over 20 was classified as in factory employment. This differs from the 36% mentioned earlier because it excludes hand-loom weavers (5%), weavers not specified (3%), and the white collar, entrepreneurial and managerial staff.
[g] Including hawkers and other itinerant traders.
[h] This group consists largely of children not yet in employment.

this topic.[29] The relevant figures are presented in Table 2. It must be emphasised that these data cover only a part of the town, and may not be wholly representative, though their broad conclusions are borne out by a mass of descriptive evidence. One major problem in interpretation is that many men who were markedly socially mobile in either direction may have moved right out of the area into other areas of the town, or to other towns.

In spite of its problematical reliability, three points in Table 2 do seem worthy of comment and probably give a broadly correct picture of the trends they suggest:

1. A high proportion of children went into textile occupations, but many left within a few years to go into other occupations. The figures under-represent the true number who went into textiles, since, in ten years, some would have moved both in and out of the industry. When they were young, children could earn more in factory occupations than elsewhere, but as they grew older, unless they

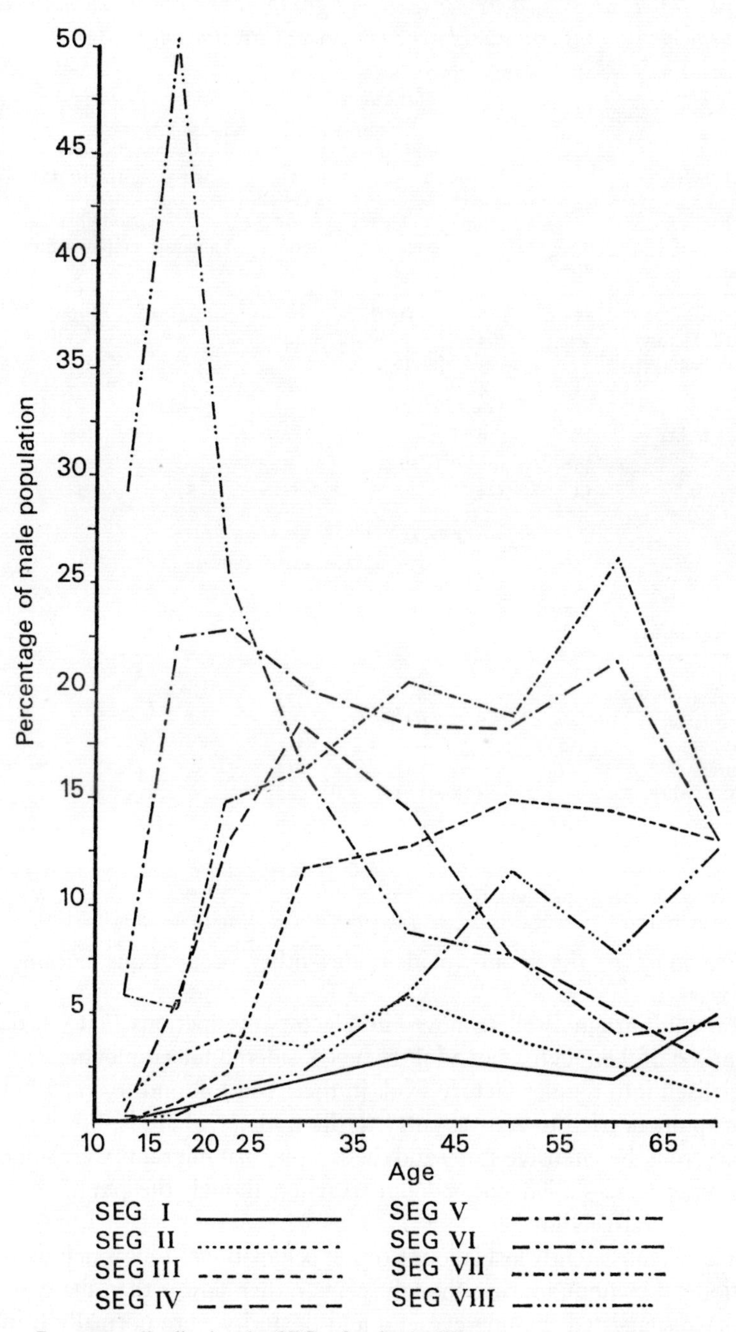

FIGURE 2. Percentage distribution, by SEG, of males in different age groups: Preston sample, 1851

TABLE 2 *Men categorised by occupational group at one census, by occupational group at the next census ten years later: one area of Preston only, 1841, 1851, 1861*

(a) All ages

	SEG at earlier census						
	III	IV/VI		V	VII	II, VIII, IX	X
SEG at later census	Trade %	Textile factory %	Other factory %	Artisan %	Labourer %	Other employment %	None[a] %
III Trade	83	6	(13)[b]	–	4	6	1
IV/VI Textile factory	–	65	–	4	7	3	42
IV/VI Other factory	–	3	(63)	–	–	–	6
V Artisan	–	4	–	89	2	–	31
VII Labourer	8	13	(25)	4	76	13	10
II, VII, IX, X Other	8	9	–	2	11	78	9
All: %	99	100	101	99	100	100	99
N	12	124	8	45	54	32	153

(b) Textile factory workers only, by age at earlier census

	Age at earlier census				
SEG at later census	10–19 %	20–29 %	30–39 %	40–49 %	50 and over %
III Trade	–	6	4	12	7
IV/VI Textile factory	54	66	73	72	57
IV/VI Other factory	8	6	–	–	–
V Artisan	21	–	–	–	–
VII Labourer	13	11	15	4	29
II, VIII, IX, X Other	4	11	8	12	7
All: %	100	100	100	100	100
N	24	35	26	25	14

[a] Includes new entrants to the labour force.

[b] Throughout the book percentages based on totals (100%) of less than 10 are set in brackets.

were promoted to the highly paid trades other occupations became more attractive.[30]

2. Few adult urban dwellers moved into factory occupations.[31] It was difficult to become skilful enough as an adult to be considered for employment,[32] many not socialised into regular factory work in their youth found it very irksome,[33] and the spinners tried to restrict entry to the trade.[34] There is, however, some evidence, from the intensive study and the sample, that migrants were sometimes able to enter semi-skilled power-loom weaving, though the pay here was, of course, comparatively low.

3. Textiles consistently lost labour to other occupations. This is in line with the predictions of contemporaries, though seems rather slower than many of them would have suggested. Failing eyesight and dexterity were normally blamed.[35] Character seems also, however, to have been important, and regular steady

employees were probably less likely to be discharged.[36] Nearly three-quarters of the men in their thirties and forties who remained in the intensive study area stayed in cotton (though it seems possible that those who became redundant might have been more likely to move away out of the survey area). Moreover, the figures do not altogether bear out contemporary opinion that redundant cotton workers could only get casual employment. Of the 14 who did leave in these age groups, only 6 went into the lowest paid occupations. One took a clerical job, and 4 became tradesmen of a shopkeeping kind on their own account. Only among those in their fifties is there a definite trend to the lowest paid occupations, though some younger men among the highly paid textile employees moved into lower paid occupations within the industry; spinners, for example, were kept on as factory labourers.[37]

Summarising this section, then, most of the population of these communities depended directly or indirectly, or at least had at some time depended, on the cotton industry, though the communities provided a wide range of employment opportunities. A large proportion of these other occupations, however, paid rather low wages and many offered only irregular employment. The prosperity of all was subject to periodic jolts when depressions hit the cotton industry. It was difficult for adult men to enter cotton, though there were good opportunities for women and children. Indeed, men gradually moved out of cotton, for various reasons, as they aged.

Family incomes, saving, and poverty

I noted in the last section that many men earned very low wages. One important result of this was that very many families lived in primary poverty, and this poverty will be shown in later chapters to have had an important influence on family structure. This section draws together available data on the extent of poverty and on its incidence.

No comprehensive contemporary survey of the extent and incidence of poverty is available for any Victorian town before the publication of Booth's report on conditions in London in the 1880s and Rowntree's on York in the 1890s.[38] Booth found some 31% of the population (40% of the working class) in poverty, while Rowntree's figures are comparable, about 28% and 43% respectively. It seems likely, however, that at mid-century in Lancashire poverty would have been even more widespread, for real wages rose markedly between 1851 and 1900,[39] and this would not have been wholly offset by the somewhat higher wage levels which could be obtained throughout the century in the Lancashire cotton towns.

The most important and most relevant modern piece of research on this topic is undoubtedly that conducted by Foster,[40] who attempted to calculate the family incomes and incidence of poverty of the population of Oldham in 1847 (a slump year) and 1849 (a 'normal' year). His calculations use the 1851 census to provide data on family composition, contemporary sources for wage and unemployment data, and for a poverty standard the Bowley revision of the Rowntree primary poverty scale, adjusted for price changes. He concluded that some 20% of the population of Oldham were on or below the subsistence line in 1849. In 1847, however, when both prices and unemployment were higher about half of the population would have been in poverty on the standards he employed.

There were, however, very great differences between occupational groupings in the incidence of poverty. Of top artisans' families only 3% in 1849 and 14% in 1847 would have been below subsistence level. For labourers' families the comparable figures were 35% and 78% and for skilled factory workers 14% and 52%. Over the life-cycle as a whole, Foster suggests that only some 15% of all working class families would have escaped a period of poverty.[41]

For the purposes of this study it was necessary to attempt for as many families in the sample as possible a similar kind of calculation of family standard of living so that the effect of poverty on family structure could be assessed. The technique used was basically similar to Foster's, but somewhat simpler to compute. The resulting data are perhaps slightly less valid than would have been obtained by a more sophisticated method, but any calculation of this kind is fraught with difficulties and based on several assumptions of a somewhat uncertain nature. For example, variations in expenditure patterns even by identically constituted families would have been large and, since only average incomes and average expenditures can be used, secondary poverty due to 'misspent' income, and variations in income due to variations in the regularity of employment cannot be taken into account. It is anyway the case that for the purposes of internal comparisons within the sample it is the relative figures which are important and these are much less affected by small absolute errors in the income and family poverty calculations.

The procedure used here was to estimate, on the assumption of a full week's work, the normal wages of all occupations for which this could be ascertained with a reasonable degree of certainty.[42] Occupations where it was difficult to arrive at a reliable estimate (hand-loom weavers, for example), and trade, middle class and clerical occupations, were excluded. So also were occupations, mainly those of women, where some worked only part-time, while others worked more or less full-time, so that no one income figure could be considered even to approximate reality (dressmakers and laundresses are the two most frequent examples). From these figures was obtained the aggregate income of each nuclear family headed by a married couple, for all nuclear families where the income of all family members could be estimated. Income from lodgers was ignored. It was assumed that co-residing children gave all their income to the family purse.

When family poverty is being considered, this seemed a reasonable assumption,[43] and certainly it was difficult to conceive of any reasonable alternative.

The consumption standard used was the original Rowntree primary poverty line based on York data for 1898–1900.[44] Taking over Rowntree's scale direct means that the figures used do not quite represent the 'true' cost of subsistence in the mid-nineteenth century, for in 1851 food prices were about 10% higher than in 1898–1900 (though coal prices, which have, of course, a smaller effect on the total index, were probably some 25% lower[45]). Thus the food values of the Rowntree scale are slightly stringent for 1851, though this may perhaps be taken to reflect a slightly cheaper conventionally accepted poverty standard than was current at the end of the century. Certainly poor law out-relief and emergency relief committee payments were seldom anywhere near 3*s*. for adults. The use of the Rowntree assumption that all children, regardless of age, consumed 75% of an adult diet probably slightly overinflates the consumption need figures for families and thus further offsets the price changes.

TABLE 3 *Relationship between poverty and life-cycle stage: married couples for whom data were adequate, Preston sample, 1851*

Relationship of weekly family income to poverty line	Life-cycle stage 1 %	2 %	3 %	4 %	5 %	6 %	All %
4*s*. or more below Less than 4*s*. above or below	17	21	52	31	5	26	9 22
4*s*. – 11*s*. 11*d*. above 12*s*. – 19*s*. 11*d*. above	31	52	34	39	13	44	32 22
20*s*. and over above	51	28	14	31	82	29	14
All: %	99	101	100	101	100	99	99
N	86	29	189	49	83	34	470

This admittedly approximate consumption standard was then compared with family aggregate income for all nuclear families for which this could be calculated (55% of all family units headed by married couples), the results being grouped into 8*s*. bands. The results are given in Table 3 broken down by the life-cycle stage (LCS) of the family.[46] In all, nearly 20% of the families for which data could be obtained were below the poverty line used here. It should be noted that, because of the use of the employment of children as one element in the classification, the variations shown here in the proportion of families in different life-cycle stages near the poverty line would to some extent be expected. The sharpness of these variations is nevertheless remarkable, even though this cycle of poverty is known in all societies and was well known to contemporaries.[47] Many families in life-cycle stage 3 had four or more dependent children, and even if the wife could work and could earn 8*s*. per week (which many did not), many labourers' families would still be in poverty, since the father's earnings would seldom exceed 15*s*. per week. Watts[48] suggests that most labourers, and also street sweepers, night soilers, policemen, hand-loom weavers, cotton dyers, railway porters, smith's strikers, and many others, would all have been in great difficulties with four or more children.[49] Power-loom weavers, and some other lowly paid factory workers, together with many less regularly employed artisans, would have been in a similar state. Few widows' families were ever far from the poverty line. Many obviously lived for years on less than an adequate diet. They seldom actually died from starvation, but they would undoubtedly have had a much reduced resistance to disease.[50] Also, like Ward,[51] they would have been unable to maintain adequate stocks of bedding and clothing.

As Foster notes, only about one in seven of all working class families were permanently free from primary poverty.[52] On the other hand, in the later stages of the life-cycle, skilled factory workers in particular lived fairly comfortably by contemporary standards, many with family earnings of at least £3 per week.[53] The earnings of children were thus crucial to the family's standard of living, though even they were of little help in the worst slump periods.

With poverty of this kind, few even in good times could afford to save anything very significant to meet temporary losses in income or for their old age, so that even short or comparatively minor crises caused severe destitution. The few with significant cash savings would mostly have been among the most skilled or sheltered sections of the working class. Although in all, in the mid-1850s, some 6,300 non-institutional depositors had over £165,000 deposited in the Preston Savings Bank 25% of these deposits were of under £5, and 40% under £10. Even assuming that the bank covered only the Borough of Preston (which it did not), and that each household had only one deposit (which, again, was untrue), only one household in every four would have had over £10 deposited, and only one in twenty over £100.[54] In practice most of these deposits belonged to domestic servants, small tradesmen, and the lower middle class, with some also belonging to the skilled factory group.[55] Savings outside savings banks probably followed a similar pattern. It seems very unlikely that many would have been able to amass significant amounts of property of other kinds.[56]

The growth of towns and its consequences

This study is mainly concerned with family life in the Lancashire towns, defined broadly as communities with populations exceeding 10,000 persons. Lancashire was considered by the census authorities in 1851 to be the most urbanised county in Britain[57] and though their definition of what constituted a town was rather vague it is indisputable that in 1851 over half of the population of Lancashire lived in the 14 towns with populations of over 10,000.[58] A community of 10,000 persons was certainly to be considered urban in the mid-nineteenth century, though by modern standards even the larger towns like Preston were very compact in area, mainly because of their high housing density.[59] The main part of the town of Preston was only about one and a half miles from east to west, and one mile from north to south. Any reasonably fit adult could thus walk to anywhere in the town in under half an hour, and this compactness has to be borne in mind when assessing the effects of residential mobility on family structure.

The population of these towns had grown extremely rapidly due both to a high birthrate, and, above all, to inmigration. With the exception of Oldham they had all been market towns of considerable importance before industry had arrived,[60] but they had been small. Even as late as 1801, only Oldham, Manchester and Salford, and Liverpool had populations of over 20,000, but in the next fifty years the populations exploded. The population of Preston in 1851 was 5.7 times what it had been in 1801, and Burnley, Ashton, Blackburn, Stockport, Rochdale, Bolton, and Bury had all grown by more than three times. The population of Preston, and also of Burnley, more than doubled between 1831 and 1851.[61]

With this rapid urban growth had come the predictable sanitary and housing problems. It should be borne in mind of course, both that bad urban housing was not confined to Lancashire but was present in almost all the larger towns in the country, and that rural housing conditions were often appalling. Nevertheless, the fact remains that the domestic environment in many parts of the Lancashire towns was squalid in the extreme.[62]

Many of the main streets were respectable enough. Behind them, however, lay a different world. There were long rows of blackened two-story terraced cottages, some built back-to-back. There were also narrow twisting lanes and enclosed courts of a dozen or fewer houses. Overshadowing all were the factory chimneys. Here and there were shops and chapels and public houses. In some areas the houses had been built so rapidly that the roads were left unpaved, unsewered and unguttered, mudbaths along which vehicles passed with difficulty. Some of the houses were so badly built that they were damp and in need of repair almost immediately. In some towns much of the population still lived in dark, damp cellars. Preston was one of the worst towns.[63]

Inside, the houses were very cramped. Two bedrooms was the rule, and beds were frequently also placed in other rooms.[64] (This would have been particularly so where these cottages were shared by more than one family.) Preston was in 1851 suffering from a severe shortage of housing. In all some 9% of houses contained more than one separate household as defined by the census authorities. Many of these secondary households had only one room or a cellar to themselves. The mean number of persons per inhabited house was 6.1; 56% of all households contained more than 5 persons, and 30% more than 7.[65]

The overcrowding and the disgusting state of many of the privies created a stench nauseating even to the residents who must have been somewhat habituated to it. Among the really poor, furniture and even bedding was sparse or non-existent. Most commentators agree, however, that the interiors of the houses, particularly those of the better paid, were as bright, tidy and clean as the poverty and the smoke and dirt of the towns would allow, though a minority, particularly the Irish, undoubtedly did live in terrible squalor.[66]

It is not surprising that, under these conditions, sickness and mortality rates were high. Minor stomach disorders must have been part of daily life, killing many infants. Occasional epidemics of more serious diseases – cholera, typhus, and typhoid – occurred, the last two probably being endemic in many areas. Scarlet fever, measles, whooping cough, smallpox, and tuberculosis were other killer diseases.[67] The average male cotton operative in his thirties could expect to be sick for at least a fortnight once in every three to four years. Among older men the incidence of this length of illness was markedly higher.[68] The death rate in Preston was said[69] to be the highest in the kingdom, and the Commission on the State of Large Towns[70] selected it for special study. A specially constructed local life table[71] revealed that almost half (47%) of all children died before their fifth birthday and 56% before they were 25, that only three out of five of those alive at 25 reached the age of 50 and only two out of five the age of 60. Other data from this life table will be produced as required in later chapters, where the uncertainties and problems created by this high incidence of sickness and death will be discussed and the extent to which kinship relationships assisted in the mitigation of the consequent distress will be analysed.

Migration

The high growth rates of many Lancashire towns, including Preston, have already been noted. In this section I present some selective background data on the migration which was the cause of a substantial part of this growth, and examine in particular where the migrants came from, and at what ages they migrated.[72]

The 1851 census revealed that in almost all large towns migrants from elsewhere outnumbered those born in the towns.[73] This was particularly true of the cotton districts. Stockport, Bolton, and Manchester all had half of their adult populations born outside their boundaries, and the figure for Preston was 70%.[74] Under these circumstances, as suggested by several of the propositions outlined in Chapter 2, the potential for the serious disruption of family relationships was undoubtedly very great, though one might predict that it would have varied somewhat depending on the distance which the migrants had come.

Unfortunately the census authorities only broke down their data on the birthplaces of the migrants by counties. For this study more refined analysis was necessary, and so the birthplace of each migrant was recorded and plotted on a map of England and Wales.[75] The birthplaces are plotted on Maps 1 and 2.

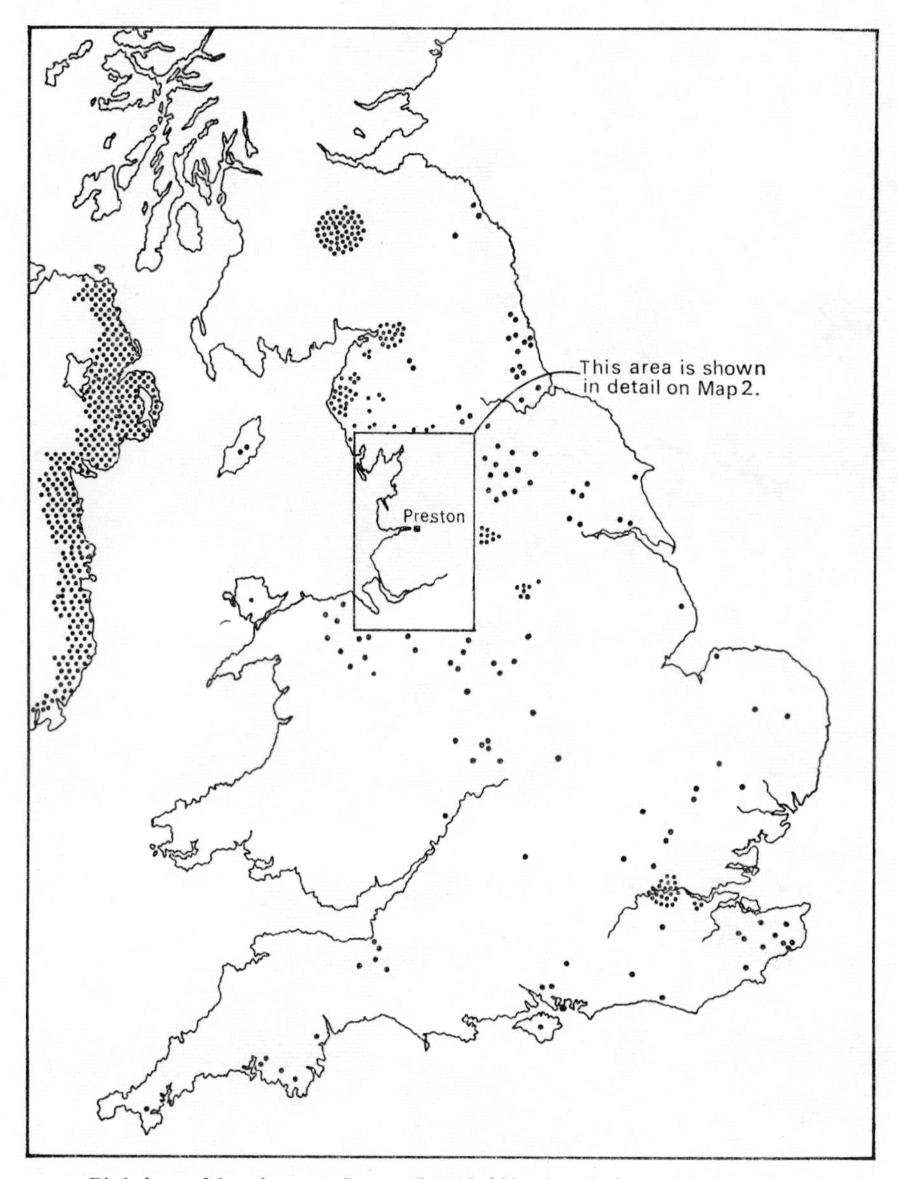

MAP I. Birthplaces of the migrants to Preston (household heads and wives only): Preston sample, 1851

Each dot represents one person. Where only the county of birth is known, this is indicated randomly within the county. Migrants from Scotland and Ireland are grouped conventionally. Scale 85 miles to one inch.

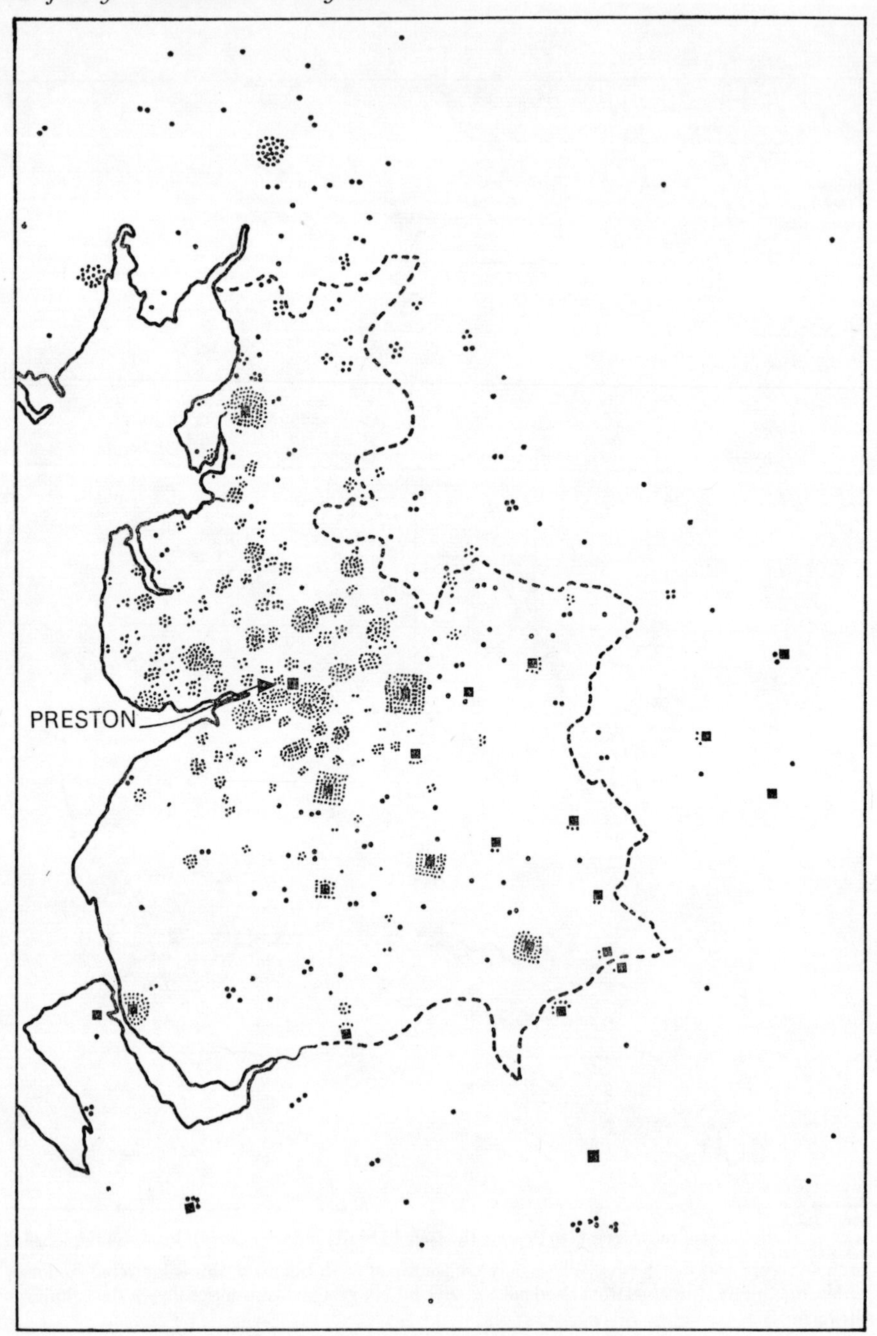

MAP 2. Birthplaces of the migrants to Preston: Preston area

Each dot represents one person. Dark squares show towns of over 10,000 people. Lancashire county boundary thus: — — — — —. Scale 15 miles to one inch.

The 3,345 migrants whose birthplaces could be identified had been born in about 425 different places. For each migrant the distance from town to birthplace was then measured. For the sake of consistency the straight line distances were used, though distances by road, track, or rail were obviously greater.

The distances from Preston to the birthplaces of the migrants are shown in Table 4.[76] These findings are in general in line with the suggestions of earlier workers that most migration was of short distance only.[77] Over 40% of the migrants had come less than 10 miles, and only about 30% were more than 30 miles from their birthplaces. Given that many people were not daunted by the prospect of a walk of 20 or more miles in a day to see kin or friends,[78] the possibility of at least intermittent contact with their birthplaces would have been open to the majority of the migrant population, though a certain degree of motivation would also have been necessary if contact were to be retained. Very

TABLE 4 *Birthplaces of the resident, non-institutionalised[a] population of Preston: Preston sample, 1851*

Birthplace	Total population %	Inmigrants[b] %
In Preston	48	..
1–4.9 miles distant	8	15
5–9.9 miles distant	13	27
10–29.9 miles distant	14	28
30 and over miles distant (other than Ireland)	8	16
In Ireland	7	14
Not traceable	2	..
All: %	100	100
N	6,741	3,345

[a] The institutionalised population are excluded on the grounds that some were not voluntary migrants Visitors are also excluded. Thus the total figure differs from the total numbers in the sample.
[b] Excluding not traceable.

few, a quarter of the migrants at most, had come so far that even occasional contact presented special difficulties. Many of these were from Ireland. Only about 2% of the sample had been born more than 100 miles from Preston but within England, Wales, or Scotland.

The data on birthplaces also made it possible to find out some details about the type of community from which the migrants had come, and this seemed important because of its possible effect on the ease with which different groups of the population might adapt to urban life, a possibility which received some support from the subsequent analysis. All migrants born within 30 miles of Preston were allocated to one of a number of community types, the classification of communities being made according to data presented in the published tables of the 1831 census.[79] Five types of community were distinguished:

1. 'Towns': all places with populations exceeding 5,000 in 1851.[80]

2. 'Agricultural villages': all villages where more than 50% of the male population over 20 were recorded in 1831 as engaged in agriculture.

3. 'Industrial villages': all villages where more than 50% of the male adult population were in 1831 engaged in manufacturing occupations.[81]

4. 'Mixed villages': all villages where between 26% and 50% of the adult male population were in 1831 engaged in agriculture, and a further 26–50% in manufacturing.

5. 'Miscellaneous villages': all villages which did not fit into one of the above categories.

Data on the type of community of birth of the sample population are given in Table 5. The most noticeable feature of this table is the large proportion of

TABLE 5 *Birthplaces of the resident, non-institutionalised population, categorised by type of community: Preston sample, 1851*

Type of community of birthplace	Total population %	Inmigrants %
Born within 30 miles in:		
towns	12	24
industrial villages	5	9
mixed villages	4	8
agricultural villages	7	13
miscellaneous villages	8	16
All communities under 30 miles	36	70
Other, Preston, and not traceable	64	30
Total population: %	100	100
N	6,741	3,345

migrants born in other towns. That most of these were, in fact, born in other large manufacturing towns is clear from Map 2. Conversely, of course, it must be assumed that many Preston born people, and many one-time Preston residents, would be living in other towns. Indeed, a number of Preston born parents in the sample had several children born in other large manufacturing towns, indicating that they had migrated away in this manner, and later returned. These would surely be only a small proportion of all those who had left the town.

Migration of this kind to other large towns seems at first sight odd, with men and women, some with families, uprooting themselves and moving away from kin and friends. This type of behaviour appears in marked contrast to the apparent extreme reluctance of members of traditional working class communities in twentieth century Britain to move away from the community of their birth,[82] particularly since much of this movement appears to have been to towns offering similar residential and employment opportunities. In fact, however, while some of this migration did occur in good times, most of it was more or less forced on men and women by unemployment during depressions, in situations where there was no acceptable means of support in the community, and where kin and neighbours were unable any longer to offer adequate assistance.[83] This topic is taken up again in Chapter 10.

Irish immigration had been a feature of the Lancashire urban scene from at least 1750,[84] but had developed only slowly until the 1840s.[85] After the famine, however, numbers rose dramatically.[86] The number of Irish born persons living in Lancashire increased from 106,000 in 1841[87] to 192,000 in 1851,[88] and Irish as a proportion of the population of Preston from 3.3% to 7.4%.[89]

When considering the possible effects of migration on family structure, two important matters need to be borne in mind, viz: the period of the life-cycle at which migration occurs, and whether the migrants come alone, in a nuclear family, or as part of a wider kinship group. Some migration occurred at all stages of the life-cycle, but it was particularly frequent among single men and women in their late teens and early twenties, and among those married couples with small families.

TABLE 6 *Proportion of the population born in Preston, by age and sex: Preston sample, 1851*

	Males		Females	
Age	%	*N* (100%)	%	*N* (100%)
0–4	86	418	85	452
5–9	73	389	79	359
10–14	66	392	66	349
15–19	54	390	52	418
20–24	39	316	40	398
25–34	30	473	33	546
35–44	25	379	32	411
45–54	25	230	25	319
55–64	14	156	13	160
65 and over	23	93	20	101

Some indication of this concentration of migration into the younger age groups can be obtained from Table 6 which shows for each age group the proportion of the sample population who had been born in Preston. Particularly noticeable are the large increments in the proportions not born in the towns which occur in the age span 10–34. So great, indeed, was the rate of inmigration in these groups that the number of girls aged 15–19 and 20–24 resident in Preston in 1851 actually exceeded the numbers aged 10–14 by 12% and 11% respectively, in spite of an annual mortality rate in these age groups of around 1% per year of life.[90]

This migration by teenagers had long been part of the English tradition, with boys and girls being sent off into service or leaving home to 'seek their fortunes' in the towns,[91] and this practice continued throughout the nineteenth century. It was reported from the Lune valley that 'Almost all our boys go off to the manufacturing districts when they are 12 years of age or earlier.'[92] The Irish, too, frequently came over as single men, and married in England.[93]

It is unfortunately impossible to measure the exact proportion of inmigrants who came in as teenagers either alone or only with siblings or friends, rather than as members of nuclear families. This proportion must, however, have been considerable. Taking boys aged 15–19 for example, one way of making an estimate would be to take the proportion of migrants of that age not living with parents on census night. This figure is 28%.[94] However, this is an overestimate of the sole element among the migrants because some children would have left home or been orphaned after they had reached Preston with their families. 14% of Preston born boys of this age were not living with parents. If the inmigrant children had had otherwise similar life histories to the Preston born, then 14% of them would also have been orphaned or have left parents voluntarily. In fact 28% were living alone so one can assume that at least 14% had migrated to Preston on their own. However, some would also have been orphaned in the country (and thus been forced to migrate alone), so the true proportion migrating alone is more than 14%. Probably, in view of the parental mortality rates of the period, 20% is not much of an overestimate. For girls aged 15–19 the figure would have been higher since 22% of Preston born and 45% of migrants were not living with parents on census night. 30% seems a not unreasonable estimate for this group.

This flood of young single persons was joined by a substantial number of young married couples. Somewhere approaching 19% of those couples whose eldest surviving co-residing child was aged under 5 must have come into the town during the previous five years, since this eldest child had been born outside Preston.[95] For those with a similar child aged 5–9 the figure was 28%. There is some suggestion in Table 7, though the differences are not significant even at the 5% level, and from data in Table 6, that, as family size increased and men aged, the tendency to inmigrate decreased.[96] Those from the country would find it difficult to get employment as they grew older, and factory workers, too, found it more difficult to obtain employment in a new town for themselves and their families.[97] With more children in work, moreover, the families of older men were probably more likely to have had some meagre income coming in in all but the worst depression periods when there was anyway little work to be had elsewhere.

There is other evidence, too, to suggest that most of those who did migrate later in life did so because they had to. Particularly to be noted are the Irish,[98] distressed hand-loom weavers,[99] and also probably widows. All these families

TABLE 7 *Co-residing children aged 0–4 and 5–9 not born in Preston, by birth order: Preston sample, 1851*

	Age of child in 1851			
	0–4		5–9	
Birth order of child	Not born in Preston %	All Children *N* (100%)	Not born in Preston %	All children *N* (100%)
1st or 2nd	17	336	27	285
3rd or 4th	13	251	22	203
5th or later	11	181	20	135

were attracted by the possibility of obtaining well-paid employment, mainly for the children, in the mills.[100]

Brief mention will be made later of other minority groups of migrants, notably a small passage in both directions of old people. But the heavy migration of young married couples and of teenagers will be of greatest interest in subsequent analysis.

Population turnover within the towns

The population of Preston, and almost certainly of the other manufacturing towns of Lancashire, contained, then, a high proportion of inmigrants, many of whom were young, many of whom had recently arrived, and many of whom would, within a few years, move away again. Migration between communities, however, with all the potential social disorganisation that it involved, was not the only source of disorganisation due to changes of residence. Even when a migrant reached the town, he did not settle in one house and remain there for the rest of the time he spent in the town. The native Prestonians, too, moved house frequently. In the intensive survey area,[101] only 14% (45/311) of the males, and 19% (75/390) of the females who were aged 10 and over in 1861 (and had therefore been alive in 1851) were, in 1861, living in the same house as they had been in 1851. Because house numbers were not given in 1841, precise comparison with the previous decade is not possible, but it would appear that, if anything, perhaps due to the deeper and longer period of depression during the 1840s, an even higher rate of turnover had occurred in the decade 1841–51.

This finding was not unexpected, and ties in with what else is known about this topic for the nineteenth century. Chadwick,[102] indeed, found that in ten parishes in York over a third of the population moved within two years, while in London over a third had moved within six months.[103] Some of the movement, of course, reflects outmigration from the community and some undoubtedly involved movement to other widely dispersed parts of the town. Both these kinds of movement might be expected to have been inimical to the growth of local family and community solidarity.

However, much of the movement was only short distance.[104] No fewer than 12% of those men[105] aged 10 and over in 1861 who were not living in the same house as they had been in 1851 were traced in 1851 to houses within 50 yards of their 1861 homes. A further 6% were traced at 50–99 yards distance, and another 8% at 100–199 yards. Thus, in all, almost 40% were found in the same house or within 200 yards of the house that they had occupied ten years earlier. Moreover, from the additional number who were traced to houses within contiguous enumeration districts, but more than 200 yards away, it seems probable that another 10–20% were living within less than half a mile. And it is of course the case that any person living anywhere within the town would only be about half an hour's walk away from his old home.[106]

Conclusions

In this chapter I have shown something of the background against which the population under study had to make their family lives. Three issues seem to stand out as potentially important: poverty, rapid turnover of population, and uncertainty both of employment and of health. In terms of a simple 'industrialisation leads to disruption' thesis, kinship relationships would surely have become minimal in such a situation. But this is to overlook the controls that kinship could still exercise and the problems that this very disruption imposed. The more sophisticated approach outlined in Chapter 2 would rather suggest a kinship system weak on trust, strong on calculativeness, but exhibiting a strong element of dependence on short run and low cost kinship relationships, and one which only in some extreme cases on the three variables outlined above would involve no kinship relationships at all.

The remainder of Part 3 describes the patterns of kinship relationships which existed, and tries to explain why and how they were maintained.

5. Urban household and family structure

This chapter and the one which follows are mainly descriptive. Their purpose is to give an initial overview of the extent and strength of family and kinship ties in the Lancashire cotton towns. They will make little attempt to assess the functional importance of these ties. That must be left until the functions that relatives provided for actors have been reviewed, and the alternative sources of provision of these functions evaluated. The main indicators of kinship strength used in this chapter are co-residence, deliberate propinquity, contact situations, and sentiment. Each is inadequate taken alone but the overall effect is of considerable interest.

Residence patterns

I begin this chapter with an outline description of patterns of residence in Preston. The Preston sample contained 1,128 houses, occupied by 1,241 households and 6,741 resident persons. Of this number 93% lived in the same household as at least one other person known or presumed with considerable certainty to be related to them either by blood or by marriage.[1] A further 1% headed households and lived either alone or only with persons not related to them. The remaining 6% lived either as solo servants or solo lodgers and were not shown in the enumerators' books as related to any other member of the household. Some of these did in fact have siblings living with them in lodgings and some few lodgers were undoubtedly related to the family of the household head, though not recorded as such.[2] The total number of persons living with relatives of one kind or another was, therefore, probably of the order of 95% of the population. On this measure, then, this was predominantly a familistic society, but yet one where a not insignificant minority appear to have lived their lives away from day to day contact with family and kin. In other words, some alternatives to the family as a residential group did exist. These alternatives and their effects will be explored in more detail later.

Turning now to more detailed household structure and composition, I first present in Table 8 data on the structure of the families of the household heads. I do this in this form, rather than in terms of the structure of households as is commonly done in present day studies, because the large number of households containing odd lodgers or servants otherwise somewhat conceal the family structure pattern.

Table 8 suggests that at a point in time most people who were not solo servants or lodgers lived with their current nuclear family only.[3] Nevertheless, that as

TABLE 8 *Structure of the families of the household heads: Preston sample, 1851*

		Percentage of all such families
Head alone, or only with unrelated persons		4
Nuclear families		73
Childless married couples	10	
Married couples or widowed persons with unmarried children	63	
'Stem' families		10
Two or more lineally related ever married persons and their nuclear families if any	9	
Ditto plus other kin	1	
'Composite' families		13
Unmarried siblings only	1	
Other combinations of kin	12	
Other (one family where the head was absent and which contained four servants only)		0
All households: %		100
N		1,241

many as 23%[4] of households contained related persons other than members of the current nuclear family of the head in as fluid society as this is obviously of very considerable importance. Clearly kinship relationships at some level were being maintained in spite of the potentially disruptive effects outlined in Chapter 4. Indeed, in comparative perspective, kinship co-residence was frequent, for, by comparison, in England and Wales in 1966 only 9% of all households contained kinsmen beyond the nuclear family. In Swansea in 1960 well under 14% of households included co-residing kin among their members, and in Bethnal Green in 1955 the figure was under 10%.[5] Thus even in comparatively highly kinship oriented communities markedly fewer households are found to contain kin of this kind, and this would prove to be the case, though to a lesser degree, even if house sharing could be included.

There is, however, a further point of great interest, for the make-up of the households with kin in Preston was rather different from that found in Swansea and Bethnal Green. Whereas some 55% of families with kin in England and Wales in 1966, and well over 65% of those in Swansea in 1960 had a 'stem' family base, this was the case in only 47% of these families in Preston. This large number of families with 'other kin' makes the nineteenth century picture of particular interest in comparative perspective, and poses interesting problems of interpretation.[6]

Within the 277 'stem' and 'composite' family units were subsumed 84 additional (or secondary) nuclear families. In only 17 households,[7] however, were there two lineally related married persons both of whom had spouses alive and in residence; in the remaining 67 stem families, therefore, one spouse of at least one of the two couples was dead or temporarily or permanently absent. This too is markedly different from the present day picture. In addition, six of the composite families contained two married couples. The sample contained just one four-generation family.

Table 9 looks at a different aspect of the same kinship picture by giving a full listing of the relationships to the head of the household of all the kin present in these households. Undoubtedly the most noticeable feature of this table is the large number of siblings, nieces and nephews, and grandchildren with no co-residing parents who were to be found living in the Preston households. This finding reinforces the conclusions of Table 8 discussed above. Just who these children were will be discussed at some length in later chapters.

Next, I turn to a further consideration of non-family members – lodgers, servants, and visitors – who they were, and with whom and how they lived. Table 10 shows the proportion of homes of members of the different SEGs containing these non-family members. 6% of all households had at least one visitor. Many of these were staying in hotels, inns, or lodging houses around the town; the remainder were scattered widely through households headed by persons in all SEGs. Some of these were genuine visitors, come to the fair which had just ended,[8] or to visit friends or relatives, but some, at least, seem to have been recent arrivals summing up the employment situation before deciding

TABLE 9 *Relationship of co-residing kin to household head: Preston sample, 1851*

	Marital status of kin			All kin	
Kin relationship	B[a] (*N*)	M[a] (*N*)	W[a] (*N*)	(*N*)	%
Grandmother	–	–	1	1	0.2
Father or father-in-law	–	–	17	17	3.3
Mother or mother-in-law	–	–	29	29	5.7
Married son or son-in-law	–	40	17	57	11.1
Married daughter or daughter-in-law	–	40	23	63	12.3
Grandchild with parent[b]	68	2	–	70	13.7
Grandchild without parent	68	–	–	68	13.3
Sibling or sibling-in-law[c]	73	8	16	97	18.9
Niece/nephew with parent	22	–	–	22	4.3
Niece/nephew without parent[b]	70	6	1	77	15.0
Aunt or uncle	1	–	1	2	0.4
Cousin	5	–	–	5	1.0
Son-in-law's father	–	–	1	1	0.2
Son-in-law's brother	1	–	–	1	0.2
Wife's brother and wife	–	2	–	2	0.4
Greatnephew	1	–	–	1	0.2
All kin				513	100.2

[a] B = bachelor; M = married; W = widowed.
[b] Including spouses of married grandchildren and nieces/nephews.
[c] 26 of these were siblings of an unmarried head.

whether or not to settle in the town.[9] Beyond these comments there is little one can say and visitors are not subjected to any further analysis.

The 187 servants and apprentices in the sample (34 male, 153 female) made up 3% of the sample population, and were found in 10% of all households, predominantly, as might be expected, in the higher SEGs. They are not of particular significance here, except that service was an important way by which country girls adapted to urban life.[10]

TABLE 10 *Proportions of all households with co-residing lodgers, servants, and visitors, categorised by sex and marital status of heads, and by SEG of the head in the case of households headed by married men: Preston sample, 1851*

Head		Percentages of all households with:			All households
		Lodgers	Servants and apprentices	Visitors	(*N*)
Married man					
SEG I	Professional and managerial	5	59	9	22
II	Clerical	3	19	–	31
III	Trade	13	33	11	142
IV	Higher factory	26	2	4	141
V	Artisan	14	4	4	165
VI	Lower factory	29	1	5	79
VII	Labourer	24	1	6	157
VIII	Hand-loom weaver	38	–	–	55
IX	Unclassified	26	2	8	127
X	Not employed	6	2	–	17
All SEGs		22	9	6	936
Other men		18	22	4	83
Women		33	8	4	221
Servants only		–	(100)	–	1
All households		23	10	6	1,241

776 persons (419 males, 357 females) were classified by the enumerators as lodgers or boarders.[11] Lodgers (including families of lodgers) made up no less than 12% of the sample, and were present in 23% of the households,[12] scattered widely through the working class section of the population. For widows, taking in lodgers was an important source of income. There is some suggestion that the poorer SEGs may have been rather more likely to take in lodgers, but this is by no means clear-cut. Indeed as I shall show later, the provision of lodgings was one important way by which members of all SEGs helped migrants to adapt to urban-industrial life. There is also some suggestion from the intensive survey data that where a family left the town children who did not go with them were often lodged with neighbours. Many lodgers were obviously friends of the landlord. Some were 'passed on' from one household to that of a relative when the

original landlord's family moved. Couples took in lodgers at all stages of the life-cycle.

Lodgers are thus a sociologically significant element in the population, because their relationship to their landlord was more or less a non-familistic one and thus an alternative (and possibly a threat) to the strength of family and kinship bonds. The reasons for the presence of so many lodgers are discussed below and their effects assessed in later chapters.

About half (48%) of all lodgers were unmarried. The rest were almost equally divided between married couples and their children (if any) and widowed persons and their children (if any). Half of all single male lodgers and three-fifths of single female lodgers were aged 15–24. Of the couples 64% of the husbands were under 35, over half were childless and over half of the remainder had only one child. In all among the lodgers there were another 126 nuclear families[13] (9% of all nuclear families).

Contemporaries were particularly concerned about the large lodging houses, which they saw as housing, in the main, vagrants, prostitutes, and thieves, as hotbeds of promiscuity and as bastions of antifamilistic and other antisocial values.[14] However, in Preston at least, these large lodging houses were in a definite minority, and the more respectable sections of the working class seem to have lodged, if at all, with a family or a widow, as individuals or as one of a small group. Thus 41% of all households which had lodgers had only one, and a further 28% two. Only 4% had more than six lodgers, and only 1% twelve or more. On the other hand this still meant that 21% of all lodgers lived in a house with more than six others, and 11% (or one in nine) in a house with twelve or more. These larger lodging houses may not have been many in number but they contained more than 2% of the population. Their potential influence cannot be completely ignored.

The following passage describes what was probably the typical living arrangements, at least as far as single lodgers were concerned: 'The actual cost in rent to a single girl living with a family, sharing their bedroom, and benefiting from their fire and lights, is from 9*d*., to 1*s*. 3*d*., a week. For a single unfurnished room in a cottage 1*s*. to 1*s*. 6*d*., would be paid.'[15] (This sum was said to include coals and candles. Washing materials and sundries were provided for another few pence). In addition 'single women ordinarily pay a sum per week for cooking of their food'.[16] The Preston enumerator referred to above[17] recorded that 'In all the district there are only seven Lodgers who take a Separate Eating-room. In all other cases the Lodgers eat at the same Table, but provide their own food, paying a Rent of from one shilling to 2*s*. 6*d*., per week for an adult.'[18] Single lodgers, indeed, were probably often treated as one of the family.[19] Nuclear families probably most usually had a separate room to themselves, but cooking was still often done by the landlady.[20] Occasionally several families lived in a house, each with a room of their own.[21] But in general, given the miserable conditions prevailing in many houses, lodging must often have been almost as comfortable, or even more comfortable, than living at home. And it was not exorbitantly expensive.

So far I have discussed only household composition. However, not all households occupied a whole house, and so sharing a house with another household may be seen in some ways as an alternative to living in lodgings or sharing with kin. In all 23% of households shared a house with one, or very occasionally more than one, other household. Unfortunately the schedules do not normally give information about the relationship, if any, between heads of different households living in the same house, but 21 households (2%) shared a house with another household whose head bore the same surname; most of these were undoubtedly relations. If affines, not traceable by this method, could be included, one might hazard that about 20% of shared houses were shared by households who were in some way related.

I turn next to a more detailed consideration of the residence patterns of certain specific groups in the population. In many ways this gives a much clearer picture of the residential significance of kinship, service, lodging, or sharing, than do the aggregate figures outlined so far.

Taking married couples first, there were for them a number of possible patterns of residence. They might head a household of their own, occupying either a whole house or only part of a house, and, in either case, they might take lodgers or kin into their own households. Or they might live in someone else's household; in this case the head might be a kinsman, or he might simply be a landlord letting them lodgings. The same options, with the additional possibility of becoming a domestic servant, were open to single and widowed persons. The extent to which married couples chose these different options at different periods in the life-cycle is shown in Table 11.

87% of all married couples headed their own households, 72% in houses of which they were the sole occupiers. Lodging and living with kin were minority patterns. On the other hand, over two out of every five couples followed one or other of these options in the period immediately after marriage, though most only for a few years.[22] Thus, while a home of one's own was normal, other arrangements were important for a large proportion (possibly at some time the majority), particularly in the early days of married life. Moreover, later in the life-cycle, some couples again gave up living in a household of their own and went and lived with others.[23]

In the discussion that follows it is convenient to break down the analysis into three parts, and ask, first, what influenced whether or not a couple headed their own household, second, if they did, what determined whether or not they had a

TABLE 11 *Residence patterns of married couples, by life-cycle stage:*[a] *Preston sample, 1851*

	Head of own household			Not head of own household			All married couples	
LCS	Occupying a whole house %	Sharing a house %	All %	Living as lodgers %	Living as kin %	All %	%	*N*
1	44	13	57	28	15	43	100	159
2	56	20	76	14	10	24	100	59
3	76	14	91	5	4	9	100	388
4	85	13	98	1	–	1	99	122
5	82	16	98	1	0	1	99	234
6	73	23	96	4	1	5	101	106
All	72	15	87	8	5	13	100	1,068

[a] For the definitions of life-cycle stages, see note 46 to Chapter 4 (p. 202 below).

house to themselves, and third, what influenced their choice of residence if they did not head a household.

Variations in behaviour pattern over the life-cycle are the result of the operation of a number of other variables correlated with life-cycle stages. One, in particular, seems important here, family size, though occupational and to some extent normative constraints were also at work.

Table 12 suggests the crucial importance of family size in determining whether or not a couple headed a household of their own. Where rents and fuel costs were high and housing in short supply (as they most certainly were in the Lancashire towns), there were undoubted advantages for the newly married, the old, and others with small families, in saving money by joining other households, regardless of other advantages which might accrue from this kind of

TABLE 12 *Residence patterns of married couples, by number of co-residing children: Preston sample, 1851*

	Number of children			
	None %	1 %	2–3 %	4 or more %
Family occupies:				
whole house	53	71	75	85
part of house	16	16	17	12
Family lives:				
in lodgings	20	9	4	2
with kin	11	4	4	1
All: %	100	100	100	100
N	235	207	314	308

sharing. Moreover, while family size was small, the inconvenience which might result from crowding into the two-storied terraced houses, or from taking an odd room in a larger house, would not have been unbearable.

Table 13 suggests that family size was also important for widowed persons.[24] It may also be noted at this point that many more widows than widowers headed their own households (often, as I showed above, partially supporting themselves by taking in lodgers), and that many fewer lived in lodgings.[25]

TABLE 13 *Residence patterns of widows and widowers, by number of co-residing children: Preston sample, 1851*

	Number of children			
	None %	1 %	2–3 %	4 or more %
Widowers:				
own household	13	43	73	100
lodgers	48	40	20	–
with kin	36	17	7	–
in service	3	–	–	–
All: %	100	100	100	100
N	90	30	30	10
Widows:				
own household	27	61	85	100
lodgers	19	20	3	–
with kin	44	20	11	–
in service	10	–	–	–
All: %	100	101	99	100
N	113	66	93	39

Table 12 showed, however, that family size but little influenced whether a couple who headed a household shared a house or had a whole house to themselves, nor was there any great difference in family size between those living as lodgers and those living with kin. For those who headed a household, the occupation of the husband seems above all to have determined how they lived. The size of one's income, which for many was perilously low as the last chapter showed, was a major determinant of whether or not one could afford the rent of a whole house. Occupation was also for the middle class associated with norms prescribing 'proper' patterns of residence, and presumably aimed at ensuring that girls lived after their marriage at a standard of living not far removed from that in which they had grown up.[26] These norms appear to have prescribed as necessary in the Preston context not merely a household of one's own but a whole house as well. For the trade group, a home of one's own was almost an essential prerequisite to one's business life.

Table 14 shows firstly that almost all of those in the professional, white collar, and trade groups did head a household of their own, while a considerable proportion of all working class groups, regardless of income level, lived with kin or in lodgings while their families were small. Secondly, Table 14 shows that the middle class groups usually also had their houses to themselves. Among the working class on the other hand income was important here and as the income of the head of the household fell, so couples, although heading households of their own, were more and more likely to be forced to save rent by sharing a house.[27]

I noted above that family size did not influence whether those *not* heading their own households lived as lodgers or instead lived with kin. A relationship

TABLE 14 *Residence patterns of married couples categorised by SEG of husband, by number of co-residing children: Preston sample, 1851*

	Number of children				
	None %	1 %	2–3 %	4 or more %	All %
White collar and trade:					
own household	98	100	100	100	99
(of this group sharing)	(2)	(6)	(4)	(10)	(6)
lodgers	2	–	–	–	1
with kin	–	–	–	–	–
All: %	100	100	100	100	100
N	42	32	53	70	197
Higher factory and artisan:					
own household	61	88	93	97	86
(of this group sharing)	(21)	(18)	(13)	(9)	(14)
lodgers	18	4	3	2	7
with kin	21	8	4	1	7
All: %	100	100	100	100	100
N	85	79	105	117	386
Lower factory, labourer, and hand-loom weaver:					
own household	63	80	89	97	83
(of this group sharing)	(36)	(20)	(30)	(18)	(24)
lodgers	27	17	6	2	12
with kin	10	3	5	1	5
All: %	100	100	100	100	100
N	71	71	113	91	346
Unclassified and not employed:					
own household	65	71	93	97	83
(of this group sharing)	(42)	(35)	(21)	(23)	(37)
lodgers	27	14	2	3	12
with kin	8	14	5	–	5
All: %	100	99	100	100	100
N	37	28	41	31	137

does emerge, however, if the proportions lodging and living with kin are cross-tabulated with the income level of the head. While 50% of those of the better paid section of the proletariat (SEGs IV and V) who did not head a household lived with kin, only 27% of the worse paid (SEGs VI–VIII) did so.[28] In fact, this relationship is mainly an artifact. Migrants were more likely to go into lower paid occupations, and, it would appear from Table 15, were also much less likely to live with kin, presumably, in part at least, because they were less likely to have kin in the town with whom to live. In this sense then, lodging was partly anyway a substitute for absent kin; as I shall show in Chapter 8, many of the migrant couples were lodging with co-villagers already known to them. A fuller table not reproduced here revealed that when migration was controlled, the relationship by occupation completely disappeared.

TABLE 15 *Proportions of married couples, in LCSs 2–5 and not heading their own households, who lived in lodgings and with kin, by migration pattern: Preston sample, 1851*

	Migration pattern		
Married couples	Adult migrants[29] %	Intermediate %	Non-migrants %
Living in lodgings	88	52	42
Living with kin	13	48	58
All: %	101	100	100
N	16	31	12

The relationship between migration and residence pattern is significant $p < 0.02$ (chi^2 at 2 d.f. = 7.579).

Couples in life-cycle stage 1 who had no children could not, of course, be included in Table 15.[30] If, however, the residence patterns of those couples in this LCS with one or other spouse not born in Preston are compared with couples where the same spouse was not a migrant, a similar relationship appears. 44% of couples whose husband both did not head a household and had been born in Preston were living with kin, compared with 31% where he had at some point in his life inmigrated.[31] For wives, the comparable figures are 53% and 29%.[32]

It is, of course, worth asking why so many non-migrant couples lived in lodgings rather than with kin.[33] Part of the answer is that some, given the high mortality rates, had no kin with whom to live.[34] Others, given the high birth rates, had no kin with space available for them. Still others had no suitable kin in Preston because all their kin had migrated to other towns. Nevertheless, just as some (though not very many) adolescents were living in lodgings to get away from relatives,[35] so some (and again it would seem not very many) young adults were undoubtedly doing so and doing so as the result of a deliberate decision to terminate most relationships with kin. The reasons for the adoption of this attitude and behaviour I explore further in Chapter 11.

Summarising, then, at least half of all couples lived with kin or in lodgings for the first few years after marriage, unless they were middle class. Which of these alternatives of living with kin or in lodgings they chose seems partly to have been dependent on whether or not they were migrants, and, therefore, presumably, simply on whether or not they had kin alive in Preston with whom to live. Some, however, seem to have deliberately decided, for one reason or another, not to live with kin. Later in the life-cycle, as the size of their families increased, most couples set up households of their own. Only the better off among the working class, however, could afford to take a whole house to themselves. Probably about one in five of the sharers shared a house with kin.

Young unmarried men and women are another group on which much attention will be focused later. For this group, living with parents, with kin, in lodgings, or in service, were all possible patterns of residence. This section seeks information on the role of age and of migration as factors influencing the pattern chosen, and the relevant data are given in Table 16.

Most children, as might be expected, lived with one or both parents as part of a nuclear family. There may have been disadvantages in such a close relationship,[36] but for most children and young persons the forces pushing them towards residence with their nuclear families outweighed the disadvantages. I shall argue below, moreover, that a large proportion of those not living with parents had no parents in Preston with whom they could live. Some were orphans; the parents of some had outmigrated; many were inmigrants who had left their parents behind in the villages or towns of their birth.

It was to be expected that migrants would be significantly less likely to be living with parents[37] and also to be living with kin,[38] since fewer of them would have had kin in Preston. Table 16 shows this indeed to have been the case. Many of those who were living with kin, moreover, may have lived in Preston for most of their lives, having come in with their parents and siblings many years earlier. Some, however, as I shall show in Chapter 10, were recent inmigrants taken in by kin, given a home in the town, and helped to find a job and generally to adapt to urban life. The rest of the migrants went into lodgings or into service, the latter being particularly preferred by girls (for whom there were of course many more opportunities).[39]

Some 10% of the 15–19 age group, however, and about a quarter of the 20–24 group, lived in lodgings, and this pattern was favoured by almost equal proportions of migrants and non-migrants.[40] These are obviously significant proportions. The factors which might lead children deliberately to leave home and go into lodgings, something which much concerned contemporaries, will be discussed in some detail in Chapter 9. It should be noted here, however, that mortality of parents, a factor seldom discussed by contemporaries when referring

TABLE 16 *Residence patterns of young persons aged 10–34 categorised by age and migrancy: Preston sample, 1851*

	Of all young persons: living with parents %	All young persons N(100%)	Of all young persons not living with parents, living: in lodgings %	with kin %	in service or apprenticeship %	All not with parents %	N
Boys							
Aged 10–14							
Migrant	88	139	44	44	13	101	16
Non-migrant	94	253	38	56	6	100	16
All	92	392	41	50	9	100	32
Aged 15–19							
Migrant	72	174	51	29	20	100	49
Non-migrant	86	202	41	52	7	100	29
All	79	376	47	37	15	99	78
Aged 20–24							
Migrant	55	134	78	13	8	99	60
Non-migrant	80	83	71	29	–	100	17
All	65	217	77	17	6	100	77
Aged 25–34							
Migrant	48	110	72	16	12	100	57
Non-migrant	39	23	86	7	7	100	14
All	47	133	75	14	11	100	71
Girls							
Aged 10–14							
Migrant	77	119	19	59	22	100	27
Non-migrant	89	230	12	69	19	100	26
All	86	349	15	64	21	100	53
Aged 15–19							
Migrant	55	185	37	20	42	99	83
Non-migrant	78	202	38	36	27	101	45
All	67	387	38	26	36	100	128
Aged 20–24							
Migrant	55	155	46	11	43	100	70
Non-migrant	73	106	52	24	24	100	29
All	62	261	47	15	37	99	99
Aged 25–34							
Migrant	45	131	26	28	46	100	72
Non-migrant	67	63	71	10	19	100	21
All	52	194	37	24	40	101	93

to the 'problem' of the lodging-houses, must have been the main reason why many teenagers went into lodgings or to live with kin. Indeed, if the mortality figures calculated from the survival tables are at all reliable (and both these and the sample figures are of course subject to some margin of error), it would seem that as many as 10% of the 15–19 age group, and 19% of the 20–24 group had neither parent alive.[41] If this was the case then the vast majority of non-migrant children who had parents alive were in fact living with them. A few, of course, were living with a stepparent only, their widowed parent having remarried and later been survived by the second spouse. It is also conceivable that orphans were more likely to migrate away from Preston, having fewer kin bonds to keep them there; it also seems likely that their own mortality would be above average. For reasons to be discussed in Chapter 9, migrants may also have been more likely to leave home in this way than non-migrants. Nevertheless, these figures do suggest very strongly that those who deliberately left home were a minority. Of those non-migrants not living with parents, half the men and a third of the women in the 15–19 age group, for example, lived with kin, which suggests that a large proportion of those who had kin but no parents in the town probably chose to live with kin. Certainly the extent of family disruption on this score can be much exaggerated. If lodgings were a threat to family life they were obviously more a threat because of their potential than because many people actually left home to live in them. This topic is taken up further in Chapter 9.

Finally in this section on residence patterns, one or two other figures may be given to indicate the importance of nuclear family and of kin in this sphere, and these do suggest that kin were very important indeed to those in real need. I noted earlier that large numbers of widowed persons lived with kin, with the kin as the heads of the households. Table 17 shows the proportions living with kin if the proportion who had taken kin into their own households are included, and suggests that kin were of considerable assistance for this group, particularly for the childless,[42] and for childless widows above all.[43] That half of all childless widowed persons found a home with kin is obviously of some significance. Kin were, however, even more important for older widowed persons. Of those aged 65 and over, no fewer than 66% of non-institutionalised widowers and 64% of widows had one or more kinsmen in the same household, and only 17% of aged widowers and 14% of aged widows had no known related person living in the same household.

TABLE 17 *Proportion of widowers and widows having kin in the same household as themselves: Preston sample, 1851*

	Widowed persons with co-residing children		Widowed persons without children		
	Living with kin %	All N(100%)	Living with kin %	All N(100%)	All with kin %
Widowers	29	70	42	90	36
Widows	31	198	57	113	40
All widowed	30	268	50	203	39

I have just noted that many more widows than widowers, particularly if they had no co-residing children, were likely to be sharing with kin. Most modern surveys find a tendency towards matrilaterality in relationships with kin.[44] In the Preston sample the data were as follows: 57% of all those married children who lived with parents lived with the wife's parents; 66% of all widowed mothers who lived with married children lived with a married daughter though 52% of widowed fathers in this situation lived with a married son;[45] 65% of those girls who lived with a married sibling lived with a married sister though 45% of boys in this situation lived with married brothers.[46]

The consistency of the trend toward matrilaterality suggests the importance of women in the maintenance of the kinship system (though only the preferential attachment of widowed parents to married daughters is actually statistically significant even at the 5% level). More interesting in some ways than the overall trend is a suggestion that men were more attached to male relatives (49% of all cases) and women to female relatives (66% of all cases). Possible reasons for such a trend, the definite existence of which would only be confirmed by a larger sample, will be suggested in Chapter 11.

In sum, then, nuclear family-based residence was the normal pattern for the Preston population taken as a whole, but a very large proportion of people in certain family statuses occupied some non-familial residential status. For the young married couple and for widowed persons (particularly the older widowed persons), kin-based residence was important. For the young married couple and for young single men and women, particularly if they were migrants, lodging was a frequent pattern. Sometimes lodgings seem to have been merely a substitute for living with kin where a person had no kin with whom he could live. Sometimes, though probably much less often, as later chapters will show, lodgings were more disruptive, posing a viably competing alternative to family and kin, an alternative which weakened family and kinship relationships. Always lodgings were in the background, as a possible escape route should family obligations become too overbearing.

This completes for the present the discussion of co-residence patterns; the next section presents the limited evidence available on who lived not *with* whom, but *near* whom.

Propinquity

Young and Willmott write: 'The couples who choose to live with parents are the exceptions. Most people do not want to live with them, they want to live near them.'[47] This comment seems equally applicable to mid-nineteenth century Preston. Kinship does not stop at the front door. There are few functions which can be performed by a co-residing kinsman which he cannot perform equally well if he instead lives next door, or even up the street. Patterns of co-residence are easy to measure. Too much emphasis on them, however, may lead to serious distortions in the analysis of family structure.[48] Co-residence of married children with parents may, indeed, turn out to be related above all to the balance between supply and demand for housing suitable for young married couples,[49] except where other factors, such as a family business or family farm, make it particularly advantageous. This section presents what limited data are available on propinquity of residence of related persons.

Stella Davies, writing about Manchester towards the end of the nineteenth century, writes that it 'was felt to be desirable that relatives should live near one another'.[50] A glance at any enumerator's book for Preston suggests the plausibility of this proposition, since one soon finds streets where several families have the same surname.

It was obviously necessary, however, to attempt to assess statistically the extent of this propinquity, and some very imperfect data were obtained from the intensive survey life histories which at least suggest the dimensions of the situation.[51]

From among the 1,700 households examined in the intensive survey it was possible to identify positively 80 as containing someone definitely related to a person traced in another household. Between them these provided 52 paired relationships for analysis. Just over half of these were married children–parent relationships (24 married sons, 3 married daughters),[52] the rest mainly siblings. Table 18 shows the distance between the homes of the members of these pairs.

Before the full import of these figures can be seen, however, it is necessary to estimate the proportion of relatives who have been traced. For the 'other related persons' group this is almost impossible, but for married sons some estimate can be made. It is known that 127 sons aged 5 and over disappeared in intercensal periods from co-residing families which could be traced in at least two successive censuses. I estimated from my mortality table that, if these sons were a representative sample of the population as a whole, given their age distribution, 116 would have been alive at the next census. On the basis of information about the proportion of the population married in any age group a rough estimate can be made of the proportions of the population unmarried at one census who have married by the next.[53] On the basis of these very rough assumptions it would appear that 50, and more certainly, under 55, of these sons who had left home in the intercensal period would have been alive and married at the later census. In 1851 the town of Preston contained about 11,000 houses. The area searched contained 1,703 houses in 1851, about 16% of the houses in the town. On this basis, if these surviving married sons had been scattered randomly over the town,[54] and even if, as seems very improbable, none had left the town at all, one would have expected to find only between 7 and 9 in the area searched. In fact, at least 9 of these married sons were traced to houses within 100 yards of their

TABLE 18 *Distance between residences of 52 traced pairs of kin: Preston intensive study, 1841, 1851, 1861*

Distance between residences	Married child/parent relationships (*N*)	%	Other related persons (*N*)	%	All (*N*)	%
Contiguous[a]	2	15	2	12	4[c]	13
0–24 yds	2		1		3	
25–49 yds	1	26	2	24	3	25
50–99 yds	6		4		10	
100–199 yds	4	44	7	52	11	48
200–399 yds[b]	8		6		14	
400 yds and over[b]	4	15	3	12	7	13
All	27	100	25	100	52	99

[a] Next door, opposite, or back to back. All other measurements are in a straight line.
[b] The search area being based on contiguous enumeration districts, not all the houses in the area over 200 yards were searched. Similarly where persons were living outside the base area, and near to the boundary of the search area, some few even within 200 yards may have been omitted. The figures in this table should, therefore, be seen as minima.
[c] After discontinuities in the numbering have been taken into account, the chances of any pair of names coming up in these positions at random is rather less than 1 in 425 (1,700, the number of houses in the area, divided by 4, the number of possible positions).

parents, and 22, or 2½ to 3 times the randomly predicted number, were found in the area searched. Many at least were not moving far on marriage.

Moreover, even within the searched area, there was a noticeable tendency for related persons to congregate near together rather than to be scattered over the whole area, even though, with one or two minor exceptions, the area was apparently remarkably homogeneous in its types of housing. This clustering tendency is most obvious if the actual distribution of related persons over the area is compared with a population randomly distributed over the same area. For this calculation all houses in the searched area were allocated a number and each half of each paired relationship was randomly plotted on a map with the aid of a table of random numbers, no more sophisticated technique being possible because the streets were not laid out on the ground in any regular pattern, so that distances between successively numbered houses varied considerably. Since at least one out of a high proportion of the pairs was living in the base area, which was in the centre of the searched area, to have plotted both houses entirely at random would have biased the results in favour of the hypothesis. To avoid this, the first number selected was always taken from a universe restricted to the enumeration district in which one of the actual residences had been located. Where one of the pair came from the base area, this enumeration district was always used for this purpose; otherwise, selection was made at random. To decrease the possibility of chance random fluctuations affecting the results, the whole set of data was worked twice. The results are shown in Table 19. The

TABLE 19 *Comparison of actual and expected distances between residences of related pairs of kin: Preston intensive study, 1841, 1851, 1861*

	Actual distribution		Expected distribution	
Distance between residences	%	Cumulative %	%	Cumulative %
Contiguous[a]	8	8	–	–
0–24 yds	5	13	2	2
25–49 yds	6	19	2	4
50–99 yds	19	38	7	11
100–199 yds	21	59	16	27
200–399 yds	27	86	38	65
400 yds and over	13	99	35	100
All: %	99	99	100	100
N	52	52	104	104

[a] See note *a* to Table 18, p. 58 above.

difference between expected and actual data appears very marked,[55] the medians being about 320 and 170 yards respectively.

There are regrettably few cases where the same pair of related families was traceable in two successive censuses, so it was not possible to trace movements by kin over time in any detail. Some interesting examples were, however, found. Thus, in 1841 James Taylor and family lived in a house in Chetham Street, while his brother Thomas (the relationship is traceable through kin co-residing in their households) lived with his family about 200 yards away in Dock Street. By 1851, however, Thomas had moved to Chetham Street as well, and lived at 21, while James and family were at 17. Another case is also of interest. In 1851 Robert Hunter and family lived with Robert's wife's parents at 8, Lower Pitt Street. By 1861 they had moved out, to a home of their own, but only to next door, where they shared a house with one of Robert's wife's brothers, John; he, not traceable in 1851, had returned with his family by 1861 to live in the adjacent house to his now widowed mother and his unmarried siblings. A number of other similar cases also appear.[56]

It seems evident, therefore, that some related persons did make positive efforts to live near one another, and to a remarkable extent succeeded. One caution is, however, in order. Some bias in favour of residence near to parents and to the home in which one was brought up would be expected even if attachments were minimal. Sons would seek homes near their work and friends, and also would be more likely to know about housing vacancies in the local area. It is difficult to see how any unbiased data could be found on this topic. It is true that the distance from their old homes of the residences of traced married sons whose parents had disappeared from the area was only marginally greater than that of those whose parents were not traceable. This increases the caution with which one approaches the propinquity figures, but, in fact, shows little, because many at least of these households would have been established before the parents died or moved away, so that attachment to kin could still have been an important factor determining the original location of the child's home.

So far, only the more stable families, those where several sets of related persons remained in the one-sixth of the town surveyed for ten or more years have been examined. This degree of stability, as I noted in Chapter 4, was by no means universal. People regularly moved around and some left the town. Many new inmigrants came in from the country over the twenty-year period from 1841 to 1861, and some people moved in from other areas of Preston. Is it possible to say anything about the role of kinship in influencing the place where these groups set up their homes?

It is usually impossible to identify positively relationships between neighbours who are only found in one census, or whose families did not split up in an intercensal period. Nevertheless, there is some evidence that very many of these families too did make strenuous efforts to live near to persons whom they knew, many of whom were undoubtedly kin. As an example, it may be noted that in the base area in 1851 there were six households (3.4% of all households) headed by persons named Eastham, and two in 1841 and three in 1861. Of the 1851 Easthams, only two families are known to have been related. On the other hand, five of these families, including the pair known to be related, had head, wife, or child born in Penwortham. In the search area as a whole, a further five families named Eastham, with a similar link to Penwortham were found. Similarly, in 1861, no fewer than five families of Wignalls, whose head had been born in Longton, were found in the western half of the search area alone. Neither of these surnames was exceptionally common in the villages in question.[57]

Individual examples of cases where people who were probably related lived in close proximity are legion. For example, in 1851 William and Fanny Pilkington, almost certainly newly wed, lodged next door to James Pilkington and family. James and all his elder children had been born in Rufford; so had William. Again, in 1851 John Clarkson, a 27-year-old linen spinner, and his family lived at 3, Back Croft Street. In 1861 they lived at 4, Birk Street, and John was now a flax mill overlooker. At 3, Birk Street in both years lived Robert Clarkson and family. Robert also was a linen spinners' overlooker, and, like Thomas, had been born in Kirkham, though while John had come to Preston before 1845 (as revealed by the birthplaces of his children), Robert had not come until 1847 at the earliest. These two pairs, and many others not cited, look extraordinarily like siblings.

In all, starting from the base area, 137 such pairs of relationships were identified, by the criteria of same surname and same birthplace used in the above examples. The criterion 'same birthplace' was restricted so as to exclude the

TABLE 20 *Comparison of actual and expected distances between residences of pairs of individuals or families with the same surname and birthplaces: Preston intensive study, 1851 and 1861*

	Actual distance		Expected distance	
Distance between residences	%	Cumulative %	%	Cumulative %
Contiguous[a]	2	2	–	–
0–24 yds	2	4	2	2
25–49 yds	5	9	2	4
50–99 yds	8	17	6	10
100–199 yds	20	37	19	29
200–399 yds	38	75	32	61
400 yds and over	26	101	39	100
All: %	101	101	100	100
N	137	137	137	137

[a] See note *a* to Table 18, p. 58, above.

Irish born and the Preston born, of whom there were far too many to make this a stringent enough test. The distances between the actual residences of members of these 137 pairs, and expected distances as calculated by the method described above, are given in Table 20. The overall results are suggestive, the medians being about 260 and about 360 yards.[58] Some, at least, of these people were related, did know one another, and did make deliberate efforts to live near one another.

It is, however, important to get the facts discussed in this section in proper perspective. Even calculating by households, and even if all the pairs covered by Table 20 were, in fact, really related, the data described here have only covered about 23% of the 1851, and 28% of the 1861 base area households. This figure is, of course, by no means a maximal one, because the very method of data collection means that some groups will be under-represented. The limitation of the 'possible relative' category to English born migrants leaves out the potentially larger number of Preston and Irish born related households, and equally significantly, the Preston born married children of inmigrant parents. It also excludes all other families where siblings were, for any reason, born in different communities. If a method more sensitive to affinal relationships had been used, this too would have increased greatly the proportion of the population of the enumeration district with a traced kinship relationship.

In sum, therefore, many, perhaps even a majority, of people did deliberately live near one or more kinsmen and many others probably tried to. This strongly suggests kinship was providing significant functions for them. However, some people undoubtedly had disagreements with kin and moved away because they had no wish to have relationships with them, while a substantial minority had no relatives living in the town with whom to interact. Kin, then, can never have provided for all the main solutions to the problems set by urban-industrial life. Nevertheless, I shall argue in later chapters that, however imperfect, they were still the most important source of assistance that there was for the mass of the population. To this I shall largely attribute the kinship bonds I have here described.

Other contacts with kin

It is obvious from the previous analysis that kinship was an important factor influencing residence patterns, both within the same house and within the local community. I have suggested that, since kin apparently made *positive* efforts to live near one another, interaction between them must have been fairly important; it was also probably frequent. This section discusses briefly some of the specific evidence on the existence and frequency of this interaction with kin.

It must of course be stressed that just because interaction with kin occurred it is no necessary indication that kinship was important.[59] The real test, which is quite impossible in any precise way in historical work, would be to examine the extent to which kinship was given preference over other relational contacts (and the reasons for this preference), and the extent to which contacts with kin fulfilled functions which were not adequately met if kin did not provide them. This section seeks only to describe kinship contacts, and suggest their frequency. An attempt to assess their relative significance compared with other primary and secondary contacts must wait until Chapters 10 and 11.

There is, then, no one-to-one relationship between contact rates and family cohesion. The positive efforts made by the Victorian Lancashire working class to maintain relationships with kin, as suggested by the earlier sections of this chapter and as supported by discussion at various points later, do suggest, however, that relationships with family and kin were seen as important and functional.

There is a mass of cases in the literature where people are noted as interacting with and engaging in activities in company and co-operation with relatives, both with their current nuclear family and with wider kin.[60] Among types of interaction noted[61] are shared leisure activities (trips to the beer shop or to the country, or just a chat over tea[62]), visiting and dropping in,[63] at holiday times outings and family gatherings,[64] parties for birthdays and weddings and mothers' day.[65] Families attended funerals and church and night school together.[66] They are recorded as begging together and as criminals together,[67] and as minding each others' children and helping in sickness and unemployment and death and old age and every other crisis and contingency.[68] Knowledge seems often to have been widespread about relationships and where relatives lived or were last heard of as living, and about their jobs and the sizes of their families.[69]

Some people at least, then, obviously had frequent relationships with kin. There is, however, no way of measuring for the population as a whole the extent of these contacts or their importance in comparison with relationships with neighbours, workmates, friends, and so on. Content analysis would, in theory, allow some quantitative estimates to be made, if one could trace enough documents describing in any detail relational patterns. Personal diaries, the most obvious source, are, however, very rare for the classes of person under consideration here and, moreover, tend usually to concentrate on political or economic matters, rather than more mundane interpersonal relationships.

One useful diary did turn up in the literature searches, however, that of John Ward, a Clitheroe weaver, which covers part of the period 1860–4.[70] Ward had no kin living nearby except a daughter who married in 1862, lived with him for a while but moved out for some unknown reason during the Cotton Famine. The only primary relationships noted in the diary are occasional letters to and from two married brothers, occasional visits to and from one of these brothers who lived in Preston, and one set of friends in Accrington. He also on three occasions notes that he spent part of an evening drinking with some workmates, though it is highly probable that not all such activities were recorded. Recorded interaction with his siblings was very erratic. Twice his brother Dan moved without either informing him or, for some time, letting him know his new address.[71] All forms of interaction with Dan are recorded on only nine occasions in four years. With his other brother recorded interaction is even more infrequent. He comments at one point that he has had no letter for eighteen months.[72]

Ward's contact with his kin was, then, very irregular. On the other hand, given the hours that were worked and the means of transport available, occasional contact is probably all that could normally have been expected between kin living ten or more miles apart. More interesting, in many ways, is the fact that Ward does seem to have felt that, when in difficulties, he could rely on his brother for sympathy and possibly for assistance. During the time he was unemployed 'I went twice to Preston to see my brother Daniel, *but* him and his family were no better off than myself, having nothing better than Surat to work at'.[73] Similarly, visits to or from his sibling Dan were obviously somewhat special occasions, involving tourist trips to the local sights, a certain amount of festivity[74] and 'a long talk about old times'.[75] The general atmosphere is of a friendly relationship, from which definite satisfactions were being obtained, in particular in the form of a possible fall-back in time of need.

The only source located which made possible any detailed content analysis was Gaulter's report of his investigations into the 1832 cholera epidemic among the Manchester working class.[76] Gaulter was concerned to establish whether or not cholera was primarily spread by contagion. To this end he analysed and described in some limited detail for each of the first 200 cases notified, all contacts with other victims of the disease or their families which occurred in the period immediately before the onset of symptoms. These data were subjected to a content analysis. In all, interactions involving 37 non-co-residing dyads can be traced from Gaulter's data, some occurring several times. 9 of these are with kin, and 28 with neighbours of various kinds. Gaulter also describes 11 dyadic interactions between fellow lodgers, or lodgers and their landlords, and 5 between co-residing kin. More interesting, however, is a consideration of the content of the interaction. This was divided into classes as given in Table 21.

TABLE 21 *Content analysis of the types of contact of cholera victims with kin, neighbours, and fellow lodgers. Data from Gaulter (1833). Listing in priority order*

		Contact with:	
Type of contact	Kin[a]	neighbours	fellow-lodgers
Assistance	8	6	6
Visited sick	–	11	1
Conversed with or transitory	1	7	4
Trade (including child-nursing)	–	4	–
All contacts	9	28	11

[a] Co-residing kin are excluded.

Most of the kin contacts, then, involved positive assistance. 'The day before her seizure she had assisted in washing the dead body of E. Faulkner (her father).'[77] 'Mother to Barlow, she put her into the sling, washed her sheets, and went to the dead house to take off her ring.'[78] Some of the neighbours provided similar kinds of assistance.[79] Thus, for example, 'Bostock's wife came into Goodwin's house on Wednesday morning, her husband being dead. Anne Goodwin took a note on the same day to Bostock's after his death.'[80] 'Waited on Bostock during the latter part of his illness.'[81] Many of these contacts with neighbours were, however, more casual, and of less functional importance, being confined to visiting the sick or a brief conversation in the street. It may also be noted that while 5 out of the 9 contacts with kin are noted as occurring on more than one day, only 4 out of the 28 neighbour interactions are noted as having done so. Finally, while in only 3 out of 7 cases of kinship interaction did these kin live within 200 yards of each other, the members of none of the other dyads lived more than this distance apart.

Material suitable for content analysis is, unfortunately, limited. What can be got out of data of this kind does, however, further strengthen the argument that kin were, for all who had them in locations where they were able and willing to provide functions of the kind required, of considerable importance.

Perceptions of kinship relationships

Finally in this chapter, I want to ask whether or not there is any evidence on the extent to which kin were perceived as members of a solidary group, sharply differentiated from non-kin, and with an insistent *claim* to recognition, in the way that some of the evidence presented below in Chapter 7 suggests was the case in Ireland and even in the rural areas of Lancashire. If not, just how were they perceived?

Inevitably, evidence on such a topic is scanty in a historical situation, and in this case in particular, the writings of novelists (who generally portray family bonds as strong[82]) cannot be considered as as reliable as on some other points. The somewhat limited evidence on affect within the nuclear family is presented in Chapter 6, where I conclude that strong bonds of affection were to be found within most nuclear families. Similar evidence of affect felt towards wider kin is also scattered in the literature. For example, Gaulter cites a woman of 86 who was 'in an agony of grief at the death of her granddaughter',[83] and a married woman of 28 'was greatly alarmed and distressed at the seizure of her father'.[84]

Besides this kind of evidence, some indications are found that kin *because they were kin*, often felt they had a claim to special treatment. In Chapter 10 I shall suggest that Irish immigrants felt they had a claim for assistance on any kinsman they could locate, and that this claim was frequently accepted. Among the English, too, those who were in better circumstances often seem to have felt that they had some duty to assist less fortunate kin, and this, in turn, seems to have been expected by their relatives. Many readers will remember how in a rural setting in Hardy's *Tess of the d'Urbervilles*,[85] Tess was sent, when the family was in distress, to 'claim kin' from a wealthy family whom they believed to be relatives. A number of cases appear in the Lancashire literature where kin, particularly nephews, are taken into the employment of better-off relatives.[86] Bamford, in the same vein, comments on a wealthy aunt who failed to assist his family when they fell on hard times, and significantly writes of his 'misnamed relatives'.[87] It appears also that it was felt that one had a certain duty to keep in touch with kin,[88] and to attend certain rituals such as funerals and weddings. The importance attributed to mothers' day in some areas has already been noted. Ward's brother Dan's visits were obviously special occasions.

One other kind of evidence may also be noted as suggesting that the family was not without importance as a unit in the definition of the life situation of the Victorian Lancashire working class. Data in the intensive study suggest that, most commonly, children were named after kin, and that where the name of a parent or uncle or aunt was given to a child which subsequently died, a child born later was often given the same name. Precise quantification of this apparent tendency is not possible with the data used, because some children of almost all families had left home or died, and the names of the siblings and parents of the children's parents are not usually known. Some kind of family reconstitution technique might, however, give interesting results.[89] Often the same name is found over several generations, particularly for the eldest son. Other behaviour patterns which could reflect a similar sentiment are the frequently expressed desire of fathers that their sons should enter the same occupation as themselves,[90] and also the considerable importance which seems to have been ascribed to heirlooms.[91]

Conclusions

Taken alone, some of the evidence presented in this chapter may appear somewhat inconsequential. Taken together, however, it does seem to suggest very strongly that, in spite of migration, residential mobility, industrial employment, and high mortality rates, most people managed to maintain relationships with their family, both the current nuclear family and the family as a web of wider kinship relationships. The very fact that migrants and the widowed and the old made efforts to move near to kin suggests that it was a functionally important unit too. Later chapters will show that this was indeed the case.

However, the picture is by no means one of unmitigated devotion to kin. Some adolescents and some married couples deserted their families, and though it is difficult to estimate numbers of 'deviants', and though their number can easily be exaggerated, their effect on the population as a whole may very well have been far greater than simple numbers would suggest. Qualitative data support this picture. The *Morning Chronicle* investigator[92] summed up the relationships between parents and children no longer living at home as follows: 'The results of the inquiries I have instituted in different quarters are contradictory and unsatisfactory. There are – if I may use the phrase – a great number of shades of family disruption. Sometimes the scattered members of the household remain in constant communication with each other. Sometimes only occasions of sickness or death bring them together. Sometimes they sicken and die without any mutual knowledge and without much mutual regard, each isolated member of the family having become part and parcel of a new circle of social relationships.' Later he even goes so far as to cite an informant on 'the lukewarm carelessness of feeling that subsists between parents and their children after the latter are grown up and doing for themselves'. In view of the data I have presented here (and notably that on co-residence of aged widows), and of other data I shall present in later chapters, this last remark seems both too sweeping and too much of an oversimplification. However, again and again in subsequent chapters I shall note attitudes and behaviour akin to what this same *Morning Chronicle* observer goes on to compare to that of the members of a joint stock company where 'as surely as the different personages of the company begin to perceive that they are contributing either in money or in comfort of situation more to the family than the family contributes to them, so surely they withdraw from the association to labour in isolation, or to form new and more profitable social combinations for themselves'. In other words, there is considerable evidence to suggest that important and functioning ongoing kinship relationships of the kinds described above were yet often set against a background orientation of calculativeness and instrumentality. In this situation non-performance of kinship roles by some of the population is an obvious corollary. It is to the understanding of this particular combination of functional relationships with kin and calculative orientations to kin, that most of the remainder of this book is addressed.

6. Aspects of relationships within the urban nuclear family

In this chapter I turn to a consideration of selected aspects of relationships within the urban nuclear family. I concentrate in particular on those aspects which have implications for the main question under review in other chapters – why should people have wanted to maintain relationships with parents and other kin, and what influenced the quality of those relationships?

I tried to show in the last chapter that most young people before and after marriage maintained some relationships with their parents and I argued that the evidence suggested that these relationships were seen as useful and important. I also showed that some people broke off relationships with parents and I suggested that many more who maintained relationships yet adopted a calculative instrumental orientation to them.

One possible interpretation of these patterns would point to unsatisfying relationships of younger children with their families of orientation as the cause of such orientations and behaviour. It would begin with the observations of a mass of middle class contemporaries[1] to the effect that the nuclear family was disintegrating and that child neglect, drunkenness, and even infanticide were widespread. It would then argue that in consequence lack of respect for parents, desertion of parents by children when in need, and a generally instrumental attitude were only to be expected. Such an interpretation would also, of course, lend support to a simple 'industrialisation leads to disruption' thesis; indeed such data have often been used by polemicists for precisely this purpose. In this chapter I try, as far as the data allow, to assess the extent to which behaviour of this to us extreme kind did in fact occur and the validity of an interpretation which perceives this as a cause of family disruption. I shall argue that such an interpretation is not wholly supported by the generality of the data. I shall suggest further that it ignores the total context of which such behaviour was a part and, by doing so, ignores the actors' perceptions of their situations and, in particular, certain factors which can be seen as counterbalancing the 'neglect' which occurred.

Firstly, then, what was the attitude of parents to their children? Middle class writers often argued that many of the working class did not want to have their children, saw them as a burden, frequently allowed them to die, deserted them, or even more or less killed them for the sake of the money they would receive from a burial club, and that in the cotton towns affection within the family was almost entirely lacking.

It is undoubtedly true that, as the size of their families grew, many mothers did view further additions to their families with some reservations.[2] It is, however, naive to assume without further inquiry that when the children arrived they were not treated with as much care and affection as the family could afford to, and knew how to give them.

Similarly, the allegation that working class people 'often appear to be very indifferent at the death of their children, and sometimes express satisfaction at it, saying that they ought to be thankful to God for taking away a child when they have so many to provide for ...'[3] shows little about the strength of family bonds. Firstly, it seems highly probable that, as a result of its far greater frequency, death was viewed with greater equanimity by the Victorian working class than it is today or was by middle class contemporaries.[4] Moreover, the rationalisation that it was best for parents and children for the new baby to die sooner rather than suffer on and probably die later had at least some justification and certainly would have helped to reconcile the parents to the loss.[5]

There is anyway at least as much evidence to suggest that, except in a minority of cases,[6] parents usually grieved heavily at the loss even of very small children. Thus there are recorded the 'gentle sorrow' of a father at the death of his child,[7] and the 'deeply distressed state' of a joiner who 'Just before the boy died ... had caught him up in his arms in an agony of sorrow and kissed him several times.'[8] In spite of the dangers, real or imaginary, not one case where a sick person was deserted in sickness by a member of his or her nuclear family has been found in the literature searched.[9]

Then again, allegations are frequently found to the effect that, because their parents were so often drunk, many children suffered severely from neglect and ill-treatment. To some extent, indeed, these allegations have some truth and, where this was so, this factor does appear to have operated to an important degree in weakening the bonds between children and their parents.[10] The nineteenth century working class world was, however, a harsh one, and much of the treatment which may seem cruel to us, and even did so to the Victorian middle classes, was almost certainly defined as much less harsh by those who administered and received it. It must also be remembered that in many cases of alleged neglect (for example, parents who gave their children no food to take to work during the day[11]), the parents were often quite literally unable to afford the food because of their large families and low wages. Similarly, the ragged clothes and insanitary state of the young urchins of the towns were as much due to ignorance and poverty as to neglect.[12]

It is of course true that examples of extreme behaviour do occur. For example, a boy and his brother were taken to a nearby canal and thrown in by their father, with, it was alleged, the express intention of drowning them. Their stepmother was said to have 'locked them up in the house, tied them up to the bedposts, and "clemmed" (starved) them shamefully'.[13] 'A boy driven to idleness by the strike was turned out of doors by the father, who was nevertheless, able to keep two cows',[14] and other cases are noted where children were '"turned out of doors" the moment they ceased to contribute to family income'.[15]

It is, moreover, also true that in many of these cases of cruelty and neglect, drink was involved. A drunken husband beating his wife until her face was 'one mass of bruises', and pawning all the furniture,[16] can hardly have encouraged the children to have much affection for him.[17] Nor can the behaviour of those men who, it was alleged, spent all their earnings in the ale-house and left their children to starve.[18] The misery caused by this type of behaviour is clear from this statement from the son of a moulder who, though he earned 36*s*. per week, 'called at the alehouse on Saturday night, and spent half his money before he came home; my mother would sit crying, not knowing how the shop bill would be paid. About twelve o'clock my father would come home as drunk as a pig; he would clap down about eighteen shillings, and with that they might have done well, but he kept on wanting drink all the week'.[19] Some mothers, too, were frequently drunk, and it was alleged that children were killed by being overlaid by mothers in their drunken stupor.[20]

Certainly, in the nineteenth century, drinking was widespread among the working classes. In 1846 Lancashire magistrates tried over 25,000 cases where men and women were charged with offences in which drink had probably been involved.[21] The intensive study suggests that there was a beershop or public house in nearly every street. Rowntree found at the end of the century in York that the average working class family spent 'not less than 6*s*. per week' on drink, which was about one-sixth of income or about 31 pints of beer (or alcohol equivalent).[22] Clay claims that a strike involving 4,000 people over 18 led to a fall in consumption of beer and spirits worth £1,000 per week which, even allowing for the downward multiplier effect on community aggregate demand, does suggest a very considerable rate of consumption, since five shillings would buy about 32 pints of beer (or alcohol equivalent).[23] Some, but a minority, of members of all SEGs were involved in heavy drinking, though some commentators believed that the better class of cotton operative drank less, and some artisan groups more.[24]

In sum, there is no doubt that heavy drinking did lead to some serious neglect of children and some brutality. Against this, however, must be set the fact that some degree of drinking by fathers was undoubtedly an accepted part of daily life and part of a child's expectations. It is also probable that brutality by fathers had the effect of increasing affective bonds between children, and between children and their mothers.[25] And it does at least seem very likely that middle class commentators tended to exaggerate both the degree of drinking that was general, and its effects, from too great emphasis on isolated cases and on misleading averages. It undoubtedly influenced the attitudes of some children to their fathers. It can hardly have been the only factor involved for the majority.

A further set of allegations that surrounded the working class family and the mother in particular was that the long hours worked by many women and the neglect of home and family that ensued (with husband and children driven to the beer shop by the unwelcoming domestic scene) were a further source of the disintegration which many imagined existed. These allegations and the other supposed detrimental effects on the healthy development of the children have been fully documented by Margaret Hewitt,[26] and so only a brief discussion is necessary here.

Women had always worked in England, but their work had usually been domestic or agricultural but seasonal and had therefore allowed them to give at least casual attention to home and children for at least part of the day.[27] This domestic employment for married women was still common in the 1850s. Women 'in certain branches of business at home render important services; such as wives of farmers, of small shopkeepers, innkeepers, shoemakers, butchers'.[28] Many families had their earnings increased by wives running a little provision shop or a beer-house.[29] Well over a third of all working wives in Preston in 1851 were employed in non-factory occupations.[30] Many others also worked irregularly or part-time in such occupations, but were not so recorded.

Mill work, however, was very different. Here women were employed all day, away from home, in a situation where they could not usually take their children with them[31] and where the needs of children and home had to a great extent to go unmet, or be provided by some other person.

In all, in the Preston sample 26% of all wives living with their husbands worked.[32] The effects of this work on the family, however, were considerably less than they might have been, both because many women (particularly those with children) worked at home, and because it was above all the younger wives and those with few or no children who were in employment at all. This is clear from Table 22.

There is evidence from the intensive study and from descriptive data[33] to confirm that these trends away from work and away from factory occupations as the family moved over the life-cycle were the results of more than a mere quirk in cross-sectional data or of a once and for all shift in behaviour patterns. Nevertheless, nearly a quarter (23%) of all wives with children worked (20% of those with children under 10), and probably (if some account is taken of 'weavers') about 15% of all wives with children worked away from home for most of the day. In all, 23% of children under 10 who had a co-residing father had working mothers; almost exactly half of these mothers worked in factory occupations.[34]

These data, taken alone, do at first sight seem to provide some basis for the proposition that many of the children suffered neglect because their mothers

TABLE 22 *Employment and type of employment of wives co-residing with their husbands, by life-cycle stage:*[a] *Preston sample, 1851*

LCS	Of all wives, proportion working %	All wives N(100%)	Of working wives, proportion in factory occupations[b] %	All working wives N(100%)
1	44	159	72	92
2	38	59		
3	28	388	52	134
4	23	122		
5	15	234	19	52
6	16	106		
All with children	23	822	52	185
All	26	1,068	52	278

[a] For the definitions of life-cycle stages, see note 46 to Chapter 4 (p. 202 below).
[b] These figures should be seen as minima as they exclude 'weavers', who made up 11% of working wives in LCSs 1 and 2, 13% in 3 and 4, and 25% in 5 and 6. Only some of these, and almost certainly a smaller proportion in the later LCSs, would have been factory weavers.

worked, though many of the examples of neglect given in the literature were undoubtedly isolated and exaggerated. Before charges of neglect can be substantiated, however, two further questions must be asked:

1. Did the mothers work because they were callous, or because they had to to improve the life chances (quite literally) of the family as a whole? In other words, is this one more example of the crucial role played by direst poverty in determining the family relational patterns of large sections of the population under study?

2. Were the persons with whom the children were left always callous and indifferent to the fate of their charges?

There is considerable evidence to suggest that the main reason why mothers left their homes and families and went out to work in the mills was because their families sorely needed the extra money to raise a standard of living which the low wages of the husband (or the occasional dissolute father[35]) would otherwise have forced below the primary poverty line. The fact that most appear to have worked until the last minute before the birth of a child and to have returned almost immediately afterwards suggests a similar motivation.[36] Only before they had their first child did many women work because they wanted to.[37] Tables 23 and 24 support the hypothesis that necessity played an important part in encouraging wives to work, and also make clear the way in which the working wife was a major solution to family poverty.

The fourth column of Table 24 shows that over 60% of the families of the wives who worked in factories would have been in difficulties[38] had they not done so. The fourth column of Table 23 shows that with the earnings of the wife, only one in six actually were. In a third of all families which would have been in difficulties without the wife's earnings, the wives did in fact work. Conversely, where the family was well clear of the poverty line, most wives appear to have worked only if they had no children who would have suffered from lack of

TABLE 23 *Relationship between family standard of living and working wives: married couples for whom data were adequate,*[a] *Preston sample, 1851*

Relationship of weekly family income to poverty standard	Of all families, families where wife worked: in factory %	elsewhere[b] %	All families (*N*)	Standard of living of families: of factory working wives %	of all working wives %
Below by 4*s.* or more	5	2	41	2	2
Below by under 4*s.* to above by less than 4*s.*	14	3	105	17	14
Above by 4*s.* to 11*s.* 11*d.*	23	9	151	41	38
Above by 12*s.* to 19*s.* 11*d.*	21	10	102	24	24
Above by 20*s.* and over	19	21	70	15	22
All	18	9	469	99 (*N*= 86)	100 (*N*= 128)

[a] For details see p. 30 above.
[b] Includes 'weavers'.

TABLE 24 *Relationship between family standard of living and working wives, when earnings of wives (standardised at 8*s.*) are excluded: married couples for whom data were adequate,*[a] *Preston sample, 1851*

Relationship of weekly family income to poverty standard	Of all families, families where wife worked: in factory %	elsewhere[b] %	All families (*N*)	Standard of living of families: of factory working wives %	of all working wives %
Below by 4*s.* or more	29	7	59	20	16
Below by under 4*s.* to above by less than 4*s.*	26	10	135	41	38
Above by 4*s.* to 11*s.* 11*d.*	17	7	134	24	24
Above by 12*s.* to 19*s.* 11*d.*	8	11	89	9	14
Above by 20*s.* and over	10[c]	10[c]	52	6	8
All	18	9	469	100 (*N*= 86)	100 (*N*= 128)

[a] For details see p. 30 above.
[b] Includes 'weavers'.
[c] All this group had either no children, or no children aged under 15.

attention,[39] and a larger proportion of those who did work did not work in factories.[40] Nevertheless, even where the family was in poverty if the wife did not work, only one-third appear in fact to have been in employment which suggests considerable affection towards children and perceived role conflict, rather than neglect.[41] It is also important to stress that, at these levels of poverty, where mothers did work they may very well have been so much improving the standard of living of their families that the betterment of the family's satisfactions outweighed in the minds of the children the greater degree of neglect suffered by themselves and by their home.

About one-quarter of all children under 10, then, had working mothers, and at least half of these had mothers who worked away from home and whose ability to care for their children was consequently diminished. It was only a minority of these children, however, who were left all day with hired nurses indifferent to their fate. While the mother was probably the best and first choice as a guardian, in her absence kin and close friends and neighbours were usually available as substitutes.[42] In 14% of all cases where the mother worked (17% of all cases where she worked in a factory) the house contained an otherwise unemployed grandmother. Most of these would have been available as guardians. In addition, in a further 7% of such cases (28% of those where mother was a factory worker) some other unemployed person in the house, usually a co-lodger but sometimes a sibling or other relative, was similarly available.

Nearly half of all the young children of women working in factories, then, were probably cared for at home by a close relative or by a friendly lodger. Many more, undoubtedly, were cared for by close relatives who lived next door or just up the street.[43] Indeed, if it be assumed that only one-half of all infants (children under one year of age) with no potential guardian in the home were cared for by relatives or friends living nearby (and this must surely be seen as a minimum figure in view of the findings of Chapter 5), then, at a point in time, less than 2% of all infant children in the industrial districts of Lancashire were being left with professional child-minders.[44] As a source of neglect and a factor affecting children's attitudes to their parents, then, working mothers were probably in fact of comparatively minor importance.

Finally, to what extent is it true, as was frequently alleged, that parents exploited their children's labouring ability, by forcing them at an early age into the labour force instead of sending them to school and bringing them up 'properly'? Thus, for example, J. P. Kay wrote: 'Too frequently the father, enjoying perfect health and with ample opportunities for employment, is supported in idleness on the earnings of his oppressed children.'[45] One may cite also the allegations, almost equally frequent, of the instrumental attitude of parents 'who will take their children away from a kind master, and place the child with another (less kind), for the purpose of getting higher wages'.[46]

It is of course true that some exploitation did occur and this was seen as exploitation even through the eyes of the working class at the time. Moreover, where this was so it does seem to have been important in encouraging children to terminate relationships with their parents.[47] Often, however, when children were sent to work before the normal age it was for a reason, such as family poverty, which was seen as justifying behaviour which might otherwise have been seen as improper, or it was because the alternatives, usually education or mischief, were seen as worse or at least were not highly valued.[48]

There is no doubt that some children were sent to work long hours from a very young age, even as late as the 1850s and 1860s. Children as young as 7 were reported from some industries,[49] while other industries regularly employed or had employed children under 10.[50] In cotton, after 1833, children were not employed so young, most beginning at about the age of 12. Table 25 shows the proportion of children of different ages recorded as in employment by the census of 1851, though one may suspect that these figures are subject to considerable under-reporting. Nevertheless, it seems legitimate to conclude that by the 1850s comparatively few parents were exploiting their children's labour by forcing them into work at a very early age, though numbers of parents still tried to evade the law by pretending their children were older than they were.[51]

Moreover, in the large proportion of the cases where young children were employed, it is clear that they were sent to work because the family was so poor that their earnings were absolutely essential if the family was to continue to function at all as an effective unit.[52] Thus a hand-loom weaver commented that 'I could not support my children except they were to bring something in.'[53] Another said his child was only employed in a mill 'because I could not make do unless he was employed: my family was increasing'.[54] Indeed, it was claimed that only the children of 'the class a little above necessity' were usually still in education between the ages of 10 and 12.[55] A spinner sent his first four children into the mill before they were ten, but the fifth he kept out of the factory until

TABLE 25 *Percentage of children aged 7–15 recorded as in employment at the census of 1851, for Manchester and Salford, and for Preston*[a]

	Age of children								
Percentage employed	7	8	9	10	11	12	13	14	15
Manchester and Salford:									
boys	1	2	4	11	23	41	60	76	..[b]
girls	1	2	3	8	14	27	44	61	..[b]
Preston:									
boys	–	–	7	13	27	39	74	88	93

[a] The Manchester and Salford data come from PP1852 XI 470–1; the Preston data from the sample.
[b] Data not available.

the age of 12 or 13, 'because our circumstances were better'.[56] Thus, again and again, parents who otherwise showed considerable affection for their children and concern to do the best possible for them were yet forced by large families and low wages to send their children to work as soon as possible.[57]

It is moreover clear that the more extreme allegations to the effect that fathers lay in voluntary idleness while their wives and children were forced into work can seldom be substantiated, though, probably where excessive drinking prevented a man from holding down a job, cases almost certainly did occur. More often, however, fathers were idle while their children worked because age had meant that they had lost their factory jobs, or because they were not qualified for a regular job and were more or less unemployable except as casual light labourers.[58]

In sum, therefore, I would argue that where children suffered from neglect or overwork, this was more usually the result of ignorance, lack of foresight, or necessity than the result of deliberate cruelty or exploitation, though both were by no means rare. Few children then, will have perceived themselves as exploited. This opinion is strengthened if attention is turned to evidence on the affectionate bonds to be found in many families between children and their parents (particularly their mother).

Thus Adshead,[59] on a general level, notes a man returning in the slump of the 1840s to 'his famishing wife and family, among whom love for their parents and love for each other seem in a remarkable manner to have survived the circumstances of comfort in which they were formerly placed'. Similarly, the agent of the Liverpool District Provident Society argued that 'It is really only the professed beggars among the Irish who will ill use their children; the respectable Irish poor are very tender to them, and will try to get them into schools, or to bring them on in the world, and do as much for them as the parents of any other country'.[60] Perhaps even more interesting is the comment of the informant cited at the end of the last chapter on the carelessness of feeling between parents and adult children. He observed that with regard to *young* children 'Nothing can be more warm and keen than the affection of parents throughout the cotton districts for children, so long as they continue children . . .'[61] It was only in adolescence that the changes occurred, and that as much as anything at the children's volition.

Many of the arguments given by the operatives in favour of the reduction of working hours in the late 1840s seem also to show their concern for their children,[62] particularly if one admits that most of them did realise that it would bring with it a reduction in their wages. Thus 'thinks she has been long enough away from her children when she has been away 10 hours,';[63] 'Much better for her children being with them in the evening';[64] 'he now has the pleasure of being more with his children, and seeing to their general wants and comforts'.[65]

Even when the children worked, parents seem typically to have treated them with as much concern as was possible, given the underlying need that they should work at all. Thus from the same source: 'has several children employed in the factories, and is thankful to have their labour limited to 10 hours'.[66] There are several cases in the literature where parents who thought their children's health was being injured by factory work quickly moved them to other employment which they believed would be less arduous.[67]

There is also considerable evidence to suggest that bonds of affection were particularly strong between *mothers* and their children, which seems to reflect both the greater role of the mother in the life of the child and also the fact that it was she above all who made sacrifices for her children and she who protected them from their father. She, in turn, therefore seems to have received from them affection and gratitude. The segregated conjugal roles which seem to have been typical of these families are probably also important here.[68] Thus, while at weekends 'the men and single women really make holiday ... the married women, who seem the slaves of Lancashire society, are then, however, obliged to set to work harder than ever ...' to do shopping and housework.[69] This pattern seems to have been typical, and applied to child care too, though some husbands, particularly in times of crisis, did help out in these tasks.[70] More usually, however, in critical times, the mother seems to have taken over complete control. 'I have sometimes thought that a family undergoing such a trial [unemployment] is like a crew at sea, short of provisions, with a limited allowance meted out day by day. Here it is the wife that is captain, she is provider and distributor. The husband under such circumstances commonly leaves all to her, and right nobly does she discharge her part ...'[71] Another contemporary comment is also worthy of note: 'An observation constantly made by the medical men, that the parents have lost their health much more generally than the children, and particularly that the mothers, who most of all starve themselves, have got pale and emaciated ...'[72]

I have already noted that drunk and cruel fathers caused considerable distress to many children. Where they occurred, wife beatings, desertions of the family, adulterous relationships, and other misdeeds on the part of the father must often have further influenced the attitude of children to him, particularly if the children had to some extent identified and developed a strong bond with the mother. Cases or general descriptions of such activities abound in the literature, though it is impossible to know how widespread they were.[73] A London case is perhaps particularly interesting since it shows the operation of the mother-child bond under such circumstances: 'Sometimes he illtreats me. If he don't with his hand, I know he does with his tongue. He has the most dreadfullest tongue ever heard of. He drinks very hard. He's drunk whenever he's the money to be so ... I can assure you I have been obliged to live upon my two shillings ... I have, indeed, sir, a very hard time of it. I'm ready to run away, and leave it very often. If it wasn't for my children, I should do it'.[74] It is not surprising that for many it was the case that 'should the mother die . . . her little ones weep indeed, as their only friend is gone'.[75]

In sum, then, the balance of the evidence on my interpretation suggests that to the best of their ability most working class mothers do seem to have been affectionate and to have done what they saw as the best for their children while they were young and that young children will have perceived this as being the case. Many fathers, too, were similarly much loved and appreciated,[76] though some were feared as intolerant or as heavy drinkers. I shall suggest later that it may have been above all the children of these parents who sought to terminate relationships with their families, but it seems unlikely that in general the attitudes and behaviour of adolescent and adult children towards their parents can simply be attributed to excessive ill treatment while the children were young.

7. Family, society, and economy in the birthplaces of the rural born migrants

Before further exploring and attempting to interpret the patterns of kinship relationships found in the Lancashire cotton towns, I turn aside in this chapter to a brief discussion of some of the factors underlying family cohesion in nineteenth century Ireland and in the agricultural areas of Lancashire.

It seems necessary to say something on this topic for two reasons. Firstly, the population of the towns of Lancashire, as I showed in Chapter 5, retained considerable links with kin outside the nuclear family, and performed important functions for the members of the nuclear family. Yet these towns were undoubtedly urban-industrial communities. The question thus arises as to whether industrialisation was having any effect at all on family structure in nineteenth century England. This can only be established if one knows what family life was like in the rural areas of the country whence the urban population was recruited, and particularly what it was like in agricultural areas not greatly affected by industrialisation. I shall suggest in this chapter that among certain groups of the population of rural England and Ireland, the family remained a strongly solidary and functional unit. I shall then attempt to establish the factors which seem to have underlain this considerable family cohesion. The analysis conducted here will thus provide comparative data based on similar sources analysed in a similar way, against which the data on the urban family can be assessed. It will also point to some of the factors the presence or absence of which in the towns may help us to understand the patterns of family life which were found there.

There is also a second important set of reasons for this diversion from the main theme of the book. When I come to explain the family patterns of the migrant groups of the population in the towns, it will be necessary to have some understanding of the patterns of family relationships in the areas whence the migrants had come. I shall suggest that men and women were able in spite of migration to maintain some important functional relationships with kin left behind in the country. In addition, I shall suggest that some of the patterns of family structure found in the towns can only be explained as hangovers from rural patterns, which, though now lacking structural support, were, for a time at least, continued in the towns. Readers should note that the family patterns described here for rural Lancashire were almost certainly not typical of agricultural areas of Britain as a whole because the whole organisation of agriculture in the Lancashire communities was very different from elsewhere.

The quantitative data on the rural areas of Lancashire presented in this chapter are mainly taken from the agricultural village sample drawn from the 1851 census enumerators' books. The universe and sampling procedure for this sample were described in Chapter 3.[1]

No comparable quantitative data are available for rural Ireland. Information on this area is thus confined to descriptive material. In particular, data are drawn from the extremely copious evidence gathered from a wide cross-section of the population of the whole country by the Commissioners of the Poor Inquiry, Ireland.[2] Data are confined to pre-famine Ireland because the famine finally overthrew an already creaking traditional economic system in Ireland and thus the structural basis on which the family patterns of the Irish born inhabitants of Preston had been built up.

The economic and social background

Ireland, culturally and to some extent economically, was a very different place from the original homes of the other cotton town inmigrants. In history, traditions, religion, and even language, it was sharply differentiated from the rest of the kingdom. The destitution of the mass of its populace exceeded anything in even the most backward areas of rural England.

In 1841, the year of the last census before the famine, Ireland had a population approaching eight and a quarter million. The country was almost entirely rural and agricultural; only 18 towns had populations exceeding 10,000 and 72% of the males over the age of 15 were engaged in wholly agricultural pursuits.[3] The exact number employed in truly industrial occupations is impossible to ascertain, but was probably well below one per cent of the population, concentrated in the area around Belfast. Since it is anyway very difficult to learn much about the non-agricultural sector of the population, attention will concentrate here on the farming community which provided the mass of the migrants.

Most of the Irish people lived in a state of the utmost destitution, often on the verge of starvation,[4] though some areas were in less distress than others. Most of the land was owned by large landowners, frequently absentees, from whom farmers rented their land either directly or through middlemen, though this latter practice considerably declined from 1815 onwards.[5] The average farm was minute, and the standard of agriculture far below that of England.[6] Some few of the farmers worked quite substantial areas. However, the majority of the land was parcelled out between small farmers of five to fifteen acres and the equally numerous classes below them, the cottiers (part labourers, part farmers, occupying 'a small lot of ground at a fixed rate, generally payable in labour'),[7] and the labourers proper. These labourers acquired for a season a small patch of land. On this they strove to grow enough potatoes to keep their families for the next season and then either laboured at eightpence to one shilling per day for enough days in the year to pay the rent for their patch,[8] or, with the same object, left their families to shift as they could and trekked to England for the summer harvest work. This group, says O'Brien,[9] 'were therefore as miserable as it was possible for any human beings to be'. Most families had in addition some livestock, a pig or some poultry, to be carefully husbanded, and the produce sold to pay the rent or for clothing. The family met most of its needs from the land – and had to. The overall picture is of severe poverty and subsistence agriculture, typically on minute plots of land.

Both in their agriculture[10] and in their social organisation, many parts of the rural areas of Lancashire had remained almost unchanged since the early eighteenth century.[11] To the north-west and south of Preston most of the population lived clustered in small villages and were in contact with the changing way of life of the towns which they provided daily with agricultural produce. In the more remote areas, however, particularly the hill areas on the county's borders with Westmorland and Yorkshire, the farms were scattered over the moors and up the valleys, and changes came only slowly and with great reluctance. In some areas, large consolidated farms using modern farming methods and employing the largely landless day labourers characteristic of the rest of the country were to be found. Most of the county, however, was typified by small farms,[12] relying almost exclusively on family labour supplemented where necessary by farm servants boarded in the farmhouse.[13] Many of these farmers were still part farmer, part hand-loom weaver.[14] Many of the smaller farms were not far above the level of subsistence agriculture.[15] In those areas where there were agricultural labourers, they were prosperous compared with those in the rest of England as long as work could be obtained.[16] Marshall[17] argues, however, that there was always some over-supply of labour in the Lancashire villages. It was anyway never easy to get work in winter, and wages were lower then.[18]

Family and household structure

The best summary comment that can be made on these areas is that their social structure was predominantly both familistically oriented and familistically organised.

In Ireland, as is usual under conditions of subsistence agriculture, farm labour was mainly provided by the family, with each nuclear family farming its own plot, though probably with assistance at certain times from neighbours and kin. True, some of the larger farms employed labourers regularly or from time to time; there was also a small class of unmarried farm servants who lived with their employers and were considered fairly comfortably placed in comparison with the rest of the population.[19] But, typically, the numerous children assisted the farmer and his wife in the farm work from an early age until marriage.[20]

Even after marriage the men did not usually scatter far, though to some extent emigration and the cultivation of marginal land meant that some did leave the close family group.[21] More typically, however, the family farm was gradually subdivided among the children as they married, and all the children of one sex at least remained geographically close to the family of orientation.

The precise pattern of subdivision followed varied somewhat from one area to another, sometimes the land being divided between the daughters as a dowry and the sons having to 'travel', but more usually the sons getting portions of the land, not always equal,[22] and the daughters marrying out.[23] But the basic pattern was nearly always the same: 'It is the general practice with them to divide their land into portions, which are given to their children as they get married. The last married frequently gets his father's cabin along with his portion of the ground, and there his parents like to stop, from a feeling of attachment to the place where they have spent their lives.'[24] Perhaps more usually, however, while both parents were alive they lived in a separate cabin, often with its own plot of land, and only moved in with a relative when widowed. Thus each nuclear family usually had its own abode, one obvious reason being that the cabins were so small (35% had only one room)[25] and could be so rapidly erected on a part of the plot. So, though the family broke up residentially and economically as the sons married, the sons did not scatter far. The daughters, however, in the more common case, moved to the plot of their husband's family, and probably became primarily absorbed into his family group. But even they probably did not move far, though it seems that more of them moved away from the family orbit than did sons, many going before marriage to the towns as servants.[26] In all, only about 5% of the population were enumerated in 1841 in counties other than that of their birth.[27] In general, therefore, interaction of at least sons with their parents and siblings (and, of course, in the second generation of subdivision, with uncles, aunts, and cousins) could be frequent.

The willingness of the Irish to share their poverty with others even worse off than themselves was proverbial, and applied both to kin and non-kin. 'When the Irish, who are a warm-hearted people, find distress near them, they approach to it, and seek to relieve it.'[28] 'There is greatest commiseration for the aged; they are never refused a meal wherever they go.'[29] Orphans, said a witness, only slightly exaggerating, 'are uniformly taken in by the neighbouring people'.[30]

Evidence of a strong family orientation among the rural Irish is clear, and hardly a word is to be found in the report of, or evidence to, the *Poor Inquiry, Ireland*, to counter this overall impression, though there are some qualifications which must be made and which will be discussed later. Thus, 'The feeling of filial affection is very strong', found the Poor Law Commissioners in one area,[31] while a witness to the *Select Committee on the State of the Poor in Ireland* agreed that 'the tie between parent and child and kindred is of particular force'.[32]

Another noted that 'instances of children wanting in affection to their parents have been very rare indeed'.[33] Numerous cases appear in the literature of unmarried children enduring considerable hardships to maintain infirm parents,[34] and conversely, of mothers overcoming the strong Irish dread of fever to attend their sick husbands and children.[35] One witness even went so far as to argue that children gave preference to obligations to their parents over obligations to their spouses.[36]

In general, this obligation to provide full support for an old man or woman was seen as limited to children,[37] but some considered it as extending also to 'brothers, sisters, aunts, and uncles, and their children if destitute orphans'.[38] Obligations to provide some small contribution and casual or short period assistance were seen as going further,[39] sometimes as far as second cousins[40] or beyond.[41] Even very distant kin were apparently seen as under greater obligation to provide assistance than were non-kin,[42] particularly to the childless destitute. In some cases 'even if not a relative, being of the same name gives a claim to support'.[43]

The Lancashire evidence is less overwhelming but suggests, particularly in the remoter mountain regions, a strong commitment to family relationships but, compared with Ireland, a greater emphasis on the stem family as a self-maintaining group, though in a setting where wider kinship was also recognised as important. Mrs Gaskell notes the northern hill farmers as 'just, independent, upright ... disliking change, and new ways, and new people; sensible and shrewd; each household self-contained, and its members having little curiosity as to their neighbours, with whom they rarely met for any social intercourse ...'[44] Garnett notes in the hills above Fylde a manly and independent and very conservative people. 'Many families have lived on the same farm for generations; and by frequent intermarriages they have become connected together almost like one family.'[45] Other writers note cases of contact, assistance, and strong bonds of affection both between current nuclear family members and between members of the same family of orientation now separated.[46]

There is also evidence of considerable knowledge of family genealogies[47] and this seems to have found concrete manifestation in the nicknames frequently based on kinship which were given to co-villagers. Waugh notes the survival of 'The old custom of distinguishing persons by Christian names alone (which) prevails generally in Smallbridge, as in all country parts of Lancashire, more or less ... Persons are often met with whose surnames have almost dropped into oblivion by disuse', and who were instead known by such names as '"Tum o'Charles o'Billy's" ... "Ab o' Pinder's", "Den o'Robin's o'Bob's o'th'Bird-stuffers o'Buersil Yed" ... "Jone o'Isaac's" ...' and so on.[48] Kinship seems also to have been the frame of reference within which a person was evaluated to establish whether or not they were a suitable person with whom to engage in relationships. The first question Waugh was asked in several places was 'Who's lad are you?'[49]

Moreover there is widespread evidence from the literature to suggest that parents were able to exercise considerable control over the activities of their children, most significantly perhaps over the timing of their marriages and over the choice of spouse.[50]

The statistical evidence from the agricultural village sample also supports the idea that family relationships were important in this society. Thus, for example, only 15% of old people of 65 and over (other than the few who lived in institutions) lived alone; all the rest lived with related persons or with spouses. Even if only widowers are considered, only 26% did not live with some related person. All of these had a household to themselves, and some probably in fact had kin living nearby. Only 3% of the whole sample lived in lodgings. The structure of the households as a whole, compared with that of Preston, is given in Table 26. Particularly noticeable here is the large proportion of composite families, and the fact that, in all, over a quarter of all rural households contained kin. In sum, kin-based co-residence among the rural population was slightly, but interestingly only slightly, higher than it was in the town.

If, on the other hand, attention is turned to the proportion of young unmarried persons co-residing with their nuclear families, the findings are, at first sight, rather puzzling. These data are given in Table 27. Overall, the proportion of young persons co-residing with their parents was considerably lower in country than town, and this was particularly true for boys. Two closely related factors are at work here.

In the towns most of the employment that was available did not offer accommodation as part of the remuneration. In these rural areas of Lancashire, on the other hand, 43% of men employed in agriculture were living-in farm servants,

TABLE 26 *Structure of the families of household heads: Preston and agricultural village samples, 1851*

	Households in:	
Household composition	Preston %	rural areas %
Head alone	4	5
Childless married couple	10	12
Nuclear family with children	63	56
Stem family	10[a]	6[b]
Composite family	13[c]	21[d]
All: %	100	100
N	1,241	855

[a] The difference between *a* and *b* is significant $p < 0.01$ ($chi^2 = 9.775$), and that between *c* and *d* is significant $p < 0.001$ ($chi^2 = 26.482$).

TABLE 27 *Residence patterns of young persons aged 10–24, by age: Preston and agricultural village samples, 1851*

		Of all, living with:							
		parents		other kin		elsewhere		All	
		Preston %	rural %	Preston %	rural %	Preston %	rural %	Preston N(100%)	rural N(100%)
Boys	10–14	92[a]	77[b]	4	6	4	16	392	296
	15–19	79[c]	56[d]	8	8	13	36	376	266
	20–24	65[e]	53[f]	6	6	29	41	217	194
Girls	10–14	86	86	10	4	4	11	349	217
	15–19	67	62	9	6	24	32	387	268
	20–24	62[g]	46[h]	6	10	32	44	261	143

[a] The following differences are significant $p < 0.001$: a/b (chi² = 36.682); c/d (chi² = 38.770); $p < 0.01$: g/h (chi² = 9.518); $p < 0.02$: e/f (chi² = 5.997).

and there were large numbers of female servants who filled both farm and domestic roles. In all, 28% of the rural sample households contained at least one servant, compared with 10% of the households in Preston.[51] Servants made up 16% of the rural sample population aged 15 and over. Most of these servants were single (94% of the men aged 15 and over), and 51% of the single men and 47% of single women were under 20.

The presence of this large servant element in the population had, inevitably, important effects on the nuclear family both as a unit of residence and as a provider of day-to-day functions to its members,[52] for it meant that in their early teens large numbers of children left home and went to live with another family in order to obtain employment.[53] This effect was increased by the fact that only a minority (25% of all servants in the sample) went into service in the village of their birth. However, including this 25%, 62% were living less than five miles from the village of their birth so contact could fairly easily be maintained if desired.

A second and partly overlapping aspect of the rural situation was also both directly and indirectly at work here. Arensberg and Kimball have described in great detail how farms were passed from father to son in pre-war rural Ireland,[54] how one son succeeded to the farm and the others were forced to 'travel', the men usually receiving a sum of money only occasionally large enough to allow them to establish themselves on a farm of their own, and some at least of the daughters receiving a dowry and marrying into other farms. A parallel scattering of the nuclear family unit occurred in nineteenth century Lancashire,[55] particularly in the north. Thus it was necessary for most of the sons and daughters of farmers to leave home and support themselves, and the large number of farm servants is also a reflection of this practice.[56] Many of these non-inheriting sons, like many of the sons of the labourers, who had nothing to inherit, swelled the ranks of the urban migrants.[57]

A very pertinent question then becomes the effect that this separation from parents at an early age had on the functionality and solidarity of bonds between members of the nuclear family, particularly where, when the child left to go into service, this was the end of his or her membership of the family as a residential and domestic unit. Evidence on this topic is, unfortunately, very sparse. It would appear probable, however, that once the nuclear family had scattered in this way, while bonds of affection and a sense of special relationship remained which could be called upon fairly predictably for temporary assistance in short-term emergencies, the family as an important functional unit crucial to the welfare of the individual became much lessened in importance.[58] It was, for example, reported from Durham (and this probably had wider applicability) that female farm servants usually saved their earnings in preparation for their marriages, rather than contributing anything much to the parental household.[59] There is also an isolated reference to a father who refused to supply any further material assistance to a son who had already been given his portion.[60] Further research on this whole topic is obviously necessary, however, before anything certain can be said on this point.

Compared with the situation in the towns, then, it does seem that there was a strong emotional and functional commitment to family relationships in both rural Ireland and rural Lancashire. This was particularly so among those who expected to inherit the farm or a portion; in such cases the parents had very considerable control over the actions of their children. The question to be asked in the rest of this chapter is how this generally strong familistic orientation can be explained.

Discussion – the normative interpretation

In terms of the phenomenal continuum outlined in Chapter 2, family behaviour in both these societies was definitely located towards the normative pole. Family relationships were almost universally maintained without question at least until the 1830s. If questioned the phenomenal justifications one gave were essentially in terms of tradition and of religion.

Thus, as an explanation of why neighbours so willingly gave help to those with no relatives, one Irish witness said, 'They think that the potatoes they have are God's, and that when one of his creatures is in distress, he has as good a right to a share of them as themselves.'[61] Several Irish witnesses referred to the obligation to assist kin as a 'sacred one'[62] and 'a religious duty',[63] one adding, showing clearly the importance of tradition of this kind in these closed communities, 'it is the law of the country to do so',[64] while another in the same vein said that 'the law of custom holds so strongly'.[65]

To say that behaviour was normatively determined is not, however, to answer the question, but only to pose it in a new way. One must then ask: 'Why could these strongly held normatively oriented patterns be maintained?' And this question can in turn be broken down into two lines of attack: (1) How can we explain the viability of a strong normatively based family system in these societies? (2) How can we explain the particular kinship patterns which existed in these societies? This section considers the first of these points. The second is taken up in later parts of this chapter. In each section the Irish data are dealt with first and then the less complete Lancashire data are considered.

Firstly, then, as I noted above, Ireland was subject to only very slow social change. In terms of the discussion in Chapter 2 there thus existed one of the principal structural prerequisites for the emergence of consensus over family behaviour. This process was helped by the relative isolation and homogeneity of the communities. In consequence alternative reference groups were almost completely lacking. Thus children would gradually and imperceptibly internalise many of the family and community values and norms, the only ones to which they had access, as they worked with and watched and modelled themselves on their parents. Under these circumstances some development of a familistically oriented super-ego was probably almost inevitable.

Nevertheless, this is inadequate as a total explanation. Every year a number of men from most parishes went to England or elsewhere for a while. Thus it seems almost certain that the Irish peasant was familiar with the fact that other people in other societies organised their family life rather differently. There were anyway enough deviants from the dominant values for alternative definitions of family obligations to be perceived at least occasionally by both child and adult.[66] Even within the communities it was recognised that some children were more willing to assist parents than were others, and one small farmer at least attributed these differences to differences in socialisation: 'I have observed that where the sons have the handling of their own wages too soon, and are allowed to spend them at fairs and markets, they grow up in extravagant bad habits and have little kindness for their parents when they grow old; but this happens particularly when the children have been reared vulgarly and without learning.'[67] Moreover, in cases where parental role models did not meet their family obligations,[68] it would seem reasonable to suggest that their children in turn will often not have internalised obligations to parents.

A second and supporting factor at work in stabilising a normative orientation, and indeed in orienting it towards commitments to family relationships, was of course the all-embracing Roman Catholic Church. Priests frequently used their influence to remind parishioners of their familial obligations,[69] and the passages quoted above showed the extent to which religious interpretations of these obligations were dominant at the phenomenal level. The church's power in the community also made it able to wield considerable sanctioning power at the structural level via its influence over the behaviour of other members of the community.

There is no doubt, then, that these ideological influences reinforced custom and were important in maintaining a strong normative commitment to family obligations. It is also clear that, when the structural forces which underpinned the old family structures began to break down, forces of this kind were important in retarding changes in family patterns, and in encouraging actors to maintain familial obligations.

Finally, these were small, isolated, homogeneous communities with low population turnover and highly intertwined kinship ties. In other words, the preconditions for close supervision of behaviour by the community and for effective sanctioning of those individuals who could not leave it were both met. Since, traditionally at least, life chances were inextricably bound up with a plot of land in a given community, few actors could easily escape without serious diminution of life chances from any sanctions which the community's members sought to impose. Indeed, given this situation, it was probably only because the sanctions were generally limited to moral opprobrium (healthy adults being apparently but little dependent in other ways on actors outside their own kinship circle) that actors could escape at all from their obligations.

Evidence on the willingness to sanction deviants in these communities is widespread. Thus, for example, 'There is in this neighbourhood a woman who has been turned out of doors by her son and the whole parish is crying out against him as an unnatural villain',[70] and a labourer is noted as saying that 'For fear it would be cast up to me, I would support my mother, my father, or even my uncle.'[71] 'Shame and fear of degradation prevents their being allowed to beg' is one further example of a common sentiment.[72] The fact that community pressures could almost always force marriage on those who had illegitimate children, may also be noted here as further evidence of their strength.[73]

There is also some limited evidence to suggest that landlords could and did exercise considerable influence in support of familial obligations. Thus, 'Before the son is allowed to take the farm which belonged to his old father, a bargain is generally made by the landlord or his agent, that the latter shall be supported from the farm.'[74]

The evidence on the operation of these forces in rural Lancashire is less voluminous and less clear cut, though it suggests similar conclusions, with, however, the possibility that some of these factors (and particularly religion) may have played a slightly lesser role. Most children, notably in the isolated northern small farm areas, grew up and were taught all they knew mainly in a family context.[75] In some areas where farms were widely scattered, as noted in the quotation cited earlier,[76] they developed in almost complete isolation from other sources of influence than the family and, perhaps, the church.

There was, however, one difference from the situation in Ireland: over the horizon lay the towns with their lure of individual freedom. How much this phenomenally affected the relationships between family members will probably never now be known, but it seems probable that it will have introduced just a note of uncertainty into family relationships, offering alternatives to bargains with family members, and thus reducing further the absoluteness of the dependency. Religion, too, was undoubtedly more important here than it was in the towns, with most of the population attending church fairly regularly and holding at least some minimal religious faith.[77]

In the Lancashire rural communities, too, and particularly perhaps in the more traditional areas, there does seem to have been a fairly strong sense of community, and sanctions in the form of gossip and of the withdrawal of community assistance in various times of need may have been not unimportant factors maintaining normative commitment to relationships with family and kin. This is suggested, for example, by a story told by Bamford[78] of a conversation between a Londoner and a Lancashire villager where, on the one hand, the peasant is incredulous because the Londoner does not know various friends of his who live in London, while, on the other, the Londoner is equally incredulous at the way the villager knows all about such private matters as the profit made at the local mill, the source being 'because Tun o'Ned's, o'Bill's, o'Sally's towd meh so; and beside I know it's true an' nowt elze, for meh feyther has lift oppo'th'Cawbook o' his lyre, an' he sesso; an' it's like to be true isno't?'. The *Morning Chronicle* reporter, speaking in particular of the hand-loom weaving village of Middleton, noted the strong neighbourhood sanctions that were imposed there. 'The sergeant (of police) . . . thinks it's quite ridiculous. He says he never saw such people. If he offends one he offends all . . .'[79] Later he notes similar pressures as operating to enforce trading with particular local shops and 'bus companies.[80] Smith,[81] describing local courtship patterns, notes that 'No "chap" might meet his "woman" on a Friday evening. If he did he would be sure to set all the old frying pans and kettles in motion, as if a thousand bees were aswarm.' Thus for those whose life chances were dependent on remaining in the community (which would above all have applied to the farmers' sons), considerable sanctions could have been brought to bear if members of the community were both motivated to seek to enforce familial obligations and in a position to know about non-performance of them.[82] On the other hand, however, it seems at least plausible to suggest that the Lancashire farms, being more affluent, were even less dependent than the Irish on community assistance. To the extent to which this was in fact the case, community sanctioning power would have been less effective.

Discussion – the structural interpretation

In the last section I concluded that, in terms of the heuristic perspective outlined in Chapter 2, in both the societies under study in this chapter the preconditions were present for the existence of a family relational pattern of a normatively specific kind.

If the heuristic framework outlined in Chapter 2 is to be viable, however, patterns which are normatively sanctioned will usually in the long run reflect the underlying structural constraints at work in the society. Even neighbourhood sanctions will only in the long run be powerful, and people will only be motivated to administer them, if the maintenance of one particular set of bargains is in the interests of the majority of the members of the society. Otherwise, it will be remembered, I suggested that subcultures supporting other courses of action would in course of time arise. Some evidence to be produced in Chapter 9 will suggest that in the towns this did indeed happen where the parental generation tried to impose on their children obligations which, at the structural level, they had not the power to enforce. The factors discussed so far also offer no explanation of differences between different socio-economic groups in at least some aspects of relationships within the family and kinship systems. These differences, as I shall show below, appear to have been related to the employment of the father and the size of the income that he could obtain. This section therefore seeks explanations at the structural level of the *form* of the relationships which emerged.

The basis of my argument is that this strong commitment to family and wider kinship bonds was due, at the structural level, to the fact that it was very difficult for any person in these societies to solve the problems with which life faced him without recourse to assistance from others, and that kin provided the source of assistance which gave the optimum bargain to actors in their relationships with others. In the rural areas, indeed, relationships with kin offered almost the only bargain at all which could be taken without very serious and even crippling reductions in life chances.

Particularly important among these needs were, on the one hand, the need to find employment which would bring in an income adequate to provide one with a standard of living at around one's customary level, and, on the other, the need to find some source of assistance in maintaining oneself in dependency states such as old age, which required assistance involving not inconsiderable expenditures for relatively long periods of time. This chapter will primarily confine its attention to these classes of needs since an analysis of the factors operating in bargains over the resolution of these needs will be enough to establish the main points at issue. There were, however, a large number of other critical life situations which the members of these societies had to face (sickness, child care, and even the provision of such things as advice and emotional support). References to the provision of assistance by relatives in these fields, which undoubtedly helped to strengthen further the structural constraints discussed here, will be given as footnotes to Chapters 10 and 11 where the operation of these factors in the towns is discussed in some detail.

Chapters 10 and 11 will suggest that family and kin were the preferred source of assistance in solving these critical life problems in the towns, and that, indeed, much of the assistance was provided by kin. Relationships with kin, and even with members of one's current nuclear family were, however, somewhat unpredictable, and some sectors of the population broke off relationships with family and kin, or were able, by threatening to do so, to reduce their obligations to those which gave a fairly immediate return. The high commitment to family relationships which was so typical of the rural areas, was not generally to be found in the towns.

The key difference between the urban and rural situations seems to be due not to a difference in need for assistance (though needs may indeed have been rather more pressing in rural Ireland for reasons to be discussed below), but rather to the fact that, in the towns, it was possible for actors to find other ways of meeting them than through familial relationships, without any great loss, and, at times, with an actual increase, of satisfactions.[83] In the rural areas, by contrast, it was only through maintaining relationships with family and kin, with all the associated obligations that this involved, that actors could hope to maximise their satisfactions under normal circumstances. A number of cases will, however, be noted where, when it became possible for actors to maximise satisfactions without recourse to kin, kinship obligations were, indeed, rejected.

One further element in this pattern seems crucially important in reinforcing and underpinning these structural pressures to maintain kinship relationships at almost any cost. In these societies those who were in a position to give assistance to those in many states of need, were themselves directly dependent on those in need for the provision of other facilities which, both at a point in time and in the future, were more or less essential for the maximisation of their own satisfactions. Children, at least if their fathers were farmers, were dependent on their parents for employment in the short run, and for their long-run future security in the form of a portion of the family estate. They were dependent in this way precisely because there were, given the current economic organisation of the society, no alternative ways of meeting these short- and long-run needs which offered anything approaching such good benefits at anything approaching such low costs. Refusal on the part of the children to render this assistance as required by their father meant refusal in turn on his part of any share in the set of rewards which maximised the children's life chances. Conversely, refusal by parents to offer rewards to their children for services rendered and to treat them in accordance with the norms of the community deprived them, the parents, of the labour they needed to run the farm now and to keep them in old age.

For this analysis to be plausible it is necessary to establish two points. Firstly, it must be shown that there was for the sons and daughters, or at least for some of them, no viable alternative to family participation if satisfactions were to be maximised. Secondly, evidence must be sought to establish as far as possible that these kinds of factors did indeed operate. The remainder of the chapter reviews data on these points.

The heuristic framework outlined in Chapter 2 would suggest that sons would only wish to become employees of their fathers if no better alternative was available to them, and the fathers would only wish to employ their sons if in this way they too maximised their satisfactions.

It is fairly clear that, for sons, the expectation of inheriting a farm of a reasonable size was, in the framework of the local community in particular, the best solution available. Indeed, concerning Ireland, comments on the acute land shortage, in a situation where every man was anxious 'to get a piece of land',[84] 'in consequence of its being the only support of the peasantry',[85] are widely scattered in the literature. To get land meant, normally, that one had either to inherit it or, possibly, since the potato meant that a family could live on the tiniest of plots, to squat on a piece of land marginal under any other form of cultivation. This latter course of action must, however, as the century progressed, have become more and more difficult as such land became almost completely occupied.[86] Such land was anyway usually inferior. Some did, however, remain available, possibly, as will be noted shortly, with significant results. Emigration, too, though it involved considerable hardship and uncertainty, was another possible solution to the problems presented by land shortage, and one which undoubtedly became more attractive as the size of plots fell and the standard of living they permitted became increasingly miserable.

In rural Lancashire, on the other hand, if the farm was of any size, it almost certainly offered the most promising long term rewards, at least to the inheriting son. The others of course would sooner or later have to travel, though for those from larger farms the reciprocal rewards for remaining at home in the way of a portion would obviously have been not insignificant. Also, given the high mortality rates, younger sons might anyway ultimately inherit the farm. Within the local community, the alternative was either a long spell in a subordinate position as an unmarried and fortuneless farm servant, or a marginal existence as a farm labourer.[87] The lure of the towns is an unknown quantity, but it seems very unlikely that urban occupations could compete in terms of economic return with the rewards derived from the inheritance of farms, at least of those of over twenty or so acres, though it probably did offer attractions to some younger sons, and was a major lure to those with little to inherit.

The farmer father, too, both in England and in Ireland, drew considerable benefit both in short and long run from an ongoing functional relationship with his children. He needed labour on his farm for which he could seldom afford to pay the cash market price,[88] and he and his wife might well need someone to look after them in their old age when they became too infirm to support themselves from the farm.[89] In Ireland there was no proper poor law provision at all for the old or others unable to support themselves, except in a few localities. In contrast, moreover, to the situation in France,[90] the father both in Lancashire and in Ireland was in a strong bargaining position to obtain this kind of support, as long as he could rely on the fact that some or all his children were dependent on the farm for both their long- and short-run optimum life chances, for in both these countries he retained an absolute discretion as to how he divided up the estate between his children.

The basic bargain was then, at the structural level, clear. In England the sons laboured for their father, and received portions in return, one son inheriting the farm, and with it the obligation to care for parents in old age and for any siblings who were not yet adult, until they reached manhood. In Ireland the practice was similar, but most sons received a part of the farm, and usually with it a part of the obligation to care for parents,[91] though the child with whom the father lived often seems to have received, in reciprocation, a somewhat larger portion.[92]

It would seem, moreover, that this line of analysis can also provide insight into the reasons for the difference between these two practices, though it would be necessary to test this hypothesis on a larger sample of societies before coming to any definite conclusions. Poverty in Ireland was greater than it was in England, and the average size of farm smaller. Thus the inducement that the father could hold out to his sons was less. The absence of a poor law on which to fall back meant that his need was also greater. His overall bargaining position was therefore weaker. At the same time the small size of the plot, and the availability of marginal land offering at least a possible alternative, would suggest that in Ireland the bargaining position of the sons was greater. The potato made it possible for the sons and the father to eke out a living on minute scraps of land so that pressures on the Irish father to allow subdivision of his land were more difficult to meet. Everything points, therefore, towards subdivision in Ireland. The argument is strengthened by the fact that before the introduction of the potato, and after the famine, single inheritance appears to have been the more normal pattern.[93] It also seems that in areas where the size of farm was larger, and among the rather better off (in other words where the inducements that the father could offer were greater), marriage was more delayed and subdivision less common.[94] The evidence on the relationship over time between changes in inheritance practices and the changes in productive power of land, suggests that the direction of causality was probably that hypothesised here.

Moreover, it is clear that the Irish at least, at the phenomenal level, did quite specifically recognise that an element of exchange was involved here. Thus, it was noted that, although a good many people were supported by relatives who had 'no property sufficient to compensate anyone for supporting them',[95] for most farmers the support 'must not be looked upon as wholly gratuitous, for the father resigns successive portions of his land to his offspring as they get married, and continues to occupy his own house until they are all settled', and so 'they give up their land as an equivalence for their support'.[96]

The above line of analysis may be taken as explaining the most likely origin of the great willingness of the Irish to support their parents in old age. This argument is strengthened, as would be predicted by the analysis in Chapter 2, by a consideration of what happened even in Ireland when really harsh poverty began to grind down the population; there is considerable evidence to suggest that as poverty increased and the return for help given became less and less, more and more people began to calculate at the phenomenal level the advantages and disadvantages of supporting parents, and, where the return was seen to be too low, to refuse support.[97] Since it was estimated that a man needed three acres to support both family and parent,[98] by the 1840s the mass of the population would already have moved away from a situation where the long-run returns outweighed the short-run costs of assistance. Parallel with this increase in poverty, it seems that the norms themselves began to undergo change so that 'a much more selfish tone is gradually, from the change in circumstances, becoming perceptible among the poorer classes of the people'.[99] Indeed it was even noted that now some of those 'who could well afford support' had begun to refuse to support their parents.[100]

There is other evidence too which suggests both the underlying exchange element at work here, and the way in which the relationship was apparently increasingly becoming the topic of conscious calculation. Short-run costs were increasingly being weighed against short-run benefits.

Usually the parents kept some portion of the land for themselves, or reserved the title to the whole plot, as a surety for their maintenance.[101] They thus were able, by their power of testamentary discretion, to enforce the reciprocal obligation, for non-compliance would meet with the withdrawal of a very significant factor in the son's life chances. Failure to retain control, however, meant that the father lost this power, and this 'has been observed to turn out unfortunately on many occasions; for, as no written contract is entered into, the old parent is consequently depending on the kindness of his son for his very existence', and 'it is no uncommon thing nowadays to see the poor old man turned out when he is getting peevish and silly'.[102] Similarly, 'formerly a verbal contract was thought sufficient but it gave rise to so many quarrels that more caution is used now . . .',[103] while a small farmer reports that those who gave up the title to the land 'were often sorry for it before they died . . . (Now that there is a contract) . . . quarrels are very rare, for if the old persons were driven out of the house, they would take so much along with them . . .'[104] and could thus play off one child against another to ensure support.[105]

A second factor, which appears to have entered into the phenomenal definition of the situation of both farmer and labourer, was that to support a relative did not only involve costs; some benefits were also forthcoming. The parent could frequently be useful on the farm,[106] and, indeed, was expected to be.[107] Moreover, men and women 'are usually useful to mind the house and children'.[108] An extreme case of the consideration of these instrumental advantages seems to be that of an old woman who was taken in even though she was not even a parent but a more distant relative. Her husband, however, who could offer nothing in reciprocation, was not cared for:[109] 'The mother lives with one of her own relatives, for whom she works, being handy and useful; but the old man is obliged to beg; he is no longer able to work as he used ...'[110] Moreover, increasingly perhaps, the norm was interpreted literally. It prescribed support. Demands for additional favours beyond this (particularly for tobacco) were then treated strictly in cost–benefit terms, and usually rejected.[111]

Finally, input–output considerations of exchange seem to have begun to operate to some extent in determining for how long, and to what extent, a son was prepared to support his parent. Obligations were not seen as limitless in time. As the parent lived on and resided for longer and and longer, the benefits forgone by the son increased, until the point was reached where the costs of the best alternative (in terms of sanctions, conscience, complaints from the wife and so on) became less than those of continued support. It seems that the old man was then sometimes at least sent away, the son considering his obligation discharged.[112]

The evidence on the operation of these factors in rural Lancashire is less voluminous, but there is at least some indication that similar forces were at work. Farmers with larger farms do seem to have been much more able to keep their children at home and thus keep support for their old age. This is suggested in Table 28

TABLE 28 *Co-residence patterns of married men aged 55 and over engaged in agriculture (family of procreation only): agricultural village sample, 1851*

	Farmers of:			
	50 acres and over %	20–49 acres %	under 20 acres %	Agricultural labourers %
Living with:				
spouse only	17	31	38	36
unmarried children only	62	58	58	64
married children	21	10	4	–
All: %	100	99	100	100
N	52	29	24	25

The differences between the residence patterns of these three groups of farmers are significant $p < 0.01$ ($\text{chi}^2 = 13.40$) at 4 d.f.

which shows firstly that the smaller the farm, the more likely it was that couples would in old age be left alone with no co-residing children to help them (a situation equally common among the landless agricultural labourers). Secondly, it would appear that the larger the farm, the more likely it was that one child would have married and be continuing to co-reside.

As the size of the farm increased the return for work put in in terms of the portions received would rise.[113] On the smaller farms it was not worth the children's while to stay at home. They left home to become farm servants or independent agricultural labourers or to migrate to the towns, all of which offered a better return.[114] If the farm was large enough, on the other hand, there might even be enough capital to set up a second son on a farm of his own,[115] and the inducement to stay was further increased.

Summarising then, I suggest that the basis, at the structural level, of the functional family solidarity found in rural Ireland (and probably also among certain groups of the population of rural Lancashire) was the absolute *interdependence* of family members such that neither fathers nor sons had any scope for alternatives to the family as a source of provision for a number of crucially important needs. The strong normative sanctions possible in these communities could then usually ensure that all members of the society conformed to these family bargains which gave them the optimum average long-run returns.

As poverty increased in Ireland, however, this structural base began to break up and poverty increasingly brought about a situation where those who provided assistance of a kind which had traditionally been in their long-run interests might even in extreme cases starve and thus not reach the long run at all.[116] Customary values began to lose their power; uncertainty increased; alternative solutions had to be sought by sons and daughters. Emigration increased and parents were not supported. Thus short-run needs and returns came increasingly to dominate bargains between parents and their children, in place of the normatively prescribed bargains offering only longer run rewards to the sons and to the fathers, which had previously been the optima open to both.

In the Lancashire villages too it may at least be suggested that the ability of the father to reward his sons for their labour contribution to the family farm at a competitive level was important in determining whether the sons stayed at home, worked the farm, and supported their parents in return in old age. Labourers' children were perhaps particularly likely to leave home and to refuse support.[117]

Finally, I should like to suggest that one other factor may have been important in rural Ireland in encouraging the population as a whole, and wider kin in particular, to provide some assistance to those in need, even when they were themselves in dire poverty.

In England no one needed to actually starve to death. There was always the Poor Law to fall back on. Thus, if a relative felt that he really could not afford to support a kinsman, and was prepared to face the consequences, if any, in the form of sanctions from the community, he could always allow the person in need to fall back on to the Poor Law. For many, indeed, this was probably the optimum alternative for both assister and assisted, given the extreme privation which would have resulted if kin had tried to care for those in need.[118] It may be noted that some witnesses did indeed consider that the norm among the labouring population, particularly in the south, ran very much along these lines.[119]

In Ireland, at least until 1838, on the other hand, there was no proper Poor Law provision for old or sick or widowed, except in a few areas.[120] Thus, assistance from relatives and neighbours was more or less the only alternative to starvation for those in distress.[121] Given this fact, persons in need would have been more insistent in their claim for assistance, and it would have been more difficult for the potential assister to argue and rationalise that his obligation was removed by the existence of alternative forms of assistance. Indeed, when the person in question would probably die of starvation if assistance was refused, there could be no easy rationalised escape. Either a man gave assistance, or he found a very good reason for not doing so and the person in need might well die. It seems that at this ultimate pole most societies do indeed develop behaviour patterns whereby all those who would not themselves die of starvation by giving assistance do in fact give it, except where poverty becomes very extreme.[122] It it easy enough to explain logically this kind of food sharing among active adults and among those who are temporarily unable (through sickness for example) to find food for themselves, but more difficult to explain why such norms should usually include the permanently dependent as well. Perhaps such norms need fairly strong sanctions to enforce them, and once categories of who shall and shall not be assisted begin to evolve the whole system begins to break down, because unless the norm is absolute, certainty declines somewhat and all actors are encouraged to take only a short-run view. Further research is obviously necessary here.

In terms of the analysis in Chapter 2 it is, however, possible to hypothesise reasons why kin above all were obligated to assist in this way. On the one hand, if this kind of mutual assistance between members of a society near the starvation line is to evolve, the net of assistance must be spread fairly widely, because otherwise at any one time no one individual or nuclear family would be able to provide enough assistance, while other individuals with some surplus would escape the obligation altogether. On the other hand, if the net is too wide, it is easier for some individuals to escape from their obligations altogether. If suspicions begin to arise that some are not contributing a fair share, then predictability of response will fall, and, via a process of disengagement, the whole solidary system will break down, and each individual will seek only to contribute in return for fairly immediate assistance. Thus the optimum system does indeed seem to be one where the boundary of the obligations to assist comes to develop at some clearly structured point intermediate between the nuclear family and the whole community.[123]

8. The phenomenal level: environmental sanctions, ideologies, and socialisation

I suggested at various points in Chapters 5 and 6 that although a large majority of the urban population of Lancashire were involved in relationships with family and kin, and although these relationships seem to have been important to them, yet the nature of their commitment tended, sometimes markedly, towards the calculative pole of what I have here called the phenomenal continuum. Still more evidence in support of these suggestions is presented as it arises in the context of the argument of Chapters 9, 10, and 11. This calculative orientation was in marked contrast to the predominantly normative commitment of the rural populations studied in the last chapter. In marked contrast, too, to the comparative consistency of behaviour revealed in the rural areas was the considerable diversity of family behaviour which was a feature of the urban scene. In Chapter 2 I suggested a relationship between these two elements. In this chapter I shall investigate some of the possible factors underlying the urban population's calculative orientation towards their family relationships. I concentrate here particularly on the normative or trust elements. A second and quite different set of structural factors which reinforced those noted here is discussed in Chapter 11.[1]

Many of my conclusions in this chapter on the normative system are similar to those implied by the writings of the urban disorganisation writers.[2] However, and in marked contrast to the suggestions of this group, this relatively weak normative orientation was not accompanied by a parallel relative absence of primary relationships of a patterned and connected kind. Indeed, not only were functional ongoing relationships with kin being maintained but men and women were also participating actively in networks of neighbours, friends, fellow lodgers, workmates, and persons born in the same village or area as themselves, and this participation, which took place both informally and in certain more formal organisations (notably friendly societies), was highly functional for many of them.

These other primary networks and organisations are, of course, of considerable theoretical importance.[3] Firstly, many of them provided precisely the same kinds of functions as did the kinship system, and were thus, logically, possible viable alternatives to a man's maintaining a strong commitment to his kin. Secondly, and by contrast, such networks could also, of course, under certain circumstances such as existed in the rural areas, have reinforced kinship commitment by negatively sanctioning rejection of kinship obligations. In practice they seem probably to have had only a limited effect on this latter score.[4]

One can posit on logical grounds that, even if an actor is a member of one or more relatively close-knit networks of this kind, if such networks are to ensure that an actor maintains obligations to kin as seen by kin, they must meet certain requirements. A network must be in a position to know about family obligations as seen by alters. Its members must have enough power over the individual to make its point of view a factor which he must consider in his choice of relational patterns. The analysis in Chapter 2 would suggest that in the long run this will normally be so only to the extent that any one part of the network (or sub-net) offers a service to the actor which he cannot obtain from elsewhere except at greater cost. However, to the extent that this sub-net is itself in an interdependent relationship with other sub-nets which also have some limited power over the actor, the true choice may be between this and several other sub-nets taken together, and the alternative. Thus, a number of subnets either fairly tightly connected or alternatively each to some extent superimposed, may together exercise considerable influence over the actor, even though each, taken individually, exercises but little control.

Thirdly, the sub-net must be motivated to attempt to enforce control on the actor in a familistically oriented way. One may suggest on the basis of the formulation in Chapter 2 that groups will typically only make strong efforts to support the performance of family roles to the extent that the interests of their individual members would appear to be threatened, either directly or indirectly, by non-performance of these obligations to third parties.

These requirements seem to imply in turn:

1. that at least one member of the sub-net other than ego must be in contact with ego's kin, either directly or indirectly.

2. that ego must be dependent on the net to such an extent that the ultimate sanctions of expulsion or withdrawal of a service or services are meaningful to him, in that no alternative source of assistance could be mobilised which could adequately compensate him for the resultant decline in his satisfactions.

3. that network members must be motivated to enforce the obligations. The analysis in Chapter 2 suggests that this is most likely to occur either if they are subject to very strong ideological or cultural influences, or, at the structural level, because they, or someone they are dependent upon, are, or expect to be, in a similar status to the kinsman seeking assistance within what is to them, in the light of their present and expected future situations, a relevant time scale. Thus, indirectly, they see non-performance of this obligation by this actor as a threat to themselves.

The major concern of the first part of this chapter, then, is to try to establish to what extent there were these non-familial primary networks, and to what extent they did meet the conditions that appear logically necessary if they were to be motivated and able to sanction non-performance of actors' obligations to third parties. Or, conversely, to what extent, by offering viable alternatives to kinship did they serve instead to weaken commitment to family relationships? Later sections consider other possible sanctioning agencies and the role of ideologies.

The role of primary networks or groups

Firstly, then, there is considerable evidence to suggest that persons born in the same place, even though not related, deliberately clustered together in the same alley, street, or section of the town.[5] These co-villagers provided a number of functions for new arrivals. They found them jobs, provided them with temporary homes, and generally helped them to adapt to urban life. In sum, these nets sometimes and to some extent provided a wide range of services similar to those which I shall show in Chapter 10 were also provided by kin. A shared past history, some shared friends and acquaintances, and, in the case of the Irish, shared religion, and in some cases a shared language different from that of the rest of the community, seem to have increased the extent to which, in a strange town, inmigrants (and particularly the Irish who were also subjected to discrimination by the English) felt dependent on, and were glad to be integrated into, a community of this kind.[6]

Most towns, as is well known, had Irish ghettoes.[7] In the intensive survey area in 1851, 60% of households in the searched area containing at least one Irish born person were next door to, or directly or diagonally opposite, another house containing at least one other Irish born person. There is also some slight evidence to suggest that this type of clustering was not uncommon among persons from the same village, though obviously it is almost impossible to separate out from these clusterings those who were in fact relatives, particularly on the female side. Nevertheless, it may be noted that certain streets do seem to have had connections over time with particular villages. Thus, for example, Birk Street had eleven houses. In 1851 three, and in 1861 four, of these were occupied by families from Kirkham, even though only one of the 1851 families was present in 1861. None of these families had the same surname or were known to be related. If it is considered that the random sample contained only 65 people from Kirkham in the whole town (about 1% of the population) and only 14 male household heads from there, the chances against this type of clustering are obviously quite high.[8] A number of other similar clusterings were also observed. Overall, however, residence patterns were not statistically significantly different from a random distribution. But an overall statistically significant pattern was hardly to be expected given the small proportion of the total population that those born in any one village comprised.

This tendency for persons from the same village to cluster together is even clearer, however, if one examines from sample data the relationship between the birthplaces of lodgers and of the family of the household head. No fewer than 20% of all lodgers aged 15 and over and not born in Preston or in Ireland had been born in the same community as a co-residing member of the nuclear or extended family of the head.[9] Even on the assumption that lodgers were only to be found in houses which actually had lodgers, a random distribution would have resulted in only 2% of lodgers having co-villagers as members of the landlord's family.[10]

It seems reasonable to conclude, then, that inmigrants did make efforts to cluster together, and Chapter 10 will present further data to suggest that these birthplace-based nets had definite attractions for their members. Moreover, such nets were obviously often in a position to be knowledgeable about an actor's familial obligations, at least in as far as they continued to have bridges back to networks in the home community, which Chapter 10 will suggest that most did. Finally, because of their mixed age composition, one might suggest that they had some considerable interest in applying sanctions on family behaviour. To the extent then that a man remained a member of such a net some normative control could be exercised. Further discussion of their potential impact appears below.

There is some evidence too of patterned and functional relational groups among workmates. Even if it were possible to substantiate this suggestion with adequate data, however, it may legitimately be doubted whether these groups were necessarily likely to encourage actors to maintain their familial obligations.[11] To a considerable extent these groups, in as far as they existed, would normally have been both age- and sex-graded, and, moreover, would not necessarily have been well informed on an actor's familial obligations. Thus, in as far as such groups were to be found, and were not superimposed on other groups which were likely to attempt to enforce familial obligations (neighbourhood or co-villager groups for example), their influence may well have been two-edged. On the one hand, they may have acted as something of a force keeping men or youths in an area of the town, with the result that other forces could be brought to bear on them. On the other hand, in as far as they were age- and sex-graded, they may well have formed the basis of subcultures encouraging actors to reject familial obligations, and, to a certain extent, by providing some of the services normally provided by the family, co-villagers, and neighbourhood, may rather have made their members less dependent on these other groups. Their potential effect seems thus more negative than positive.

The same appears likely to have been true to an even greater extent of the groups of young men and women who lived in the large lodging houses. These groups, composed to a considerable extent in the opinion of most writers of persons who had largely terminated relationships with kin, do appear to have offered not only support for the rejection of familial values, but also some degree of companionship and mutual assistance.[12] Their existence was made possible largely by the size of the community which allowed segmentalisation of one's relationships, and by the high individual wages paid to young men and women which allowed them to purchase all the means of subsistence, and thus made possible, at least in the short run, the termination of all relationships with parents and kin. In many of these large lodging houses no questions were asked, no moral enforcement imposed. Family values, indeed, seem often to have been systematically attacked.[13] The existence of these groups, even though their actual membership was small, must then be seen as a threat to the predictability of, and thus commitment to, relationships (particularly long-run relationships) with kin, even among those who did not actually leave home.

The possibility of high commitment to functional primary groups developing among some church members cannot be discounted. Since, however, organised religion appears to have had only a rather tentative hold on the mass of the working class in these towns,[14] these groups are unlikely, generally, to have been of great importance. Master–servant relationships, too, and also relationships between landlords and lodgers who were friends of the family, though undoubtedly potent forces in a limited number of cases, cannot have been very important over the population as a whole.

Neighbours and friends, however, were probably of somewhat more widespread importance. There is considerable evidence that structured primary groups and dyadic relationships developed in these communities between non-kin, and of the fact that these relationships did provide important assistance to many people. The sense of community that seems sometimes at least to have built up in these communities was probably reinforced by the fact that neighbours, workmates, co-villagers, friends, and even fellow church members, would usually have been the same people, so that the attractions and solidarity which developed in one relationship would reinforce the others and make it that much more difficult to break community norms, since so many different kinds of satisfactions might all have to be foregone at the same time.[15]

Further details of the kinds of assistance provided by neighbours under certain circumstances are discussed in Chapters 5 and 10. Here I simply want to present some of the contemporary comment on neighbourhood solidarity. 'In most places', wrote Parkinson[16] about towns like the cotton towns, 'even in most large towns of some antiquity, there is such a thing as neighbourhood, for the poor as well as the rich; that is there is an acquaintance with each other arising from having been born or brought up in the same street; having worked for the same master; attended the same place of worship; or even from having seen the same face, now grown "old and familiar", though the name and even the occupation of the individual might be unknown altogether, passing one's door at wonted hours, from work to meal, from meal to work, with a punctuality which implied regular and steady habits, and was of itself a sufficient testimony of character.'

Even the continual residential mobility of these towns seems to have only rippled the surface of this neighbourhood feeling. True some people came and went, and some had little or no contact even with their immediate neighbours. 'But this migration', wrote Booth,[17] and he could equally well have been writing of Preston forty years earlier, 'rarely proceeds outside the little charmed circle of alleys where "old pals" reside: it is rather of the nature of a circular movement, so that at the end of ten years a man is as near his birthplace as at the beginning, having perhaps lived in each of the neighbouring streets in the meantime.'

The extent of contact on a fairly familiar basis between neighbours is frequently commented on in the literature.[18] Thus 'In most cases the doors of the houses stand hospitably open, and younger children cluster over the thresholds and swarm out upon the pavement ... Every evening after mill hours these streets ... present a scene of considerable quiet enjoyment. The people all appear to be on the best of terms with each other, and laugh and gossip from window to window, and door to door. The women, in particular, are fond of sitting in groups upon their thresholds, sewing and knitting; the children sprawl about beside them, and there is the amount of sweethearting going forward which is naturally to be looked for under such circumstances ...'[19] Many other sources describe children and women popping in and out of each others' houses, chatting and drinking tea. For the women, while the husbands were at work, the neighbourhood and kin gossip group was undoubtedly an important source of satisfactions, company, and confidences.[20] Segregation of conjugal roles, and the callousness of some husbands, probably increased this dependence of women on the neighbourhood group.

There are also many other scraps of evidence which seem to support this suggestion that neighbourhood solidarity was often quite strong. There is some evidence of neighbourhood endogamy.[21] Two sources note the attachment of the working class to particular local shop-keepers.[22] Waugh observes that few working class people would ever beg near their homes during the slumps, for fear of damage to their reputations in the eyes of the neighbours.[23] Also worth noting is the way Bamford's neighbours rallied round him and resisted those who had come to arrest him.[24]

Moreover, there is evidence that where they knew about a person's failure to meet family obligations, sanctions and pressures of various kinds were at least sometimes imposed. In particular the reactions of the neighbours to the man who threw his sons into the canal and whose case was discussed in Chapter 6 may be noted. 'So unpopular had he become on account of his brutal conduct, that he narrowly escaped being roughhandled when removing his goods from —Street. The neighbours had assembled to publicly mark their detestation of his conduct.'[25]

There are some suggestions also that from among their neighbours and workmates most people selected a few closer friends, perhaps those they had known particularly long, had exchanged assistance with particularly often, and with whom particularly strong bonds of trust had been established. It seems to have been to these friends, particularly when one had no kin at hand, that one turned in times of crisis.[26]

It would seem then that the neighbourhood, like the cluster of co-villagers with which it sometimes seems to have overlapped, could and did exert some pressures on family members to carry out obligations to each other. It could do this because it did perform some important functions for its members, and because it was in a position to have at least some information about obligations due. Moreover, its sex and age composition was such that it might have been expected to have had some interest in trying to encourage actors to carry out obligations which gave only a fairly long-run return. Thus it does seem very probable on balance that these community and kin-based neighbourhood networks tended to bias bargains in favour of family and kin obligations and away from alternative patterns of relationship as long as people were willing to remain members of them.

However, it would also seem that the extent to which they could do this was somewhat limited, and probably more limited than it would have been in the rural areas. Firstly, there was always a minority of people in these towns who were recent arrivals, who had no kin to assist them and who therefore needed some other source of help. There seem to have been enough of these people to encourage the development of networks willing to provide assistance to new migrants regardless of kinship or community association. These groups would have had to be able to integrate new members without any real knowledge of the person's past; in other words, commitment to them, such as it was, would have been based on experience of successful exchange relationships over time.[27] The point to be stressed, however, is that as soon as networks exist which will admit members on this basis, without much, if any, reference to their past history, but simply on the basis of services exchanged (and there is little doubt that many of the neighbourhood, friendship, lodging-house, and workmate networks discussed above were partly of this origin), then such groups can be joined not only by those who have no kin in the town, but also, as long as relationships can be segmentalised, by those who have broken off relationships with their kin. In as far as these groups offer similar services to the services offered by kin, they become an alternative to kinship. Even if they are not[28] a wholly viable alternative, they yet have no sanctioning power over those who have terminated relationships with kin for some personal reason.

Thus the first factor limiting the power of neighbourhood networks to enforce family obligations seems likely to have been the fact that if they attempted to interfere too much, any person dependent on them rather than on kin could with rather little long-run loss of satisfactions move to another neighbourhood and join, within a comparatively short period of time, a new neighbourhood network, providing similar services but less informed about his kinship obligations. The uncertain economic situation meant that some people had anyway to do this from time to time if they could not get a job elsewhere through the kinship/community net.

Two other factors may also be noted briefly. Firstly, although co-villagers would have been reasonably well informed about a man's kinship obligations, many neighbourhood groups would not. Thus one would expect anyway that their influence would have been limited mainly to nuclear family relationships, and to relationships with kin who happened to reside within the neighbourhood. Secondly, in these rapidly changing communities containing people from a wide range of backgrounds, there must have been considerable uncertainty as to just what was the optimum line of conduct to follow, and just what obligations one should attempt to enforce.[29] Thus one might expect that to some extent neighbourhood pressures would have been limited to sanctions for non-performance only of very obvious obligations, like, for example, the gross ill-treatment of children as in the case cited above. Further evidence on these as on some earlier points is, unfortunately, lacking.

Sanctions from formal organisations

If the role of primary groups was probably somewhat reduced compared with the rural areas, what about other sources of sanctions? Children were, as I shall show in Chapter 9, largely independent economically of their families, and so were kin, but this would have been to no avail if third parties had been able and willing to sanction negatively in a meaningful way those who rejected family obligations. The same would have happened had these third parties refused to provide some needed service to actors except as members of nuclear families as a whole. Some employers, as I shall show in Chapter 9,[30] had in the early days attempted to employ whole families and, to some extent, to supervise their moral welfare, but this had gradually broken down with the concentration of industry in the town and the fact that the technology employed demanded a workforce with an age and sex composition different from that which the employment of whole families could provide.[31]

Another agency which might have been in a position to wield enough power to ensure that family obligations were maintained was the Poor Law, to which many of those dependent on family assistance to maintain a standard of living adequate for survival would have been forced to turn had relatives refused to support them. The law did indeed still lay on individuals the duty of maintaining their parents, grandparents, children, and grandchildren,[32] and attempts were made from time to time to enforce these statutes.[33] Systematic enforcement was, however, made almost impossible by two factors. Firstly, the extreme mobility of the population made the tracing of individuals who refused to meet their obligations very difficult.[34] Secondly, such was the poverty of the population and the heterogeneity of its life situations that it was very difficult to define by statute the circumstances under which any given person could really be expected to pay.[35] In practice, then, the Poor Law's sanctioning power was limited, though probably still of some importance in extreme cases.

One remaining agency which might possibly have exercised some control was the friendly society, membership of which was very widespread among the Lancashire proletariat. Contemporary writings have little to say on relationships of friendly society members with each other and with their society, except in the context of the drinking bouts which occurred at the meetings of many lodges.[36] It seems, however, highly unlikely that any kind of formal sanction could have been brought to bear on members by their society, since any attempt to do so would have contravened their rules and thus have laid them open to legal action. As far as informal sanctions are concerned, the situation is less clear. Once a man became a member of one friendly society lodge it was usually disadvantageous (or, as he got older, almost impossible) for him to change to another, unless he obtained a formal transfer. Such a process could therefore have provided a basis whereby information about a man's rejection of role obligations could be spread around a group small enough to apply informal sanctions effectively. Since he did not usually *have* to participate in lodge activities, however, this information could only have been fully effective if used via a neighbourhood sanctioning system. No evidence of any kind suggests that either stage of such a process did in fact operate, though this is only really what is to be expected regardless of the true case. However, the overall effect of any such action is unlikely to have been very significant, even if it did occasionally occur.

More importantly, perhaps, friendly society membership did provide a possible structured alternative to kinship as a means of meeting crisis situations. Its efficacy in this regard is further considered in Chapter 10. Its role as a source of affective relationships, and thus as an alternative to family relationships, while possibly of some limited importance, cannot now be assessed.

Ideologies

The third group of factors which I want briefly to consider here is the independent influence that ideologies formulated and administered from outside the system may have had on the working class man's orientation to his family roles.

The first and most obvious of these ideologies is religion.[37] Religious attendance in the northern manufacturing towns was among the lowest in the country, and contemporaries were unanimous in their belief that it was above all the working classes who failed to attend church. The published results of the 1851 religious census are very difficult to interpret, but the figures for Preston (which are subject to some margin of error[38]) give a minimum figure for census Sunday (including Sunday school attenders) of some 18% of the population,[39] and a maximum of 27%.[40] The figures for the other Lancashire manufacturing towns were slightly higher, but the maximum figure seldom exceeded 40%, or the minimum 27%.

On this single Sunday, then, not much over 20% of the population of Preston attended church. 6% of all household heads fell into SEGs I and II, and 21% into SEGs I, II, and III. Though obviously by no means all of these did in fact attend, attendance among these groups will undoubtedly have tended to be high. Moreover, it is known that one section of the working class who do seem to have been more regular attenders were the Irish Roman Catholics, most of whom were in working class occupations. It is notable that on the assumptions made here, Roman Catholic attendance in Preston made up almost half of the total on census Sunday. It is true that Preston had a substantial native Roman Catholic population.[41] Nevertheless it is inconceivable that a high proportion of this Roman Catholic attendance was not made up of working class persons of Irish extraction.

It is obvious, of course, that more of the working class attended church occasionally than would be revealed by a survey taken on any given Sunday. Nevertheless, it does seem clear that religion can have seriously touched the lives of only a minority of the working class, probably, except for the Irish, above all the most prosperous sectors. It was noted that many of the working class 'have not even a traditional faith',[42] and several commentators observed that even when they went to church, its moral influence was often low because ministers were not in proper contact with their flock, and because much of what was said was totally irrelevant or beyond their comprehension.[43]

The other main agency, education, by which middle class familistic values might have been inculcated into the working class, seems generally to have been equally ineffective. Few parents seem to have valued education very highly, and for some at least it was seen only as a form of useless idleness liable to deter children from learning the virtues of work,[44] or at best as a good way of ensuring that the children were kept out of mischief.[45] Many parents anyway found it very difficult to keep their children at school at all.[46] The teachers, moreover, were often ignorant, and only in a few schools was any attempt made to instil morality and a 'proper' appreciation of family responsibility into the children.[47] Educational provision was anyway very inadequate,[48] and the higher SEGs generally made up a disproportionate section of the classes.[49] A minority, but probably a sizeable one, never had any education at all, and many more had little that was of any use.[50]

Summarising then, familistically oriented definitions of family roles were undoubtedly encouraged for important minorities of the population by these ideological influences,[51] and where actors were sure that their family and kin had internalised these values then one might expect that considerable commitment to family relationships did develop.[52] For the majority, however, these factors cannot have had more than a minimal independent and consistent influence.

Child-rearing and socialisation

Finally, a few words, all that the data will allow, can be said on the subject of the development of the superego and internalisation of familistically oriented values. No general assessment is, of course, possible, but I think one may suggest that in some segments of the population superego development was probably seriously impaired and few familistic values internalised. Very few indeed of the population seem likely to have approached the state of a 'fully socialised man'.

Inkeles has usefully summed up the literature on superego impairment in a passage which might, from the limited evidence available and presented in Chapter 6, almost be describing the patterns of socialisation of some sectors of the Lancashire working class: 'Inadequate superego development can be expected in the absence of the parent, or where only intermittent, irregular, and inconsistent parental demands are met. In our culture, the effects are likely to be marked if it is the father who fits into this pattern, especially when this is linked with insufficiency of female nurturance. Inadequate superego development is also likely where the parental treatment is very harsh, especially physically, and unmixed with affection and love . . . Again, where the parent is extremely weak or seemingly lacking in capacity, power, prestige, or general adequacy, the consequence is likely to be weak superego development following from barriers against the internalisation and valuation of the parents as role model.'[53] Similar findings are summarised by Klein.[54]

I noted in Chapter 6 some neglect by mothers, including absence from home for large parts of the day, and the fact that harsh and brutal fathers were not uncommon. I think one may suggest, too, that many fathers had rather low status, particularly in the eyes of their sons, due to their inability to obtain well-paid work, or from their losing their well-paid jobs in middle age. The poor performance by some parents of family roles towards their children, seems hardly likely to have encouraged the child to develop familistic values even where the parent was taken as a role model. Under these circumstances reactions to situations by many people were more likely to take place at the ego level than at the superego level. This, in turn, would have almost inevitably resulted in a much more calculative orientation in relational behaviour.[55]

Conclusions

Summarising, then, the forces discussed in this chapter seem likely to have played in comparative perspective only a limited role in encouraging actors to maintain relationships with family and kin, because their sanctioning power was severely circumscribed. The lodging houses allowed the existence of viable (at least in the short run) delinquent subcultures; alternative neighbourhood primary groups, ignorant of an actor's past history and other obligations, were also fairly readily available. No group was able to exercise strong normative control, and indeed it is doubtful whether there would have been any great consensus over exactly what lines of conduct were to be encouraged, beyond a number of fairly basic principles. All actors, as I shall show in Chapter 9, could if they wished break free from economic dependence on parents and kin and though there were disadvantages in such a step many of the population had anyway to be in this situation. In consequence, if family demands became too pressing, escape to another town or part of a town was always possible, and many were anyway forced by economic constraints to make such moves from time to time. Third party ideological and superego controls were weak. Under these circumstances, and given the fact that rejection of family obligations was undoubtedly common enough for most to know of at least one case, considerable uncertainty would be predicted. Willingness to perform role obligations became for many something to be tested by trial and error, not something to be taken for granted. Under these circumstances some development of a more calculative orientation to family relationships would be expected from the analysis in Chapter 2. Such a development did apparently occur, yet such relationships were maintained. I discuss the factors leading to this situation in Chapters 9, 10, and 11. In Chapter 11 I also discuss a second and very potent set of factors pushing people towards such a calculative orientation.

9. The economic influences on urban family structure

I argued in Chapter 7 that in Ireland and in the countryside around the Lancashire cotton towns family relationships were of crucial importance for a considerable section of the population. The organisation of the economic system was such that many youngsters had little or no alternative but to remain in close relationships with their families if their life chances were not to be significantly reduced both in the long run (through loss of inheritance) and in the short run (through loss of employment). In turn, their families were to a great extent reciprocally dependent on them, particularly in Ireland where there had been no Poor Law. The need for assistance in many other ways reinforced this interdependency.

Moreover, considerable normative pressures could be put on the individual by third parties from whom he could not easily escape, and there was in these small communities little scope for competing subcultures. The family operated largely as a closed socialisation system. Few alternative definitions of family obligations impinged seriously on to the view of most young men and women in early life.

The last chapter suggested that these sanctioning pressures were much weaker in the towns. This chapter explores the role of relationships with the economic system as a factor influencing family cohesion in urban areas.

In Ireland and the rural areas, for the farmers in particular, the economic and family systems were but little differentiated. In general in the towns, differentiation went much further though its extent varied widely from trade to trade. Moreover, even where the father was employed in a relatively undifferentiated occupation, some alternatives were available to the child, the taking of which only slightly reduced, or in some circumstances may even have improved, his life chances, particularly in the short run. Differentiation, therefore, reduced considerably the dependence of children on their parents at times when their parents were, or were likely soon to be, dependent, for different reasons, on them. It also, of course, was an important factor giving family members access to different influences and subcultures and, thus, to the possibility of new and alternative definitions of family roles. I outline first some of the varieties of this differentiation and their implications, before going on to assess their relative distribution in the population as a whole.

Undifferentiated systems in the towns

Few urban occupations offered even the possibility of a complete superimposition of family and economic roles. Looked at in terms of the SEG classification employed in this study, only the trade group, most of the hand-loom weavers, some artisans, and some of the middle class were in this position. At most, therefore, one-third of parents with children aged between 10 and 19 were likely to have ever been able to consider offering employment to their children or kin in enterprises which they themselves controlled.

There is considerable evidence, however, that many of this third did offer this employment, and that family members were encouraged to, and did, enter the family concern. For the commercial and industrial middle class Dorothy Crozier has shown in a fascinating paper the 'not uncommon' existence in London of family businesses based on 'patrinominal kin nuclei'.[1] In Lancashire, similar partnerships seem to have occurred among the entrepreneurs,[2] but kin also seem often to have been recruited as employees. Gaskell notes how, in the earlier days of the factories, upwardly mobile entrepreneurs brought their relatives into the mills.[3] This kind of employment seems also to have been not infrequent in trade occupations. Thus George Salisbury left a cotton factory and 'spent some time as an auctioneer in the service of another of his uncles'.[4] Samuel Bamford and his wife 'went to reside with my wife's uncle and aunt, she assisting the old people in the house and shop ...'[5] Jonathan Ambray worked as a muffin seller for his sister.[6] The sample contained many similar cases. Ann Davis, a childless pawnbroker, for example, had taken three nephews, William Parry, Joshua Cunliffe, and Charles Stoney, into her business as assistants. I shall suggest later that many of these kin were orphans or children of siblings fallen on bad times, and that the taking of these relatives into one's employment was one important way in which one assisted kin who needed help in crises.

Not only kin, of course, were employed. Far more frequent was the employment of one's own children. Just one example is John Patterson and his wife who ran a drapery shop in Preston in 1851. Their two eldest sons were 'Drapers' also, while the 16-year-old son was described as 'Draper (Bookkeeper)', and the 14-year-old as 'Draper (Errand Boy)'. Their eldest daughter was described as a 'Dressmaker'. Many other similar family businesses were found in the sample among those in the business and trade SEGs.

Domestic and artisan occupations, too, gave scope for the employment of children and kin. It is obvious from the census that numerous artisans, self-employed or working on a putting-out basis, employed their children as assistants, or as formal or informal apprentices. Commissions of Inquiry noted the employment of children in this way by, among others, hatters, fustian cutters, heald knitters, and also nightmen, besides, of course, hand-loom weavers.[7]

Not all children of artisans, however, followed their fathers' occupations, any more than all children of tradesmen worked in their fathers' trade. Indeed, I shall show later that, taken overall, those who did so were in a minority. Thus, for example, while James Eastham, flagger and slater, himself employed one of his sons, his other adult son was apprenticed to a spindle maker. Such cases are relatively common. Sometimes, however, the children seem to have had few alternatives to family employment, and were given little choice of occupation by their parents. In these cases, brought up to and put to a trade, often for long hours, from an early age, they had no other skills and had nowhere else to turn for equally remunerative employment. Moreover, although the hours and working conditions of those in employment in these families were frequently appalling,[8] one would expect that some feelings of trust and mutual dependence of not inconsiderable strength would have developed from this continual interaction, which might in turn have further biased bargains in favour of family obligations. Obviously, however, there is no hard evidence on this point.[9]

Thus, in the towns, some relatively undifferentiated systems were still to be found. Viable alternatives were, however, much commoner than in the country particularly for the less affluent groups, and, compared with the rural areas, these opportunities could usually be taken up with less disruption of one's life, if, whether as a result of ill-treatment, or for economic reasons, one believed one could obtain a better bargain elsewhere. On the first of these reasons, ill-treatment, evidence is obviously difficult to obtain, but a good, and certainly not unique case is recounted by Stella Davies.[10] Her grandfather's sons were trained in the family business, but later broke away. 'Grandfather had hoped and expected that they would follow him as master builders and so extend the business, but none of them did. He was a stern, irascible man, hard, self-willed, and autocratic ... I think his sons found him difficult to get on with, for they all escaped from him in early manhood ... Jim worked under his father until he was married when, feeling perhaps that he had had enough, he told his father that he had got another boss.[11] My grandfather was wrath, and never really forgave him.' The second, the role of economic factors (particularly poverty) in determining whether or not sons followed the parental trade, will be taken up again later.

Semi-differentiated systems

So far, analysis has been confined to the minority of the population for whom to some extent and in principle the family and economic systems were superimposed in a way not dissimilar to that already discussed for farmers in rural areas. One may imagine that this must have had its effects on the bonds uniting family members, even though this is almost impossible to establish with absolute certainty with the kinds of data available. For the majority of the population, however, the family and economic systems were more differentiated, though the differentiation was seldom, perhaps never, complete.

Probably the least differentiated form of factory-based economic organisation is where the employer only recruits the principal employees, and leaves to them the engagement and payment of the necessary assistants. Thus family heads may recruit and employ children or kin, and also others, under their surveillance and economic control. This form of organisation, akin to subcontracting among artisans, was common in the nineteenth century in a number of trades, and its operation in the cotton industry is discussed in some detail by Smelser.[12]

It is important to note that, in addition to changes that it brings about in the authority position of the father and in his role in socialisation, this method of organising production differs in three important ways from a pure domestic system, ways which might be expected to have an effect on family relationships.

Firstly, under a pure domestic system, the scale and organisation of production can, to a considerable extent, be adjusted to the size of the available family labour force. Under a factory system, on the other hand, the size of the labour force employed is not usually discretionary. Instead the number of assistants is specified by the requirements of the productive process. If a man has no suitable children or kin, he must seek them in the general labour market. This, in turn, opens up an alternative to family employment in the same industry, and using the same skills, even for the children of those in the trade. As a result, parental power must inevitably, it would seem, be subject to some counter-bargaining on the part of the children. In particular, individual children must be kept content with what they, as individuals, receive, instead of their interests being to a considerable extent automatically subordinated at the decision of the father to the interests of the family as a whole.

Secondly, since this system lacks a property base, the relationship is almost inevitably a short one. After a few years children become adults, and independent workmen. The children do not therefore remain dependent until marriage or the death of the parent, as they frequently do in a farm, trade, or business relationship.

Finally, the factory provides a whole new basis for interaction and a broader reference group for its employees than that provided by the domestic system, where most of the relationships a child has will be with his family. This, in turn, is likely to mean that solidary relationships outside the family may arise, entered by the actor as an individual. As a result obligations which conflict with obligations to the family may develop in a situation, moreover, where the family's control over the socialisation of the actor is at the same time reduced.[13]

In cotton, this 'subcontract' system of factory employment had long been established, with spinners (and some rovers too[14]), usually paid by the piece, hiring their own assistants.[15] It was estimated in 1816 that 54% of the children under 18 in 13 mills in Preston, and 59% in 11 mills in the country around

Preston, were paid by the spinners and rovers.[16] Though by no means universal, where adult male spinners were employed the practice continued widely throughout the period under review.[17] In throstle spinning, however, which gradually supplemented and partly replaced the mules, and where, anyway, the principals were more often women, child assistants were usually paid by the masters. In power-loom weaving, on the other hand, the tenters (assistants to the weavers) were often employees of the weavers,[18] though the weavers were as often women as men.[19] In all, in 225 mills in the southern half of the cotton districts in 1833, 48% of all children under 18 were employed by the operatives. 88% of children engaged in mule spinning were in this position, 29% of those in weaving, 16% of those in preparatory processes, and only 1% of those in throstle spinning.[20] With the gradual relative increase of throstle spinning and power-loom weaving, the overall proportion paid by the operatives would have declined somewhat further by the 1850s, though probably a high proportion of the youngest groups still spent their early years in the mills in this relationship to a principal. Many, however, would later have moved to other branches where this practice was not found, or have left the mill altogether.

Where this system was in operation, parents could obviously employ their own children as assistants, and many did.[21] This was advantageous to the parent because he could extend his control and authority over the child, and train the child to a trade under his own eye.[22] He could also ensure that most of what he was paid went into the family purse. In addition, it was usually advantageous for the child because the parent would normally be a more sympathetic master, though the amount of wages that the child received to spend at his or her own discretion might well be below what might have been retained from a free market relationship.[23]

It is essential to note, however, that, even in spinning, by no means all of these child assistants can ever, *at any period*, have worked under a parent, nor can all spinners ever have had even some of their own children among their piecers for their whole spinning careers. This was because, at any point in time, only a minority of spinners can ever have had enough children of the right age. The most thorough, though small-scale investigation by a contemporary into this topic was that conducted by Shuttleworth in the early 1830s. He found that 837 fine spinners in 19 Manchester mills had an average age of 32. 47% were under 30, and 65% were under 35.[24] Thus, even if this group had an average age of marriage of 21 (which looks not unlikely from Shuttleworth's data), very few of the spinners under the age of 30 would have had even one child old enough for factory work and, given the mortality rates of the period, fewer still (even of those under 35) would have had two.

In this context it is interesting to note that in the Preston sample for 1851, 29% of all male spinners other than throstle spinners were under 25, and 66% under 35.[25] Only 7% of the under 35s had co-residing children in employment.

Many were not even married. Of the spinners of 35 and over, on the other hand, 69% had at least one co-residing child in employment, though many even here had only one.[26]

The crucial point to note, therefore, is that this practice of allowing operatives to employ assistants, though widespread, can *at no period* have resulted in a predominantly parent–child pattern of employment, on the ideal-typical artisan and subcontract pattern,[27] though, of course, when a spinner became the father of children of a suitable age, he could at all times offer them this kind of employment. A further implication may also be noted. Since almost all spinners had to employ children who were not relatives, children, even if their father was a spinner, could theoretically at least find an alternative employer in the cotton industry. On the basis of the analysis in Chapter 2 one would expect this to have had a weakening effect on parental control and to have given some freedom of choice to the child. Later discussion will confirm this expectation.

In the Preston sample 46% of all spinners with at least one child at work had a child whose occupation was given as a piecer. In most cases it is reasonable to assume that this child was employed by his or her father. Many of those not employed as piecers were engaged in other better paid factory occupations, though, as I shall show shortly, this was by no means always the case. Some of the exceptions may have been allowed by their parents to take less arduous employment outside the mill,[28] some probably had fathers who were not at liberty to employ their own piecers, and some were probably either too young or could earn substantially more in an alternative employment. It seems not unlikely, however, in view of some of the evidence to be presented later, that some had in fact taken the opportunity offered by other employments to bargain their way out of a subordinate relationship somewhat against the will of their parents.

There is, moreover, some limited evidence to suggest that, at the phenomenal level, conscious calculations on this basis did at times enter the parent–child relationship. One example, which must suffice for the present, is the case of Abraham Docker, a 40-year-old rover who told the Factory Commissioner[29] that a year previously 'the sons and me agreed to separate because I was unwell, and I could not perform the same quantity of such work'.

Where the spinners had no children to employ as assistants they sometimes employed younger siblings or other kin; children of neighbours and lodgers were also taken on.[30] Where non-relatives were employed they were sometimes brought into the spinner's household in some kind of quasi-familial relationship.[31]

Of the 62 spinners in the Preston sample with no children at home in employment, 4 had co-residing relatives who were piecers, 2 had piecer lodgers, one a piecer in the family which shared the house, and one had a wife who was a piecer. Many others probably obtained some at least of their piecers from among the children of relatives living nearby. There are cases in the literature of piecers working for brothers,[32] uncle,[33] and brother-in-law.[34]

Just what proportion of factory children were employed by family and kin it is difficult to say for any period; but it was not high. The only published figures available for the early years are found in the Factory Inquiry of 1816,[35] which suggest that some 12% of persons under 18 in 13 Preston mills, and 17% in 11 mills in the country around Preston were employed by parents, brothers, and sisters.[36] The only other published figure that I have traced is in Shuttleworth's 1830s study.[37] He estimated that 15% of the 3,233 piecers of his 837 fine spinners were relatives of the spinners.

In the Preston sample of 1851 households, of all piecers other than throstle piecers 10% had a father who was a spinner. A further 6% had a co-residing relative or husband so employed, and another 6% a lodger, fellow lodger, member of the landlord's family, or someone else in the same house. 30% of piecers aged under 15, however, had a parent or co-residing relative who was a spinner. In addition some piecers undoubtedly worked for non-co-residing kin. It is obvious, then, that there was in 1851 and had always been considerable employment of non-kin. Indeed non-relatives had probably always been a majority even though kin were probably preferred as being more reliable,[38] and also less expensive since, instead of being paid a living wage, their earnings could be merged into the family purse.[39]

So far, discussion of this semi-differentiated employment system has been confined to cotton factories. In fact, however, it was to be found in most trades where young assistants were required by principals. It was usually convenient for the employers, and it gave the employees the opportunity to train their children to a trade and to supplement the family income without giving too much independence too early to their children. It was quite frequent in fustian cutting where this was not still on a domestic basis,[40] in some Manchester plate glass works,[41] often in lucifer match making,[42] in brick making,[43] in tobacco manufacturing,[44] in pinmaking in Warrington,[45] in some branches of engineering,[46] and in metal working[47] and file cutting.[48]

In most of these cases, the relationship was more like the pure artisan system than it was in spinning. The assistants enabled the principal to produce more than he could otherwise have done alone, and, since wages were paid by the piece, to raise family wages; but the number of these assistants, and even their existence, was not firmly fixed by the inexorable demands of the production process (compare also to some extent, the employment of assistants in power-loom weaving).

Among other trades where assistants were more definitely needed by the process (and where, therefore, while opportunities for the employment of children and kin undoubtedly existed, there will also presumably have been a higher proportion of assistants who were *not* relatives of the principals), were metal manufacturing and forging teams[49] and some lithographic printers.[50] In mining, too, it was widespread practice for colliers to pay their own draw boys or girls, who pulled the coal from the face to the bottom of the shaft. The masters preferred this scheme because of the difficulties of supervising drawers underground.[51] As well as children, other kin were sometimes employed. There are references to a daughter-in-law,[52] cousins,[53] a nephew,[54] and wives.[55] An analysis of accidents involving both a collier and his drawer(s) at the same place and same time in the pits of the Bridgwater Trust from March 1838 to March 1841, revealed that colliers and drawers, or just drawers, had the same surname in six out of the eight cases, which certainly suggests a high rate of family-based employment in the pits.[56]

One other form of family-based employment, also of an only partially differentiated nature, occurred at least occasionally in these early factory towns, and merits a brief note. Under this system the family was not necessarily employed on the same operation, but the whole family was engaged as a family and wages for the whole family were paid to the family head.[57] This system had been much used in the early mills[58] but in later years appears to have been largely confined to the contracts given to the small number of Parish Assisted Migrants.[59]

This system, had it been universally adopted, would have meant that, in spite of the fact that they were employed in factories, children would have remained dependent on their parents in a way not very different from that found in the rural areas among the farmers. Fathers would have controlled the family funds, and no viable alternatives would have existed. In fact, this form of employment seems to have been rare in later years. It was probably not pushed further because mills had great demands for some classes of labour, notably children, but little for others, notably adult men. Thus there was no scope for the employment of all members of the families of the employees.[60]

Semi-differentiation and occupational recruitment

So far, the discussion has been confined to the *employment* of relatives by relatives. Relatives were, however, also economically dependent on each other in other ways and this was particularly so when it came to obtaining a job. Many employers consciously set out to recruit whole families, or all the younger members of families as they reached working age, or at least welcomed especially relatives of their employees. An employer of Parish Assisted Migrants noted that he could 'now, without any trouble, supply myself from Bledlow, by mentioning to my Bledlow hands that I am ready to take more.'[61] Henry Ashworth too had a definite policy of recruiting all the children of his hands.[62] The recruitment of whole families by masters in the early days has already been mentioned,[63] and the relieving officer of Hyde noted approvingly that 'when their family work at the mills, some light job is generally found for the old people likewise'.[64]

Even where employers did not follow a deliberate policy of recruiting family members, workers, particularly if they were reliable, could often obtain places for children and other kin in the firm on a preferential basis. Thus, in cotton, where the father was not in a trade where he could directly employ his children, it was 'customary upon the part of a father that you employ to make application to you, when a child is of the age of eight or nine years, to take him into a factory'.[65] A Parish Assisted Migrant wrote to her brother 'if you think you would like to come, send us word, my husband will try for you'.[66] Compare also 'My uncle in Failsworth had been employed there for years as a silk warper, and he was the means of getting room made for me in the warehouse belonging to Messers. J. T. & T. Walker, Silk Manufacturers, York Street, the manager of which concern was a younger uncle',[67] or 'a warehouse in which my elder brother had worked wanted an apprentice. I applied, and because they had been delighted with my brother, they gave me the job.'[68] Numerous other cases appear of persons in all stations of life soliciting employers for jobs for friends and relatives.[69] Indeed, at a time when the demand for jobs frequently exceeded the supply so that employers could take the pick of the field, this seems to have been the usual way of getting a job, and one which will obviously have reinforced kinship bonds to some degree.[70] A number of cases appeared in the intensive survey which suggested that men had found jobs for inmigrant and unemployed kin in their own trade. Cotton and flax mills, foundries, warehousing, railways, and even the post office, are among the employments involved.

In some trades employees tried to take this even further, thereby strengthening their economic position in the trade and also increasing their hold over their children. A number of trades made and tried to enforce on the employer rules restricting to certain close relatives entry to the trade, or, more commonly, entry into training to its better paid branches. In this way, those found jobs by kin would undoubtedly have got the best jobs.[71] Cotton spinners had tried to institute such rules before 1800.[72] The inaugural meeting of the 'One Grand General Union of Operative Cotton Spinners' ruled that 'No person be taught to spin except a son, brother, or orphan nephew of spinners and the poor relatives of the proprietors of the mills',[73] and this was confirmed at the 1830 meeting,[74] and again in 1838.[75] Piecers, however, could come from any source.[76]

Similar restrictions on training applied at various times in the century to power-loom weavers (sons only to be trained),[77] warpers (son or brother),[78] silk and felt hatters (sons).[79] Sons were to be given special preference among mill-wrights and joiners,[80] and Manchester plasterers.[81] The Openshaw dye works had an unsuccessful strike about 1840 when 'The dyers insisted that the masters should employ none but the sons of men connected with the business.'[82] However, these attempts to enforce formal kinship preference, which had never probably covered even a majority of trades, gradually declined, and by the end of the century kin were only expected to receive formal preference in a handful of small unions.[83]

Thus, even where men did not employ relatives directly, they were often in the mid-nineteenth century instrumental in getting them employed.[84] However, in those trades where apprenticeship still operated or even operated in an atrophied form the parent played an even greater part in the hiring, being actually a partner to the contract and responsible for the son's good conduct. Under these circumstances children were obviously to a great extent dependent on their parents should they wish to enter many more or less desirable occupations, though only, of course, for a few years. Contracts of this kind do not seem to have been made only in traditional trades;[85] some parents contracted their children's labour with employers in different ways and for different reasons in some manufacturing trades too, in pinmaking, fustian cutting, and metals and engineering, for example.[86]

Kin, then, were perhaps typically responsible for getting a man a job. This practice had, however, a reverse and far less attractive form, though one which must have strengthened at least the motivation to try to control the behaviour of kin. This is best shown in operation by one of Waugh's stories where a character is of a different political persuasion from his employer, and is threatened with discharge if he votes according to his beliefs in the forthcoming election. His wife reminds him 'that our Sarah an' our Mary, an' our Ailse, an' our Sam, an' his childer (children), – they o' wortchen (work) at his mill; an' as sure as ever thou votes for tother side, they'n every one get th' bag!'[87] At least two cases appear where as a result of operatives giving evidence to Parliamentary committees, they were discharged, and 'Their relations were turned away as well as themselves',[88] while an employer is recorded as saying on a similar occasion 'his Two Brothers, yonder, when they have done their work, may follow him if they please; they shall work here no longer'.[89]

Summarising, then, at the structural level, it would seem that children were much less dependent on their parents for employment than among farmers' families in the rural areas because alternatives were available which they could take if they wished. Nevertheless there were still considerable advantages to be obtained by maintaining relationships with parents because the jobs one could obtain in this way would be better. For kinsmen moving to a community where they were not known the advantages were even greater. Thus bargains were still biased towards the family.[90] The analysis in Chapter 2 would predict, however, that the greater flexibility which existed in the towns would make possible some weakening of commitments to family relationships and would allow a decline in the willingness to meet automatically, normatively prescribed obligations towards family members. In later sections I shall suggest that, at the phenomenal level, conscious calculation of the advantages and disadvantages in economic terms of maintaining relationships even with nuclear family members occurred not infrequently.

Employment patterns of family members

So far discussion has been limited to establishing the nature and implications of undifferentiated and semi-differentiated employment. In this section I shall review quantitative data on employment patterns to try to obtain some indication of the incidence of family-based employment in the population as a whole.

Taken overall, witnesses differed in their opinions as to how often all the members of a family were, in fact, employed in the same mill,[91] though, as was noted above, some employers had a definite policy to this end. Since this practice was also apparently preferred by the workers,[92] it must have been common for several members of the same family to work for the same employer. Some figures on recruitment of kin as assistants have already been presented. The literature is full of quotes like 'Father used to grind here too; he died of it';[93] 'His father was a joiner on the works, and his brother, of 15 years of age, worked in the mechanic's shop.'[94] Some families had obviously worked in the same firm for generations. Analysis of the 83 names of employees at the Sandy Vale print works[95] showed that 46 had the same surname as another employee, so a good proportion of workers there were obviously related even if affines are excluded. It may be noted, however, that only 9 out of the 29 teenage children of employees appear in the list.

No general data are available on the employment of related persons by the same employer, but the extent to which Preston sons were employed in the same trade or industry as their father in 1851 is given in Table 29. This table is, of course, biased to an unknown degree by the possibility that sons would have been more likely to remain at home if they were in the same occupation as the rest of the family. Nevertheless, a number of points appear to merit brief attention.

Among the self-employed, the sons of tradesmen seem to have been particularly likely to follow their fathers' occupations. Artisans, on the other hand,

TABLE 29 *Proportion of sons in the same trade or industry as their fathers*[a] *(co-residing children only), by SEG: Preston sample, 1851*

		Sons aged under 20		Sons aged 20 and over	
	SEG of father	%	*N*(100%)	%	*N*(100%)
I and II	White collar	42	12	(17)	6
III	Trade	37	43	58	31
IV	Higher factory	73	55	60	15
V	Artisan	22	60	35	20
VI	Lower factory	86	21	50	10
VII	Labourer	11	72	44	36
VIII	Hand-loom weaver	4	45	54	13

[a] e.g. if father is in cotton, son in cotton; if father in flax, son in flax; if father a wheelwright, son a wheelwright; if father a labourer, son a labourer. Obviously some occupational groups are larger than others, and at the margin decisions may be a little arbitrary, but this seems unlikely to bias the results significantly in any direction.

seem to have been less likely to bring up their children to their trade, probably because their sons could earn so much more working in the mills, at least until their mid-teens, while hand-loom weaving was even more affected at least in the younger age groups, not only because the children were unlikely to want to follow the family trade, but also because the family could not afford for them to do so.[96] Among the self-employed, then, only the trade group seem to have escaped the impact of industry, and this because of their relative affluence. They could offer more to their children in return for work in the family business, and the marginal return to the family from their contribution was more likely to equal that obtainable from factory employment.[97]

Turning to factory occupations, two points of some interest emerge from Table 29 and from a rather different analysis in Table 30. Firstly, it appears probable that it was above all the children of skilled factory workers who were likely to be kept on in the mill after about the age of 20. The proportion of their children employed in mills after the age of 20 was higher relative to the proportion employed under the age of 20, than was the proportion for any other group.[98] Secondly, a higher proportion of their children in the 20 and over age group were employed in the better paid (SEG IV) occupations than were the children of any other group.[99]

Thus, here too, close association with parents was undoubtedly of considerable value to the child. These skilled factory workers were both in a better position to train their children to a trade, and also probably wielded greater influence with the employer.

Trade and artisan occupations, and to some extent skilled factory occupations, also offered opportunities for the employment of relatives and might, therefore, have been expected to lead to these groups being more likely to take

TABLE 30 *Proportion of sons of different ages employed in factory occupations (co-residing children only), by SEG of father: Preston sample, 1851*

	Age of sons				
	Under 20		20 and over		
SEG of father	Proportion employed in SEGs IV and VI %	All under 20 N (100%)	Proportion employed in SEGs: IV and VI %	IV only %	All aged 20 and over N (100%)
III Trade	19	43	–	–	31
IV Higher factory	79	55	67	27	15
V Artisan	48	60	35	15	20
VI Lower factory	95	21	50	–	10
VII Labourer	67	72	39	14	36
VIII Hand-loom weaver	82	45	23	8	13

TABLE 31 *Proportion of households containing kin (other than married children and their co-residing nuclear families and than parents), by SEG of household head: Preston sample, 1851 (households headed by married men only)*

SEG of head	Proportion of households with kin %	All households *N* (100%)
III Trade	16	146
IV Higher factory	14	147
V Artisan	10	198
VI Lower factory	7	86
VII Labourer	8	167
VIII Hand-loom weaver	14	56
III and IV[a]	15	293
V[b]	10	198
VI, VII, VIII[c]	9	309

[a] The relationship between groups *a*, *b*, and *c* is significant $p < 0.05$ ($chi^2 = 6.306$ at 2 d.f.).

relatives into their households.[100] There is some suggestion in Table 31 that this may indeed have been the case. Note that artisan households prove less attractive than trade or higher factory households, presumably because of their lower economic position. The reason for the figure for hand-loom weavers, if it is not a statistical irregularity in a small population, is unclear.

Some further evidence that the ability to offer employment to kin was probably of not inconsiderable importance for the higher SEGs is that while 56% of the co-residing kin of men in SEGs III and IV were employed in the same industry or trade as their household head, this was true of only 30% of the kin of men in SEGs VI and VII. The difference is not quite significant at the 5% level; the cell values are rather small. Nevertheless, that there were some overall economic advantages for some people in maintaining relationships with family and kin seems clear. That there were not advantages for all, and that, in consequence, relationships were not always maintained, I shall demonstrate in the rest of this chapter.

Economic position and commitment to family relationships

I suggested in Chapter 7 that in the rural areas the ability of parents, at their discretion, to hold out inducements of significant gifts or inheritances and to offer employment was, both at the structural and at the phenomenal levels, important in binding children of certain SEGs to their parents and, indeed, that parents had in consequence considerable power over them. In the towns, by contrast, as I noted in Chapter 4, few of the working classes owned any significant amounts of property, so property can largely be discounted in the urban situation. As I have just shown, many did have influence over employment opportunities, and indeed it would appear that there were for their relatives significant advantages to be gained from maintaining family and kinship relationships if they wanted a secure and well-paid job. Nevertheless, many did get jobs without the influence of kin, and for those whose parents were in lower SEGs in particular, the jobs one could get for oneself would be no worse and possibly even better than those which one's kin could help one obtain. The analysis of Chapter 2 would thus lead one to expect that the strength of this source of commitment to family bonds would in consequence be much lower in all groups (but particularly among the lower paid) than it was in the rural areas. It would also lead one to expect that the children of the lower paid in particular would have been more liable to break away from their families when their other life chances seemed maximised in relationships outside the family system, since they had most to gain and least to lose by such a step. This section presents some evidence which suggests very strongly that this was the case.

Suggestions that children frequently manifested independence from their parents, and that the high wages that they could obtain from mill work was a principal cause of this insubordination, are found in almost any contemporary work on the factories and working class life. For example, Arnold believed that 'Children frequently leave their parents at a very early age in the manufacturing districts. Girls of sixteen, and lads of the same age, find that they can enjoy greater liberty, and if not greater comforts, that at least they can have their own way more completely in a separate home, and these partings cause little surprise or disturbance.'[101] Another witness commented that children at age 16 to 18 were frequently earning as much as they would ever earn, and 'this premature independence too often induces them to quit their parents' houses, that they may be more at liberty to follow their own inclinations'.[102] 'The result of this precocious independence', wrote another, 'is, of course, the utter relaxation of all bonds of domestic ... control. Within Mr Lawton's recollection, a spinner working in the mill, often with his family about him, received their wages, and kept them under proper control.'[103]

There are, then, frequent suggestions from well-informed persons that the possibility existed for children actually to break away from parental influence in the cotton towns, and that this was directly attributable to the high wages they received, paid to them on an individual rather than a family basis.

There is no doubt, moreover, that children by their late teens did earn enough to support themselves and that many earned as much or nearly as much as they would ever earn, and more, often, than their parents. Average earnings for a boy of 16 in Lancashire cotton factories in the early 1830s seem to have been of the order of 7*s*., rising to over 13*s*. by age 20, but these are average figures, and many would have earned considerably more. For girls, the comparable figures from the same source are 6*s*. and 8*s*.[104] Other estimates are rather higher or lower, but most witnesses agreed that wages, particularly for girls, were at high rates relative to future expectations.[105] For labourers too, strength was the most important qualification, and so youth was a period of relatively high wages.

Moreover, it was easy in the towns to find somewhere other than the parental home in which to live. As I noted in Chapter 4 boys and girls could leave home and go into lodging houses, and it was indeed to these lodging houses that many of those who left home were believed to have gone.[106]

There seems no doubt, then, that it was practically possible for children to break away from parental control and leave home, should they for any reason be motivated to do so. No statistical data on this matter are, however, to be found in contemporary discussions, and so it seems essential to attempt to make at least some very rough estimates of the frequency with which children left home in this way, and of the groups most affected.

Most contemporaries seem to have noted the large numbers of teenagers living in lodgings (somewhere over 10% of the 15–19 age group, for example), and concluded that most of these had deserted their parents. In fact, however, as I showed in Chapter 5, many of those in lodgings were inmigrants, and many more were orphans. In all it seems very unlikely that more than two or three per cent, at least of the Preston born, did in fact desert their parents and remain unmarried.[107]

It is not possible to explore this matter further statistically with data from the general sample. In particular there is no way of using general sample data to suggest the social factors within the nuclear family which might have influenced a breakdown in relationships. The total number of children (present and absent) in any family is not known, nor is it possible to estimate this adequately.[108] Nor is it possible to ascertain from the census for those children who had left home, the relationship between the occupation of the father and that of his son or daughter.

Instead I attempted to explore this matter further by using data from the life histories compiled from the intensive survey. This material is, of course, of very uncertain reliability, though the fact that it seems to tally fairly well with other related material on the same topic does give some grounds for at least limited confidence. Nevertheless, before these conclusions can be regarded as anything more than tentative a much larger scale survey will have to be undertaken. Thus the results presented here must be viewed with great caution.

Of 670 children of families some members of which were traced in two successive censuses, 346 were traceable in these families in the earlier but not the later of the two censuses in question. These children had therefore either died in the intervening period, or had left home either to marry or while unmarried to set themselves up independently of their parents.[109]

Table 32 gives some of the data on the 'rates of disappearance' of these children. The figures here appear to suggest that boys (who were better paid and therefore potentially more independent) were more likely to leave home and renounce

TABLE 32 *Percentage of children, categorised by sex and various social characteristics of their parents, disappearing from home in an intercensal period, by age: Preston intensive study, 1841, 1851, 1861*

Social characteristics of children and families (earlier year)	Age of child in earlier year				
	0–4	5–9	10–14	15–19	20+
	Percentage disappearing				
Boys	22	19[a]	56[c]	79	59
Girls	23	10[b]	42[d]	76	50
Father widower	40	18	50	77	84
Father married	21	14	56[e]	85[g]	53
Mother widow	25	12	36[f]	63[h]	40
Father widower or married:					
boys	18	19	58	81	70
girls	21	10	51[i]	86[j]	53
Mother widow:					
boys	13	19	50[k]	75	33
girls	31	8	22[l]	50[m]	46
Occupation of child:					
factory	..	..	55	77	56
other	..	..	60	79	67
none	23	14	47	(0)	33
Occupation of father:					
'lucrative'[n]	15		60		60
other	18		69		68
All disappearing	23	14	50	78	56
Expected mortality and marriage[p]	23	14	35	69	69
All=*N*(100%)	136	136	112	73	42

[a] The assumptions for chi² are not met in this table (see note 55 to Chapter 5, p. 206 below.) It may, however, be noted that, had they been, the differences *a/b*, *c/d*, *e/f*, *g/h* and *k/l* would be significant $p < 0.05$; and *i/l*, *j/m* would be significant $p < 0.01$.

[n] This group comprises factory and trade workers.

[p] These figures are the expected rates of disappearance on the assumption that these children had marriage and mortality rates equivalent to those of the community at large, in as far as these can be estimated from the data available. The rates of mortality derived from the Preston survival table are as follows: 0–4 group: 22.5%; 5–9 group: 11.8%; 10–14 group: 7.4%; 15–19 group: 9.7%; over 20 group: 11.7%. For marriage rate assumptions see note 53 to Chapter 5.

familial obligations than were girls, but that widows were more likely than were other parents to receive sympathetic treatment, particularly from girls. Most children left home only in their late teens, the very early twenties being probably even more popular. Contrary to what might be expected from contemporary comment, there is no suggestion from this table that factory children were particularly likely to leave home. Rather, it seems possible that the children of lower or more irregularly paid parents were the most willing to leave home.

The descriptive material discussed at the beginning of this section suggested that children were, at the phenomenal level, tending to adopt an orientation towards their nuclear families which was based essentially on short-run calculative instrumental individualism. A number of references in Chapters 5 and 6 may be recalled here as suggesting that some parents adopted a similarly instrumental orientation to their children's contribution to the family's purse. Several other sets of data also appear consistent with a situation where a considerable section of the population were making a conscious calculation of the advantages and disadvantages, in terms of the standard of living which they could enjoy, of, on the one hand going on living with parents, and, on the other, of setting up on their own.

The data presented earlier suggested the importance of the level of income of the child in *making it possible* for children to leave home should they have disagreements with their parents. Thus, essentially, the parent–child bargain came to be on more or less equal terms. Any slight swaying of the balance away from the family would, if short-run considerations only were being taken into account, increase the likelihood that children would break away. As one would expect, one factor influencing the balance seems to have been the treatment meted out to the children by the father. I noted earlier how Stella Davies's grandfather and his siblings gave up the chance of succession to the family business, and indeed in one case broke altogether with their father, because of his harshness.[110] A number of other cases of a similar nature appear. Thus, for example, a youth commented that 'I worked at the factory two years, and was then earning 7*s*. a week. I then ran away ... but I should have stayed if my mother hadn't knocked me about so.'[111]

More generally under this heading it was agreed that parents had to be very careful if they wished to correct their children. The girls 'are so independent, that if they are blamed or kept in at all by their parents, they will leave them, and go, three or four of them together – young girls of 16 and 18 – and take lodgings with some old woman to keep house for them.'[112] Many readers will remember also how Esther in *Mary Barton* began her downfall by leaving home as a result of a dispute with her brother-in-law over her behaviour.[113] Summarising, the *Morning Chronicle* reporter suggested that 'I do not think it is at all usual for the girls to leave their parents' houses until they are married except in cases where fathers or mothers-in-law (stepmothers) do not prove kind',[114] and a witness is reported as saying that after the age of 14 'a father would not inconsiderately beat his son, lest he might drive him away from his control'.[115]

It is to differences in this factor, in part, that differences in the attitudes of girls in particular towards their mothers, reflected in their apparently greater willingness to stay at home with widowed mothers than with widowed fathers, and also their greater willingness than their brothers to do so, may perhaps be ascribed. I noted in Chapter 6 that the treatment which fathers meted out to their children was very often much harsher than was the treatment which children received from their mothers. Indeed, mothers seem frequently to have made considerable sacrifices for their children and to have protected them from the fathers' brutality to the best of their ability. If one assumes that it would above all have been daughters who identified with their mothers in these situations, then one might suggest that it would above all have been daughters who would have been biased in their relational choices towards helping their mother when she in turn was in difficulties. Sons would have identified less, and therefore have been less sympathetic. Fathers, in contrast, would have been due for little sympathy, and would have been more likely to be deserted if other factors were also unfavourable.[116]

A second strand of evidence may be obtained by turning attention to the age at which children broke away, and to the size of the contribution made by children to the family purse.

I noted in Chapter 4 that, according to the Rowntree scale, the cost of subsistence for an adult living alone was around 7*s*. per week, though the cost of an additional adult living as part of a nuclear family was only 3*s*. 8*d*., and of additional children only 2*s*. 10*d*. Thus, a child could be making a very substantial net contribution to the family budget while he or she still had a wage inadequate to support him or herself living alone. The Rowntree figures must, of course, only be considered the roughest of guides to the cost of subsistence in mid-nineteenth century Lancashire. Nevertheless, if one assumes subsistence food costs as 3*s*. 3*d*.,[117] and adds to this 2*s*. for rent and heat, and 3*d*. for washing materials and sundries,[118] the cost of a minimum subsistence in lodgings would have been about 5*s*. 6*d*., even when replacements for clothes and odd extra payments (for washing or an occasional drink, for example) are excluded. To live adequately in lodgings probably cost, then, something of the order of 6*s*. to 6*s*. 6*d*. per week.

Now in a situation where actors were engaged in a pure exchange relationship based entirely on instrumental considerations, a sum of this order would then become the maximum equilibrium contribution made by a child to the family, on the assumptions that other side benefits and costs were the same in all possible relationships under consideration. A child earning over this sum and required to contribute more than this, would be better off in lodgings; a child earning less than this would have no viable extra-familial alternative, and it might be expected that such children would hand over most of their wages to their parents as a contribution to the family purse.

Each of these aspects can be considered separately. It was suggested by the data on disappearance rates that few children left home before they were in their late teens, and this seems to tally with some of the other data cited earlier which generally seems to mention 16 to 18 at least as the relevant ages.[119] The data in Table 32 also suggested that boys were probably more likely to leave home than were girls, though this appears to have applied particularly only when mother was a widow. The wages paid to a factory boy of 16 in 1834 averaged about 7*s*. per week rising to 13*s*. 6*d*. at age 20, while the figures for girls were

6*s*. and 8*s*. respectively.[120] It would seem, therefore, both that boys received more than girls in the relevant age groups, and were, therefore, freer in structural terms to break away, and that, for boys in particular, it was above all in their very late teens and later that income reached a level well above the maximum equilibrium contribution. It appears, moreover, to have been precisely in these age groups that breakaway was most likely to occur among boys.

There are also data to suggest that while most younger children seem to have handed the whole or almost the whole of their earnings to their parents,[121] by the age of 14 'many of them begin to have strong desires for finer clothing, or for other things, and they frequently stipulate with their parents for some portion of their wages',[122] and 'when they receive as much money as will more than pay for their living, they contract with their parents for board and lodging, and put the rest in their pockets ... and (become) thoughtless and independent'.[123] Independence at the structural level was thus also reflected to some degree at least in independence at the phenomenal level.[124] There is even some suggestion that many children handed over to their parents somewhere about the equilibrium bargain figure (5*s*. 3*d*.), rather than simply the 2*s*. 9*d*. to 3*s*. 9*d*. which the child actually cost the family, or the higher sum that they earned.[125] Much more evidence on this area would, however, be necessary before such a precise confirmation of this point could be established from data such as these.

The data in Table 34 provide a third strand of evidence in support of this proposition of short-run instrumental individualism. The hypotheses which underlay the setting up of Table 34 were as follows. If the children were adopting an orientation based on instrumental individualism, then they would leave home above all under certain sets of circumstances. Badly paid fathers would be unable to support their families at as high a standard of living as would the better paid. They would thus be able to offer to their children less of a margin of benefit over the rewards obtainable from living in lodgings. Thus, controlling for the occupation of the child, children of badly paid fathers should be more likely, on the basis of the assumptions being tested here, to leave home than were the children of well-paid fathers. Moreover, well-paid children would be able to afford, if they lived in lodgings, a better standard of living than more poorly paid children, and the most poorly paid might not be able to afford to live in lodgings at all. Thus well-paid children, controlling for the occupation of the father, might be expected to leave home more frequently. The predictions which result from a combination of these two propositions are that the rates of disappearance would be ranked in the order listed in Table 33. This hypothetical ordering is further suggested by the probability that highly paid children of poorly paid fathers would be put under considerable pressure to contribute more of their wages to the family purse than would the well-paid children of well-paid fathers, so that this pressure would be likely to be a further source of dissatisfactions to this group.

TABLE 33 *Comparison of hypothetical and actual ordering of rates of disappearance adjusted for marriage and mortality (for data see Table 34)*

Wages of child	Wages of father	Predicted order (see discussion)	Actual order
High (factory)	Low (other)	1	1
High (factory)	High (lucrative)	2 or 3	2
Low (other)	Low (other)	2 or 3	3
Low (other)	High (lucrative)	4	4

It is unfortunate that, because of the rather small size of the sample used here and because censuses were only conducted at ten-year intervals, the data in Table 34 refer to the age group 10–19 at the first census. Thus, by the second census, some of this group would have been in their late 20s. These data thus only hint at further support for the hypothesis under discussion here, but the coincidence between prediction and actual data seemed sufficiently great to make worthwhile their inclusion here. It seems not unlikely that the figures partly reflect differences in the age of marriage between different groups. The next section suggests, however, that very similar factors influenced the decision to marry, as influenced the decision to break away from parents to live in lodgings.

In the first part of Table 34 the actual data are presented. In the second part the figures expected in the light of expected mortality and marriage rates are

TABLE 34 *Proportion of children in factory and other occupations disappearing from home in an intercensal period, by occupation of father, and comparisons with the numbers to be expected if the groups had had the same marriage and mortality rates as the general population: 10–19 age group, Preston intensive study, 1841, 1851, 1861*

		Occupation of child in first period			
		Factory		Other	
	Occupation of father in second period	Proportion disappearing %	All *N*(100%)	Proportion disappearing %	All *N*(100%)
Actual rates[a]	'Lucrative'	72	43	60	10
	Other	78	30	75	12
Expected mortality and marriage rates[a]	'Lucrative'	49		60	
	Other	54		58	
Adjusted actual rates[a]	'Lucrative'	45		–	
	Other	64		40	

[a] For full details see text.

given, and in the third part the data are adjusted in accordance with these expected figures to give some indication of the possible true rates of break-away when mortality and marriage rates are taken into account.[126] Note that the overall orderings only differ between the actual and adjusted cases in the second and third (and thus indeterminate) rankings.

Finally, some descriptive data may be noted which further supports this line of argument. Thus an ex-collier, asked 'Do the children generally stay with their parents after they can earn enough to support themselves?', replied 'Yes, usually, especially if the father is in middling circumstances; but if the father is badly off, and does not do well to them, the children generally take advantage of it and leave him.'[127] Clay also noted the comment of a man who came out of prison to find 'my wife and the younger children in the workhouse; those who were old enough to get their own living had left her'.[128]

Summarising the above argument, then, there does seem to be evidence which would at least suggest rather strongly that many young men and women adopted an instrumental orientation to their families, requiring reciprocation for their contribution in the very short run, this orientation being present at the phenomenal level. Neale summarises well even if perhaps a little strongly: 'Where industrial employment had been procured for them, the parents found themselves dependent, to some measure, for support upon their children's earnings. How these were to be appropriated became a new source of contest and bickerings; for the parents would appropriate the greater share for domestic purposes, the children would spend it in enjoyments; hence, from these feuds, an alienation was produced between the parents and their children and the latter, feeling their own independence, voluntarily withdrew themselves from the domestic roof, and became unrestrained masters of their destiny and actions at a period of life when they were most likely to be led away by the illusion of pleasure, the force of passion, or even companionship.'[129] Compare also Gould: 'The children that frequent factories make almost the purse of the family, and by making the purse of the family they share in the ruling of it and are in a great state of insubordination to their parents.'[130] Finally, and perhaps most convincing of all, it was observed of a Parish Assisted Migrant that 'the eldest of her children (a girl earning 6*s*. 6*d*. per week) now refuses to help to maintain the younger Branches of the Family unless you will allow us something for the three youngest until they are able to work. We shall remove the Mother with the younger branches of the family, as the elder children will leave the Mother.'[131]

Thus, children's high individual wages allowed them to enter into relational bargains with their parents on terms of more or less precise equality.[132] If, as was usually the case, a bargain could be struck which was immediately favourable to both parties, then all was well, and the relationship continued, though the degree of commitment to such a relationship must often have been low. If a better alternative was obtainable elsewhere the child could take it. The contrast between the choice element in these relationships between urban children and their parents, and the situation in rural areas outlined in Chapter 7 is very marked. In the rural areas even in the short run, child and father entered a bargaining situation with the child at a very considerable disadvantage, because the father had complete control over the only really viable source of income.

Economic influences and the age of marriage

Before this chapter is concluded, one other important sign of major structural changes in family relational patterns resulting from the changes in the organisation of production, may briefly be noted, viz: changes in the age of marriage and the proportion of the population marrying.[133]

I noted in Chapter 7 that, in Ireland and in the rural areas, the age at which a farmer's son could marry was largely determined by the age at which he could persuade his father to allow him some share from the family plot. I suggested that, as a result of this, marriage was late in rural Lancashire where there were rather few alternatives available to the son which could ever hope to offer him as large a return as a share in the farm. In Ireland, however, where more alternatives were available, and among the labourers and poorer farmers even in Lancashire, parental control was that much weaker, and the age of marriage might consequently be expected to have been lower.

It seems probable that there was on the part of the Lancashire working class a considerable motivation to marry and thus to move to a situation where one was the chief person considered in a family and not a subsidiary and heavily contributing part of a larger system whose interests by no means always tallied very exactly with one's own. The evidence on the manifestations of independence from parental control discussed above seem to lend some support to this view.[134]

The high wages obtained by many men in the Lancashire towns made it easy for them to support themselves and at least a small family while relatively young. This early independence, coupled with the fact that subsequent expectations were likely to be of a fall rather than any much greater rise,[135] of wages, seems to have persuaded most that it was safe and even best to marry young.[136] This was made easier by the possibility of going into lodgings or sharing with parents after marriage, so that little saving was necessary and a housing shortage did not need to deter couples from marriage.

Thus a relatively young age of marriage was to be expected among members of the Lancashire working class. It was also to be expected that a high proportion of the population would ultimately marry. Evidence on the proportions never married at different ages for the whole urban and rural samples is presented in Table 35[137] and this shows in fact that the proportion of the population of Preston ever married at any given age was consistently higher than the proportion for the rural areas. The fact that the proportions for men were considerably higher than for women in the towns, and the converse in the country is largely

TABLE 35 *Percentage of the population never married, categorised by age and sex: Preston and agricultural village samples, 1851*

Age group	Males		Females	
	Preston	Rural	Preston	Rural
15–19	98	100	97	100
20–24	69	94	71	79
25–34	27	50	36	41
35–44	12	27	16	18
45–54	6	20	10	15
55–64	5	8	8	9
65–74	4	9	6	6
75 and over	–	12	10	11

[a] The chances that the sampling process would lead to the differences between urban and rural results being all except one in the same direction (and that the exception should be equal) are $p < 0.005$ by the sign test, when the equal exception is, following customary practice, ignored (cf Blalock (1960) 130–1).

due to urban–rural differences in the population sex ratio. Thus, for example, for the 20–24 age group, the female–male sex ratio for Preston was 0.86, while for the rural sample it was 1.18.[138]

That, for men, this trend is a result of early independence and not of other factors is supported by two further sets of findings. The first, shown in Table 36,

TABLE 36 *Percentage of the population never married, 25–34 age group, categorised by sex, for various classes of registration districts, 1861*[a]

Registration districts	Males %	Females %	Sex ratio, females: males
7 agricultural labour	31	27	1.06
7 small farmer	49	40	1.00
5 Lancs cotton	25	29	1.19
3 Lancs rural	36	40	1.19
2 metals industry	24	19	1.00
4 traditional	28	36	1.28

[a] From PP1863 LIII. Details of the districts selected are:

Agricultural labour: over 60% of the population in 1851 employed in agriculture; under 12% of those in agriculture, farmers; over 75% agricultural labourers (R.D. numbers 209, 196, 185, 181, 140, 124, 263).

Small farmer: over 50% of the population employed in agriculture; over 25% of those in agriculture, farmers; under 45% agricultural labourers (R.D. numbers 574, 569, 573, 487, 529, 530, 572).

Lancs cotton: of all Lancashire R.D.s those with largest percentage of men employed in cotton (other than Haslingden which had a predominance of hand-loom weavers), viz: Oldham, Blackburn, Ashton, Bury, and Burnley.

Lancs rural: of all Lancashire R.D.s, those with largest percentage of men employed in agriculture; viz: Garstang, Ormskirk, and Fylde.

Metals industry: Eccleshall and Sheffield.

Traditional: Norwich, Salisbury, Exeter, Canterbury.

is that early marriage was not just a matter of rural–urban differences. Areas where most of the population were agricultural labourers, and where, therefore, independence, such as it was ever likely to be, was attained quite young, had marriage ages only a little higher than those of the Lancashire towns.[139] Conversely, rural areas like those of Lancashire, where independence came late because their agriculture was based on small farms, had delayed marriages. Similarly, other manufacturing towns where independence was early had earlier marriage, while towns relying on traditional artisan and trade occupations had more delayed marriage, and higher non-marriage rates.[140]

Secondly, if the Preston sample is subdivided by SEGs, it is clear that marriage was earliest in those SEGs with high incomes for younger men relative to their expected adult incomes and with a good expectation of continued high income, and later for those, including lower paid factory workers, for whom this did not apply. It seems probable that these factors would have had particularly great effect in the Lancashire cotton towns because a very high proportion of the young women would have worked in factories and have had similar incomes and expectations. Thus, within the working class, the better paid would have been particularly favoured as husbands. Data on this topic are presented in Table 37. Inmigration by single men only able to obtain lower paid occupations slightly, but probably not importantly, biases these figures against the lower paid workers.

Conclusion

In sum, then, one crucial way in which urban-industrial life in the nineteenth century affected family cohesion was by offering to teenage children wages at

TABLE 37 *Percentage of the population never married categorised by age and SEG: males, Preston sample, 1851*

SEG		Percentage never married at age:				
		15–19	20–24	25–34	35–44	45 and over
I and II[a]	White collar	100	87	29	6	11
III	Trade	100	57	17	6	10
IV	Higher factory	95	56	14	4	–
V	Artisan	95	69	21	7	1
VI	Lower factory	99	75	37	27	4
VII	Labourer	100	68	38	17	6
VIII	Hand-loom weaver	100	75	60	27	6
IX and X	Other	100	65	27	15	5
All		98	69	27	12	5

[a] For delayed and non-marriage among the nineteenth century upper-middle class cf also e.g. Crozier (1965) 18–19; Banks (1954).

The following differences are significant at the $p < 0.05$ level by the sign test: I and II/IV; IV/VI; IV/VII; IV/VIII; V/VI; V/VIII.

such a level that they were able to free themselves from total economic dependence on the nuclear family. Because normative controls were weak and because housing, food, and other day to day necessities could be obtained on the open market, many could, at least as long as only short-run instrumental factors were considered and as long as they could remain employed, live as well or better than they could with kin or parents. Some children did desert their families and I have presented some evidence which suggested that even where they did not do so many children were conscious of the existence of this possibility and the alternatives it offered, and used it as a way of bargaining a highly independent relationship with their families. The family came to be seen by many even at the phenomenal level as a group of individuals choosing whether or not to continue their membership, and contributing to it only what was necessary to obtain reciprocal services; in sum, in the words of the *Morning Chronicle* reporter, it was seen as akin to a Joint Stock Company.[141] Yet, in spite of the widespread existence of this attitude and in spite of the possibilities for disruption that this economic independence offered, most people continued to maintain important relationships with family and also with kin, both before and after marriage. The job finding function, discussed in the first part of this chapter, seems inadequate alone to account for this, particularly for those who were already established in the urban labour force. The next chapter looks for factors in other areas of life which might have encouraged people to remain a part of a functioning kinship system.

10. Critical life situations as a factor in family cohesion

The theoretical importance of critical life situations

In the last two chapters I have suggested that in nineteenth century Lancashire most members of the resident urban working class over the age of about 18 were able, if forced or wishing to, to obtain and hold down a job, to find a home, and to obtain satisfaction of most day to day domestic needs, without the assistance of family or kin. Those with family and kin assistance could, it is true, often obtain jobs, home, and domestic life which would give them somewhat more satisfactions than they could otherwise have obtained. These somewhat marginal advantages fail, however, at the structural level, to explain why such a large proportion of the old (who often could not render even these services) were apparently supported by their children. They fail to explain why assistance was so often given to siblings and to other kin, notably orphans and widows, who were also unable to help in these ways, or, indeed, in the short run in many cases to render any real service at all. They fail to explain why so many married couples should wish to live with or so near to their parents. Nor, I have argued, does it seem likely that normative factors can have played any very great independent role, except possibly to reinforce pressures resulting from elsewhere within the system.

The resident urban working class in nineteenth century towns, above all in the rapidly expanding factory towns of Lancashire, were thus not crucially dependent on others for some of the basic needs of life – a home, work, and the company of others. In this chapter, however, I want to argue that they still needed various other kinds of help at sufficiently regular intervals to make them in great need of some reasonably predictable and regular form of assistance.[1]

Every family in all societies faces from time to time what I have here called critical life situations. Sickness, unemployment, death, or disaster remove the basis of the family's support, leave orphans and widows, require families to make temporary or permanent arrangements for the substitution of roles, cause worry and distress. Old age, marriage, and childbirth, too, all frequently mean that those undergoing them are in need of help. Finally, there are many pressing day-to-day problems; finding someone to care for the baby while the wife works, someone to look after the key while one is out, someone from whom to borrow some small amount of a necessary item of food when the supply suddenly and unexpectedly runs out.

In mid-twentieth century Western industrial societies, the more serious critical life situations occur only rather rarely for each individual family, and their worst financial and welfare consequences have been somewhat moderated by the impact of the welfare state or other bureaucratic source of provision, or forestalled for most families by insurances of various kinds. Moreover, as the standard of living of the mass of the population has gradually risen, the economic impact of all forms of contingency has become somewhat less pressing.[2]

Under these circumstances, help from non-bureaucratised sources of assistance – neighbours, friends, and kin – of a kind which demands a considerable expense of time or effort, is only absolutely necessary in rare cases, in what Litwak[3] has called idiosyncratic events, where there are gaps in the bureaucratised provision, or where this becomes temporarily overloaded.[4]

In nineteenth century towns, on the other hand, not only were these major crises more frequent, but bureaucratised means of assistance were either inadequate, or provided only at the cost of serious concomitant deprivations which tended to some extent to cancel out the benefits received. Moreover, I shall argue here that of the non-bureaucratic sources of support only the family had a framework within which reciprocation could occur which was sufficiently clearly defined to provide an adequate guarantee of assistance in the major crisis situations. It was thus advisable, or even well-nigh essential, for kinsman to make every effort to keep in contact with and to enter into reciprocal assistance with kinsman, if life chances were not to be seriously imperilled.[5]

Bureaucratised forms of assistance

I showed in Chapter 4 that most of the people under study here lived at times below or near to the primary poverty line, and few had any substantial savings to fall back on in time of crisis. Under these circumstances, any happening that removed, even for a short time, a person or family's means of support was potentially very serious indeed. For the person without any other form of assistance the only universal bureaucratised form of help was the Poor Law. Some also could use friendly society benefits where available.

However, there is considerable evidence to suggest that, in Lancashire, the Poor Law was seen by the mass of the population only as a refuge of last resort. This phenomenal definition seems to have coincided, moreover, with what an assessment at the structural level would lead one to conclude. Comment is widespread to the effect that few Lancashire operatives could swallow their pride and submit to the degradation, as they saw it, of appearing before the Guardians and being interrogated about their family means: 'The much dreaded workhouse.'[6] 'I'd as soon ha' gone to prison as do it ... just go up there before the Board, – see what they thinks of poverty there; then, maybe, you'll know why we working men had rather clem (starve) than trouble them.'[7] 'Descending to the pauper rank, a fate which the operative class generally regards with a repugnance somewhat morbid! Almost invariably they speak of the workhouse as the "Bastille", and to be taunted as a "pauper" would be by many regarded as the most opprobrious of epithets.'[8]

There is also evidence to suggest that when the operatives said that they would rather starve, they meant it nearly literally.[9] Almost all seem to have made every effort to try any and all alternatives, before making an application. It was well known that the Lancashire poor rates were the lowest in the country except in times of severest distress (and even then they were below average),[10] though higher wages, favourable population age compositions, and low unemployment helped here. Nevertheless, surveys both at the beginning and the end of the century found lower pauperism among the old than the national average, even though employment for old men and old women was not easily obtained.[11]

Also crucial, however, in a population composed largely of migrants, was the fact that migrants could often not obtain relief in the community where they and their families were at the time living. They had a 'legal settlement' elsewhere, and only there did they have any legal right to receive relief. The able-bodied could often in spells of temporary distress obtain relief in the town though they had no legal right to do so. But large numbers of widows and of aged and infirm persons and their families were periodically removed to the town or village of their birth. The Irish, most of whom had no legal settlement in England, were even more reluctant to apply,[12] for removal for them meant being dumped in any Irish port often far from their birthplaces, where anyway they might well not have lived for twenty or more years.[13]

Poor relief was, then, for most, a last resort because of the extreme dissatisfactions it brought with it. Friendly society membership,[14] on the other hand, was widespread among the Lancashire proletariat, even more widespread indeed than among the rest of the population of England.[15] It seems probable that by the early 1870s rather over 420,000 out of a Lancashire population of 2,800,000 were members of friendly societies proper and almost a million more were making payments to burial societies.[16] In other words, rather over half of all adult males[17] were insured in friendly societies, and about half the population were insured in burial or friendly societies.

These are fairly impressive figures, even taking account of the fact that they mean that half of the population, the richest but also most of the very poorest, were not covered. On the other hand the benefits of friendly society membership, though important, were limited. Few friendly societies paid anything for crises other than sickness and death of the insured and his wife. The payments for sickness, 6*s*. to 13*s*. (usually 7*s*. to 10*s*) were only one-third to one-half of the already inadequate average wage, and even these usually only continued for about six weeks before they fell to a lower rate of (normally) half the full figure.[18] Death benefits were up to about £10, but that was all a widow could usually expect. Thus, while these societies undoubtedly helped to alleviate the suffering of sickness and bereavement, and kept many off the Poor Law for a time, even these crises were still times of severe economic deprivation. Moreover, the human problems remained largely unmet. So, too, did the other critical life situations – old age, unemployment, childbirth, migration.

The rest of this chapter will examine a number of these critical life situations, and will attempt to investigate the part played by the different alternatives to the formal agencies in meeting them.

The young married couple, and the old

The first set of critical life situations which I shall examine involves the problems facing, on the one hand, the young married couple, and, on the other, the widowed and the old, and the linkages which emerge between them. It seems, in fact, that people phenomenally perceived this as a sphere where the maintenance of relationships led to a mutual increase of satisfactions in the form of fairly short-run and instrumental returns, regardless of other considerations, and that the prospect of these mutually advantageous returns was an important factor in the retention of the relationships.

I noted in Chapter 5 that in the first years of marriage few couples, particularly among the lower paid, lived in a home of their own. Most of those who could live with parents did so, the rest living instead in lodgings. In the later stages of the life-cycle, most couples headed their own households. Some of these, however, had parents living with them (some 4% in LCSs 3–5), and others lived only a short way away from their parents. Table 38 shows that in all no fewer than 32% of old people aged 65 and over lived with a married or widowed child, and a further 36% with unmarried children.

TABLE 38 *Residence patterns of persons aged 65 and over, by sex, listed in priority ordering, and excluding those in institutions:*[a] *Preston sample, 1851*

	Males %	Females %	All %
Living:			
with married child	31	33	32
with other child	38	34	36
with spouse	17	10	13
with other kin	–	10	5
as lodger	11	3	7
as servant	–	3	2
with no other person	3	8	6
All: %	100	101	101
N	93	101	194

[a] If allowance is made for non-Preston residents on a basis proportional to population (the workhouse served the whole registration district, not just the borough), the inclusion of persons in institutions would add about four women and two men to these sample figures.

Stehouwer[19] found that about three-quarters of the population of 65 and over in the three modern Western countries which he studied had at least one living child. A calculation was made on the basis of assumed mortality rates and marriage ages,[20] which suggested that only some 67% of the persons of 65 and over in the Preston sample would have been in this position had they been a random sample of the population. There is obviously some margin for error in this latter figure, but it does certainly suggest very strongly that there were few old people who could not find one among their children prepared to give them house room in old age, if they actually had any children alive.

I also noted in Chapter 5 that few households contained two married couples of two succeeding generations. It was thus, above all, widowed parents who actually shared with married children. This is clear from Table 39.

TABLE 39 *Residence patterns of persons aged 65 and over, by sex and marital status, listed in priority ordering, and excluding those in institutions: Preston sample, 1851*

	Widowed		Married	
	Male %	Female %	Male %	Female %
Living:				
with married child	50	41	15	17
with other child	27	34	50	42
with spouse	..	..	35	41
with other kin	–	10	..	..
as lodger	18	4	..	..
as servant	–	3	..	..
in other residence patterns	5	7	..	..
All living with children	77	75	65	59
All: %	100	99	100	100
N	44	70	46	24

The difference between the proportion of married old people living with married children, and the proportion of widowed old people in this position is significant $p < 0.001$ ($chi^2 = 16.351$). This group are, however, somewhat older, so this is in part to be expected, but widowed persons were also significantly more likely to be living with any kind of child, in spite of their greater age ($p < 0.05$ on a one-tailed test; $chi^2 = 3.831$).

Thus, it was above all the fact of being widowed and alone, rather than old age itself, which was crucial in leading to co-residence of married children and parents. These widowed persons were almost all old people who either had no income of their own, or had only a very much reduced one. Some were undoubtedly becoming rather infirm. For them the advantages of the arrangement are obvious enough.[21]

Apparent advantages to the couples can be summed up under four heads:

1. In Chapter 5 I noted a strong relationship between family size and whether or not couples headed their own household. Saving of rent seems to have been of crucial importance here. Rents for a whole cottage started at 2*s*. 6*d*. per week. The couple would also, if both worked, have had considerable difficulty in doing their housework, washing, and cooking, and might well have had to pay something further for this.[22] In lodgings these latter problems were solved, though at a price, and rent was perhaps only 1*s*. 6*d*. or 2*s* per week. Sharing with kin meant, however, that this sum would instead have gone into the family purse to the mutual advantage of parents and kin. The best statement of this motive for sharing with parents though in this case stressing the economic advantage to parents is to be found in the *Report on the condition of frame-work knitters*,[23] where a Leicester framework knitter noted that he went to live with his wife's parents 'because they could not afford 2*s*. 6*d*. a-week for a house'.[24]

2. Operatives married young. Few seem to have had many savings. They were thus unable to buy even the minimal scraps of furniture necessary for a home of their own.[25] Sharing or lodging helped them solve this problem too.

3. Germani[26] noted that housing shortages were an important factor encouraging co-residence with parents by young married couples in Buenos Aires.[27] No direct evidence on this point emerged from the descriptive material, but the very considerable housing shortage in Preston and the other cotton towns was noted in Chapter 4. Even if these couples had wanted a house of their own they would have had some difficulty in finding one.

4. I noted in Chapter 6 that although many mothers worked, many of them had their mothers or other relatives available at home to care for their children in their absence.

I would argue that one explanation of the large number of stem families noted by Foster[28] in Oldham when compared with the other towns he studied may well be that married children were only too willing to take in parents or other kin who were prepared to perform this service and thus allow the mother to work. When, later, their families became too large to make actual co-residence possible, the possibility of obtaining this assistance seems likely to have been a strong inducement to married children to live nearby. Some sources suggest that it cost up to 3*s*. 6*d*. or even 5*s*. to pay a nurse for a week, though these higher figures usually included the cost of some kind of feeding.[29] Even if the net cost were 1*s*. 6*d*., probably a minimum, a parent or other unemployed relative living in the house and performing this service was making an important contribution towards her keep, and this was increased if she also saved the family from the need to pay someone to do the cooking.[30] Table 40 does show, moreover, that if there was a grandmother in the house, the mother was significantly more likely to maximise her earnings by working away from home.[31]

TABLE 40 *Relationship between the employment of mothers and the co-residence of non-employed grandmothers and other persons: all mothers with children under 10, Preston sample, 1851*

	Mother works:			
	in factory[a] %	elsewhere, place uncertain %	at home %	Mother does not work %
Household contains:				
co-residing grandmother	16	11	5	5
co-residing other person	31	27	23	22
no co-residing other person	54	62	72	73
All: %	101	100	100	100
N	84	37	43	482

[a] It is never possible to be absolutely certain about where mothers worked, so these allocations may contain a very small amount of (presumably random) error, which actually works against the hypothesis and thus makes the trend shown here, if anything, an underestimate.

29% of those with a grandmother in the house and children under 10 worked, and 58% did not work at all. Of those with no grandmother or other non-employed person in the house, the figures were 12% and 76% respectively.[32] These figures are highly suggestive of some link between grandmothers, child care, and working mothers.[33] In part, however, this link may be one of co-variance rather than causation. The proportion of mothers who worked fell over the life-cycle, and so too, as the parents died, did the number of married couples with co-residing parents. So also, however, to some extent, did the proportion of couples with a child under 10. Unfortunately, any further break-down of these figures reduces the values in some of the cells so much that no conclusions of any validity can possibly be drawn. It may however be noted that the proportion of working mothers fell particularly sharply in LCSs 3 and 4. In these LCSs, poverty was, however, at its worst,[34] so one could at least hypothesise that mothers were forced to stop working in these LCSs just because there was no longer a grandmother available to care for the children. A much larger sample would be necessary to test these suggestions.

Clearly, then, the quantitative data can take the argument no further. The proposition gains added support, however, from the descriptive data. Firstly, as I noted in Chapter 6, there is much evidence that children were frequently left with kin and friends, both those living in the house and those living nearby.

Secondly, there is evidence that the exchange element in this element of the parent–married child relationship was valued and recognised. Indeed, a number of cases appear where it is consciously cast into money terms.

The most clear-cut case of this exchange evaluation is cited by Waugh, and does not actually refer to a relative at all.[35] He refers to a household which contained, besides a family with an infant child whose mother worked, an old lady of 70 who 'was no relation to them, but she nursed, and looked after the house for them. "They cannot afford to pay me nought", continued she; "but aw fare as they fare'n, and they dunnot want to part wi'me. Aw'm not good to mich, but aw can manage what they wanten, yo see'n."' 'It is very common', said another commentator,[36] 'that when a young man and woman marry they have parents, and that they may both work in the mill, they get one of their mothers to keep house.' Sometimes, indeed, payment was actually made for this service even to kin. The young married son of a Parish Assisted Migrant and his wife had had a home of their own in Princes Risborough. When they got to Staleybridge, however, he and his wife moved in with his family of orientation and are noted as paying 3*s*. per week to them 'towards the rent, for house room and nursing the child'.[37]

It was, moreover, precisely this exchange argument that was put forward as one explanation of Lancashire's low poor rates. 'Even the aged members of a manufacturing community have a different social position from that of the same class of persons in many of the parts of England . . . Many . . ., especially aged females, afford a service very appropriate to their condition, and of not inconsiderable value, by keeping house and taking care of the youngest children, while the working part of the family are absent at their work . . . With such assistance in the care of her household, during her absence at the factory, many an industrious married woman is enabled to add 8*s*., 10*s*., or 12*s*. weekly to the income brought in by her husband and the elder of her children. It is not uncommon for aged females to become domesticated for the purpose of affording service of this nature in the families of those who have no elderly relatives to support.'[38]

The ability of old women to perform these services seems, then, to have been of great importance. It was even noted that 'elderly persons ... come with their children, who support them, and they take care of the house, and cook'.[39] It would seem that for migrants to bring in parents to help them out in this way may not have been a rare phenomenon.[40]

In this connection I also made a comparison between the proportion of old people on relief in Lancashire and the proportion in other industrial and mining communities with similar proportions of persons in the 15–64 age group on relief but where there was little employment for married women, using data prepared by Booth on the situation at the end of the century.[41] This analysis did indeed suggest very strongly that, either because they were able to support themselves better, or because they were supported for the reasons outlined above, old women (though not old men) were much less likely to be on poor relief in Lancashire than elsewhere. The same appeared to be true also for other areas where women were habitually employed away from home.[42]

The feeling that parents who were supported should make some specific reciprocal contribution to the family's finances comes out in other ways too. Thus 'I took the beer-house, thinking as my father and mother-in-law had nothing to do, they might make a little by selling beer.' This family was also dependent on the mother-in-law for caring for the children, for the wife was a cripple, and so the mother-in-law's death was 'the worst shock I had ever experienced'.[43] A number of cases also appear where support was willingly given to dependent parents, but only on the condition that the Poor Law authorities provided some assistance also.[44]

In sum, it does seem that in Lancashire towns married couples and their parents could often each maximise their satisfactions by engaging in relationships with each other, that these mutual advantages were specifically appreciated by both parties, and that this was an important factor in the maintenance of these relationships.

Widows, widowers, and 'deserted' wives

I noted above that it was above all when they were widowed that old people began to reside with their married children. Widowhood, however, raised critical problems regardless of age. For men it necessitated help around the house and in the care of children. For women, particularly those with children, the removal of the principal wage-earner by death could rapidly throw the already impoverished family into the most grinding of poverty unless some means of reducing or sharing necessary expenditures could be found. Table 41 suggests very strongly that widowhood at whatever age was very likely to lead, as a partial solution to these problems, to co-residence with kin, though this, perhaps strangely at first glance, was particularly so for those with no children still living at home.

However further consideration suggests interesting reasons why it was not those most in need who shared a home with kin. I suggested in Chapter 5 that the main reason why it was the childless who lived with kin was that the co-residence of two large families would have led to serious overcrowding in the small cottages. One widowed child or sibling could relatively easily be accommodated. If he or she had two or three children as well, it became much more of a strain on the principal family's solidarity. But a further point, which I shall pursue in Chapter 11, was probably also important here. Because co-residence would usually involve a kinsman in supporting or helping to support a widow and family, and because the expense of so doing would increase with the size of the family, this would logically in turn increase the reluctance of a man with several children of his own to take on this extra burden. A childless widow would have been well able to support herself, and also make some contribution to the family budget. Few widows with more than about two children, however, would have been in a position to do so. The extent to which this motive was important

TABLE 41 *Relationship between widowhood, categorised by sex and presence of children, and residence patterns, by age: Preston sample, 1851*

	Age:			
	under 25 %	25–44 %	45–64 %	65 and over %
Husbands with children present:				
living in own household	65	93[a]	98[b]	96
with kin	14	3[c]	–	–
in lodgings	21	4[d]	2[e]	4
All: %	100	100	100	100
N	43	517	256	46
Widowers with children present:				
living in own household	(–)	43[f]	70[g]	88[z]
with kin	(100)	13[h]	7	6[b′]
in lodgings	(–)	43[i]	23[j]	6
All: %	100	99	100	100
N	1	23	30	16
Widows with children present:				
living in own household	(25)	69[k]	90[l]	87[d′]
with kin	(63)	20	4[y]	6[g′]
in lodgings	(13)	11[m]	6[n]	6
All: %	101	100	100	99
N	8	61	98	31
Widowers with no children present:				
living in own household	9	6[o]	25[p]	14[a′]
with kin	36	32	10	57[c′]
in lodgings	45	55	65[r]	29
in service	9	6	–	–
All: %	99	99	100	100
N	11	31	20	28
Widows with no children present:				
living in own household	18	17[s]	39[t]	29[e′]
with kin	47	34	32[v]	59[f′]
in lodgings	28	31[w]	18[x]	8
in service	6	17	11	5
All: %	99	99	100	101
N	17	29	28	39

[a] By the chi² test the following pairs of relationships are significant:
$p < 0.001$: *a/f*; *b/g*; *d/i*; *e/j*; *k/s*; *l/t*; *y/v*; *z/a′*; *b′/c′*; *d′/e′*; *f′/g′*.
$p < 0.01$: *g/l*; *i/m*; *j/n*; *f/o*; *j/r*.
$p < 0.05$: *c/h*; *f/k*; *m/w*; *n/x*.

in the specific case of widows is unclear but this interpretation fits with the general drift of the data presented here, and if this interpretation is correct it is another example of the instrumentality which seems to have been so important in these communities and which is a principal topic of Chapters 11 and 12.

In sum, then, kin do seem to have been a major source of assistance for widowed persons and particularly for those in not too much need. Indeed, a number of cases appear in census and intensive study data which suggest that persons who had moved away from Preston returned to live with or near kin when they were widowed, which again suggests that kin did often meet very important needs for widowed persons.[45]

Not only widows, however, could depend on kin for assistance in time of need. So, too, it would seem, could many of those whose husbands had left them to go on tramp or overseas in search of work, or who had deserted them more or less permanently. These are of course amalgamated with widows in the figures given above, but a number of cases appear in the literature which suggest,[46] and a glance at the enumerators' books supports, the idea that women whose husbands were away often lived with their parents or with other relatives, thus saving on rent and also presumably obtaining important emotional support.

Not all widowed persons left their own homes and went and lived with others when widowed. Some, particularly women, carried on heading their own households. If they did so, however, they were very likely to bring relatives into the household to join them, to keep them company, to keep house for them, and perhaps also to share the rent and even to help support them. This was above all true of those with no co-residing unmarried children of their own, 48% of whom had kin living with them, compared with 25% of the widowed who had children, 23% of married couples with no unmarried children in the house, and 20% of those with children. In about half of these cases the co-residing relatives were married children or parents, but 15% of all widowed persons had a relative other than a married child or parent in the household.[47]

Most of the co-residing kin who were not either parents or married children were siblings of the widowed person. Crozier[48] noted this practice among her upper middle class Highgate sample, and she suggested that these siblings often acted as surrogate parents and spouses, caring for home or children, and presumably providing also appropriate sex role models[49] for the children. This seems less likely to have been the crucial fact in Lancashire both because this pattern was particularly noticeable among those with no children present (19% compared with 13%),[50] and also because it was above all widows not widowers who had these co-residing kin (82% of all cases). Other factors, particularly the saving of rent, the company, and on-the-spot assistance in time of need, were probably more important in Lancashire.

For many, then, in widowhood as in old age, kin were an important source of help. For the old, in particular, there were few alternative sources of assistance which offered equal rewards with fewer dissatisfactions. Moreover, as I have shown, the advantages of close relationships between the old and their married children were immediately mutual, and this was probably also the case in the relationships between many of the widowed and their kin.

But widowhood and old age were only two of the crises which struck the members of these communities, only two of the occasions when assistance from kin was asked for and given.

Aid in illness and death

Sickness and death came frequently in these communities,[51] but this did not lessen the need for help to alleviate the worst of the suffering which resulted. Death in the family raised urgent problems of organising and paying for a funeral, of caring for orphaned children, and of comforting the bereaved. Sickness meant loss of vitally important income in a situation where there were seldom savings to tide the family over the crisis. It meant also that someone must nurse the sick person. If the mother was the sufferer, someone else had to step in to replace her in the performance of domestic functions.

As I noted in an earlier section of this chapter, some of the financial burden of these crises was alleviated by help from the sick clubs and friendly societies and burial clubs though only for a few weeks, and only for the two-thirds or so of the working class population who were members. Nevertheless, the fall in an already precariously low income was usually considerable. For those who were not members, the financial problems were likely to be acute. For all, the human problems remained.

In times of need of this kind, however, the sacrifices made by the poor to help the poor struck middle class contemporaries as quite remarkable. 'Their charity', wrote the mayor of Clitheroe, 'is unbounded. Let anyone be in want from sickness or any other cause – there are fifty kind Samaritans to comfort and relieve them with both food and personal service.'[52]

Kin were obviously among the most active of those who provided this kind of assistance in times of crisis. Some of Gaulter's material on assistance by kin has already been discussed in Chapter 5, but there are numerous other cases too. For example, a sick Irish widow is noted as 'going home to Ireland to be with her own friends'.[53] A number of blind and infirm persons are noted in the census as living with kin. Money was borrowed from kin to support the family while the chief wage-earner was ill.[54]

Neighbours, too, some of whom were also undoubtedly kin,[55] are also recorded as giving liberal assistance. A few examples best bring out this general willingness to help others. For example, a weaver's wife, Nancy Beswick, recounted[56] how when a neighbour had been ill her husband had escorted him home, she had fed him, taken his wife to the overseers about the possibility of getting relief, visited her, and assisted her in all kinds of ways. Gaulter, too, as noted earlier, has many examples of neighbours helping the sick.[57] Nunns,[58] writing primarily of Birmingham, noted that 'Day by day, yes, and month by month, have I known the younger children of a sick and dying parent fed at the different neighbours' tables, and fed willingly, as members of the family. The patient's daily food has been derived from the same source;– delicacies have been found for him where necessaries have scarcely been had at home;– he is nursed by them, and attended by them.'[59] A woman in labour, too, could rely on neighbours for assistance.[60] Workmates, on their side, often took up a collection for the sufferer.[61]

To the sick, then, neighbours and friends were often a great help. A Roman Catholic priest from Liverpool noted that the Irish 'assist one another a good deal . . . whether relations or not'.[62]

There is, however, some rather sketchy evidence which at least hints at some differentiation between neighbours and kin in these matters of assistance, though many may well have had close friends from whom assistance was as readily forthcoming as it was from kin. Some people, moreover, do seem to have fallen through the net of neighbourhood assistance. Newcomers with no kin to take an interest in them probably more often suffered crises alone.[63] When the disease was believed fatal and infectious, some were left to suffer uncared for,[64] or driven away to relatives.[65] A poor widow in great distress regretted migrating to the towns, for in her old agricultural parish 'there was not a house where I could not have had a meal for asking for, both for me and my children; and now in yonder large town, if I ask for anything everybody takes me for a thief'.[66] Some further data on this topic are presented in Chapter 11, when patterns of reciprocation in general are dealt with in more detail.

If the sick person died, too, kin are found ready with comfort and assistance. They are portrayed as washing and laying out the body and sheets, as helping to pay for and arrange the funeral, and, of course, as attending the funeral and offering emotional support to the family of the dead man.[67] Neighbours, too, were apparently similarly solicitous, particularly perhaps, from the cases examined, when the person had no kin,[68] though once again much more evidence would be necessary to be sure of this point.

Orphans

Death left orphans, or deprived children of at least one parent. The survival tables suggest that nearly a third of all children could expect to lose one parent, and 8% both, before they were 15. Yet hardly any orphans grew up in the workhouse.[69]

There is, once again, evidence that neighbours frequently took pity on those with no kin of their own, and, helped by the Poor Law authorities, frequently brought up the child.[70] This kind feeling exhibited towards orphans is the subject of a touching and quite probably realistic passage in Gaskell's *North and south*[71] while in *Hand and heart*[72] a character comments that 'An orphan is kin to everyone'.

It was above all, however, kin who took on the care of orphans, and, under the old Poor Law at least, the authorities always tried to board them with kin wherever possible.[73] Grandmothers are the commonest guardians found in the literature, but some are also noted as living with usually the more affluent among their aunts and uncles, and with other relatives.[74] The inclusion of orphaned nephews in trade union recruitment rules was noted in Chapter 9.[75] One or more children of a family which had lost only one parent, particularly if it was the mother[76] and particularly if the survivor remarried, and those whose fathers were particularly dissolute,[77] seem often similarly to have been brought up by kin, uncles, aunts, and grandparents again dominating the list of relatives. Illegitimate children, or those whose parents had moved away, were also apparently often cared for by kin.[78] If the parents died but some of the children were already fairly grown up, they seem often to have taken on the responsibility for their younger siblings.[79]

This adoption of orphans, then, is probably one major factor explaining the presence in so many households of the odd grandchildren, nieces and nephews, and siblings which were noted in Chapter 5,[80] and particularly their presence in the houses of childless widows. It is worth noting that Foster[81] found similar proportions of these composite families in all his towns, and this is probably one important explanation. The motives for adopting orphans in this way were probably at the phenomenal level mainly normative, and the spontaneity of many of the cases cited is certainly notable. At the structural level, an element of 'There but for the Grace of God go my children' may quite logically have entered in, for there were no real alternatives to pauperism and early death for the orphaned child. In the absence of firm data, this suggestion must remain somewhat hypothetical. However, a number of positive structural factors may also be noted which may have increased the willingness of actors to take in orphans. Their support would seldom have directly cost the family adopting them very much because the Poor Law authorities seem generally to have been willing to make at least a small payment in these cases.[82] For those who had no children of their own (and these seem to make up a good number of the cases which appear in the literature), an adopted son or daughter might also provide some company, some affection, and even possibly some assistance in old age and times of need. For those with a business of their own and no children of a suitable age and for those in un-differentiated occupations, orphaned kin were simply a substitute for a non-relative employee, with the added advantages that they might be paid less and might also be more easily sanctioned. Certainly a number of cases occurred in the sample where old persons with no co-residing children were apparently being supported by co-residing grandchildren or nieces or nephews.[83] Many of these old people were in trade occupations.[84] As might be expected, however, evidence on this whole topic is a little limited, and so no absolutely firm conclusion can be drawn.

Unemployment

I noted in Chapter 4 that, periodically depressions hit the Lancashire cotton towns, throwing thousands out of work. For individuals, of course, there were also periods of transitional unemployment, and enforced idleness through injury or the closure of a firm, or from migration. I further noted in Chapter 9 that relatives played an important part in finding new jobs for those who were thus temporarily unemployed, and more data on this topic appears later in this chapter. This section discusses some of the other forms of assistance which relatives provided for those rendered unemployed.

The problems of the unemployed increased with the time they had been without work, and with the proportion of the community affected. In good times, and at the beginning of a depression, 'if one artisan is out of work, he subsists and gets aid from his relations, connexions, or his fellow workmen; he will get credit; he will continue hanging on a considerable time before he will sell his goods, and be off to another town' or apply to the Guardians.[85] Assistance from kin was a major source of assistance at these times,[86] and, of course, where members of families were employed in different mills or only some in cotton at all, then some would often (though by no means always) be willing to support the others until, as the depression deepened, they too were thrown out of work.[87] The amount of time that a man could live off his friends and kin in this way was, however, definitely limited,[88] and, as time went by, other solutions became necessary. One was to go off on tramp round neighbouring towns in search of work or to emigrate.[89] Another, for migrants, was, it seems almost certain, to return to the village of their birth for a while until things improved.[90]

As the crisis worsened and involved more and more of the population, 'huddling' increased. More and more houses became empty, and more and more had two families sharing the rent and fuel and pooling their resources. Almost every commentator notes this pattern of behaviour.[91] Always a large number of houses were empty in bad years. In 1841 no fewer than 10% of the houses in Preston and 15% of the houses in Little Bolton were empty, though it seems likely that this was also, in part, the result of outmigration, and of speculative over-building in the previous boom, since the mean number of persons per occupied house was in 1851 actually higher than the figure for 1841 in almost all the cotton towns.

Wherever possible, the sharers seem to have been kin who had been evicted or forced to leave their old homes, but others were also taken in in the frantic attempts to minimise domestic costs.[92] Furniture and clothing was pawned or sold,[93] savings, if any, soon run down.[94] Relatives appear usually to have helped each other as well as they could, but their own nuclear families seem definitely to have been given priority so there was little to spare except from the fortunate families where not all were employed in cotton and who were in consequence rather better off and often continued to give at least limited help to needy kin.[95]

For months, then, the operatives lived mainly off their own resources and those of their friends, neighbours, and kin. Gradually, however, as the downward multiplier spread through the community and resources were run down, more and more were forced to go on to poor relief or to seek assistance from the charitable funds which gradually took over the major burden of the relief.[96] Even then the operatives, by sharing homes and any meagre earnings with neighbours and kin, supplemented and stretched to the limit the relief which they received. Kinship and neighbourhood simply could not cope alone with this kind of depression, though it could help to alleviate some of its misery.[97] In December 1862 over a quarter of the population of Lancashire was in receipt of poor relief or charitable aid.[98] Faced with need on this scale, extensive help from outside was inevitably necessary.

Other crises

When attention is turned to the less catastrophic though still critical day-to-day problems facing the populations of these communities, it becomes more difficult to find evidence in a historical context. Gaulter,[99] as I noted in Chapter 5, provides some limited evidence on this topic, and kin and neighbours seem heavily involved. The novelists (and particularly Mrs Gaskell) also suggest that neighbours and relatives were of great help when others had to face these many minor problems of life,[100] and some of the evidence presented in Chapters 5 and 8 points in the same direction.

In addition, one may note for example Stella Davies who writes of 'the obligation to "weigh in and help" in times of trouble', and goes on 'there was much asking out to tea, especially high tea on Sunday. Children's clothes as the wearers got too big for them, were passed on to smaller children; discarded clothes were given to the more impecunious members of the family ...'[101] Other odd incidents appear. Weavers build houses assisted by kin,[102] a man is fined, and borrows money from his sister to pay it,[103] and so on. In sum, kin were involved, but just how heavily is not wholly clear.

The overall effect of kin

All in all, then, the impression one gets (and it can only be an impression) from the literature, is of frequent functional interaction with kin.[104] It seems plain that kinship was important in the lives of many at least of the members of this society, but it is difficult to be sure on the basis of only positive data just how important it was. Limited additional evidence on just how crucial it could be can, however, be obtained from another line of approach.

Townsend[105] has shown that, by looking at the kinship relationships of those who end up in old people's homes, some further insight can be obtained into the operation of kinship in modern industrial societies. More generally, if it can be shown that persons who have no close relationships with kin are likely to find themselves in a decidedly worse position than those who have such relationships, then kinship is obviously of functional importance in the society. If they are not, then this is not so.

In areas with good surviving poor relief lists some statistical analysis of this topic could probably be undertaken, particularly if it were to be combined with a much fuller collection of family life histories by intensive survey methods than was possible with the time and resources available for this study. In the absence of this kind of data more indirect indicators must be used.

Firstly, then, as was noted in an earlier section of this chapter, almost all those who had reached the age of 65 and who had children alive were living with them. This would seem to suggest very strongly that most of those who found their way into the workhouse or on to poor relief must have been those without children alive, and thus that most old people had at least one child who was prepared to continue a functional relationship with them.

Secondly, there is also some limited descriptive data which suggests that those without a closely functioning kinship network were more likely to find themselves in severe difficulties. One source[106] notes that many of the girls living in lodgings were orphans, and that their health was much worse than those who lived with 'friends'. Waugh also comments on a girl who 'was an orphan, had no relations here, and was tossed about from place to place till she found her way to a brothel'.[107] Bamford, too, notes, 'the pale and desolate-looking Alice, who was always alone, and who had not a relation in the world'.[108] Waugh also notes the problem of the old 'lone' women. He mentions an old lady 'ill, and thinly covered in rags with a dirty cloth tied round her head . . . starving, with "naither husband nor son, nor chick nor child, nor bit nor sup, barrin' what folk that has nothin' themselves can give to her"'.[109] Further data on what happened to migrants who had no kin in the towns is given in the next section and further supports this proposition that, with all its limitations, kinship was yet an important factor mitigating at least much of the worst of suffering.

Kinship and migration to the towns

The crises discussed so far faced the whole population. There was one other set of critical life situations, however, which affected only one (though that a very large) group of the population, the migrants. I showed in Chapter 5 that, in spite of this high rate of inmigration, a high proportion of the population lived with kin and that many more lived near them and were engaged in highly functional relationships with them. Also, migrant young married couples, while slightly less likely than the natives to be sharing with kin, were nevertheless very likely to be able to find a home with them.

Migrants were also quite likely, indeed as likely as were the Preston born, to have living in their households kin who must either have preceded them, come with them *as kin*, or come to join them in the town.[110] 12% of adult migrant married couples and 13% of non-migrants had kin of this kind in their households. It seems clear, then, that *positive* efforts were being made by migrants to build up and maintain kinship bonds in the towns.

These data, based on co-residence, may, and indeed probably do, somewhat tend to bias the findings in favour of the migrants. Since migrants did face problems in adapting to urban life,[111] one might well expect that they would have been less able to set themselves up in independent households and have tended, therefore, more than their Preston born peers, to cluster into the homes of kin, rather than to move out to homes of their own nearby. In this case the overall web of kinship of the non-migrant would in fact have been stronger, though it would not appear as such from the figures on co-residence. It will almost certainly also have been the case that migrants, taken overall, had fewer kin in other houses in the neighbourhood, even though many, as Chapter 5 showed, did apparently have kin living nearby. Moreover, functional assistance to a niece or nephew was more likely, for migrants, to mean that the child, whose family did not live nearby, had to be taken into the household instead of continuing to live at home.

It is not, then, justifiable to assume from the co-residential data alone that migration was making no difference at all to urban kinship patterns. One can, however, justifiably deduce that even the migrants were able to build up an important kinship web in the towns.

This might seem at first glance slightly surprising, in view of the widely held view that migration is a key source of disruption of kinship bonds. This view is, however, an over-simplification even if only the rural situation is considered. If the urban context is also taken into account then the common belief is often even more erroneous.

There is no doubt that most of the migrants from rural areas who came to the Lancashire towns did cease to perform important functions within the ongoing family system in their birthplaces, though it may be noted that some did send sums of money, from time to time, to families and kin in the home village or town.[112] The migration of at least most of the farmers' sons and daughters to the towns did not, however, seriously upset the rural kinship system, because that system was anyway based on the assumption that only one son in each generation would retain important kinship obligations; the rest had always 'travelled', and now merely went to the towns instead of into service round about. Moreover, there is some limited evidence to suggest that kin who were left behind and who fell into situations of need were not infrequently helped by either they or some of their children being brought to the town.[113] There is also some evidence to suggest that considerable contact was maintained, and that some reverse migration may even have occurred.

It is, however, an interesting question to ask why even first generation migrants made such efforts to build up a functional kinship system in the towns.

An answer may apparently be suggested by reference to two complementary sets of factors. Firstly, all the reasons why residents found it useful to maintain a kinship system in the towns applied equally or with even greater force to migrants, who probably had fewer established friendships in the towns.

Secondly, however, migrants had reasons specific to themselves for wanting to build up and maintain kinship links, for migration in all societies presents special problems which must be met if the migrant is to adapt to a new life in his new community. He needs information about prospects and conditions to help him decide whether or not and where to go. If he goes, he is faced immediately with the problems of finding somewhere to live, of finding a job, and of adapting himself in hundreds of other ways to the new community. In the nineteenth century there was no bureaucratised provision designed to provide this kind of information and assistance. In addition, because, for example, the job market was controlled by primary relationships, help was even more necessary in some ways than it is today. I here argue that kin were by far the most important source of assistance available to most migrants.

The migrants from other parts of Lancashire, except for those from some of the remoter parts noted in Chapter 7, would already have been at least partly familiar with most of the aspects of urban-industrial life.[114] Some, of course, were only migrating from one town to another. Some of those from villages would have visited the larger towns for markets or fairs. Most would at least have been familiar with the concepts of employers and wage labour. Even factory life itself still protruded into parts of the countryside in the shape of the scattered rural mills.[115]

For some of the migrants even from England, however, the shock when faced with the need to make one's way in a large town must have been considerable, and all probably found their first days in a busy mill town somewhat bewildering. Kay, moving families from an area with little contact with factory life, took care to put them into industrial villages rather than the larger towns, so that 'the Change should be accomplished with as little Alteration in the Habits of the Labourers as possible . . .'[116]

However, besides this generalised knowledge of the facts of urban-industrial life, the migrants required and received other kinds of information. Those who had gone before sent back information advising when, where, and how to go to the towns, and gave advice about jobs, prices, wages, and the difficulties that the migrant was likely to encounter. Thus a young man in the 1780s 'received a letter from his brother, relating his own circumstances, and informing him of a situation in which he might have constant employment in Lancaster. This letter determined him to go.'[117] This kind of practice seems to have continued throughout the nineteenth century. Many of the Parish Assisted Migrants are noted as summoning their kin. Thus, 'He has written to his friends to induce them to come, and hopes that some of his near relatives will.'[118] The Irish were believed to be particularly efficient in this regard, information about changes in employment prospects being rapidly transmitted home.[119] Employers frequently used this grapevine to obtain more labour.[120] Co-villagers, equally, benefited from this service, often getting references to the relatives of friends,[121] and friends seem to have been used to take messages and even children, back and forth to relatives.[122]

If the potential migrant decided to come, he often had to find food and shelter on the journey. This was equally a problem for all those who wished to go on a visit more than a day's journey away. There are enough references to kin and friends giving a bed for the night to those on the move to suggest that this was the preferred and probably the normal procedure for those who had kin or friends somewhere near their route.[123] For the traveller who would often only be on the move because of his straitened circumstances the cost of alternatives would anyway make staying with kin highly advantageous.

When the migrant arrived in the town, he was immediately faced with a number of problems. He needed a roof over his head, a job, and someone to help him adjust to the new environment. Kin and co-villagers were his main recourse. The literature is full of references to inmigrants coming into the town, seeking out relatives or friends, and being sheltered and assisted by them. Thus 'I know that the Irish constantly invite their friends and relations in Ireland, and when they come, receive and entertain them in their habitations for a certain period, or until they obtain work.'[124] A Parish Assisted Migrant wrote home to the effect that 'if my brother John would like to come with you, there is plenty of work ... and my wife can cook and wash for him'.[125] Stella Davies records that her father left Rossendale when he was twelve, and went to Manchester. 'His Uncle Jabez Spencer had preceded him to Manchester and he and his wife, Sarah, found the lad a room in which to sleep in their cottage in Hapurhey ... My father lived with his uncle until he was eighteen.'[126] It seems clear that at least the appropriate addresses of relatives in the town were usually known.

In this connection it is of considerable interest to remember that inmigrants had a large number of co-residing siblings, cousins, and nieces and nephews in their households, many of whom were almost certainly receiving assistance of this kind. It is possible, however, to go even slightly further. Table 42 suggests, though the figures are too small to be significant, that the proportion of households containing siblings, cousins, and nieces and nephews was rather lower among households where the head was born in another town than it was when he had been born elsewhere. This is interesting, because kin born in other towns were probably less likely to migrate in this way and certainly would often have needed less of this kind of assistance if they did come.

Clustering and co-residence obviously eased the migrant over the culture shock such as it was. For the Irish, indeed, for whom the shock may have been particularly great, encapsulation into the urban Irish subculture seems to have been almost complete, and many contemporaries noted how slowly they adapted to English ways of life and began to enter primary relationships with the native

TABLE 42 *Proportion of households headed by married couples containing co-residing siblings, nieces or nephews, or cousins, all without co-residing parents, by birthplace of the household head: Preston sample, 1851*

	Of all, proportion with these classes of kin %	All N(100%)
Adult migrant:		
from English villages[a]	9	102
from towns[a]	4	46
from Ireland	8	36
other[b]	6	50
All migrants	7	234
Intermediate, all	8	429
Non-migrant, all[c]	10	121

[a] Within 30 miles only.
[b] Including those from more than 30 miles.
[c] The figures for this group may reflect above all care being given to orphans, but some of these kin, too, were migrants from villages around about and from other towns.

town-dwellers.[127] The 'fact that those that come from Ireland being entire strangers to the town, there are parties here that take it upon them to initiate them into every practice of applying for relief ...,'[128] which so aroused the indignation of the witness, was but one example of this. Muggeridge, too, noted the 'comfort and assistance' derived by Parish Assisted Migrants 'from having a neighbour to whose habits and feelings their own are assimilated; and particularly in cases of sickness, or temporary distress from any cause, the advantage has been peculiarly felt, and very thankfully admitted'.[129] This concluding comment is also, in the light of earlier discussion, of great interest.[130]

Those who lacked someone to help them in this way, seem, like those who lacked kin to help them over the other crisis situations, to have had greater problems in adapting to urban life, though there is little direct evidence on this topic. A migrant in one of Waugh's stories notes that 'I keep lookin' up an' down to see if I can leet of onybody fro our side, – but I can find noan. I'm like as I wur born alive an' kin to nobry.'[131] Parkinson too notes the problems of a migrant widow with no friends or kin in the town.[132] One may also suggest on the basis of the analysis in Chapter 5 that many of the migrant lodgers in the large lodging houses probably had no kin or friends in the town, and this group seems to have suffered badly, to have been less likely to receive careful attention should they fall sick[133] or 'from want of connections, [to] waste their small stock of money, without procuring employment, and sink under the pressure of want and despair'.[134] It was generally agreed that if they were going to fail to adapt, most did so within the first year.[135] It seems, in view of some of the discussion here, that absence of kin or friends to help them may well have been a major source of their difficulties. Inmigrants could not expect to make friends immediately on arrival. Thus they were highly dependent on kin and co-villagers and other persons already known to them or with whom they had some pre-existing connection.[136]

The new arrival also needed a job. In this sphere, unless he was qualified for a middle class job or had a trade which was in demand, he was likely without some assistance to be in extreme difficulties for he lacked at least the skills and often also the contacts necessary to obtain any but the most menial factory jobs.[137] Table 43 suggests that migrants in general found it difficult to get well-paid jobs. Many more were in labouring occupations, many fewer in the well-paid factory trades.

TABLE 43 *SEG of household heads, married couples with at least one child, by migration pattern: Preston sample, 1851*

SEG of household head		Adult migrant %	Intermediate %	Non-migrant %
I, II, III	White collar and trade	13	21	17
IV, VI	Factory	19	28	35
V	Artisan	18	20	23
VII	Labourer	28	15	8
VIII, IX, X	Other	23	15	17
All: %		101	99	100
N		234	429	121

Taking SEGs IV and VI, and SEG VII as separate samples, the difference in their distribution is significant ($p < 0.001$) by the Smirnov test (chi^2 at 2 d.f. = 21.183).

Table 43, however, conceals important differences between migrants born in different *types* of communities. For example, 60% of adult migrants born in Ireland, 38% of those born in agricultural villages, but only 11% of those born in towns, and 15% of those born in industrial villages, were in labouring or other similar occupations. Conversely, the proportions in factory occupations showed an opposite trend, being 2%, 3%, 32%, 35%, respectively. It was, then, as might be expected, above all those who came from areas with no experience of industry, and with, in consequence, no training for the well-paid urban jobs for which an early training was essential, and who also had no skill except their strength, who had most difficulty in obtaining any other than casual employment in the towns.[138]

It seems probable also that those who had kin to come to stood a better chance of obtaining a better job. The difference between the 27% of lodger migrants aged between 15 and 34 who were in labouring occupations and the 17% of migrants living with kin in this age group who were labourers, while not significant, is certainly suggestive. Kin were certainly often instrumental in obtaining jobs for inmigrants, just as they were for people born in the towns. Thus 'A brother who was then living in Bolton persuaded his father to obtain Timothy to a Wesleyan friend in Bolton who was a taylor and draper. This friend was in need of just such a boy, and his brother was of the opinion that this was a good opening',[139] and, in Birmingham, 'They are very charitable one to another when a new one comes; an old hand will sham sickness to put in a relation or friend newly arrived till he gets into the way of the place.'[140] Numerous cases in the census also suggest this practice.

Finally, the other side of this coin may be noted. One observer commented that it was very difficult for the unemployed to get a job in other towns since they lacked the necessary 'influence with an overlooker or other person in authority at the mill'.[141]

So far, the advantages to the incoming relatives of this process have been made clear. The advantages to the relatives making the effort to receive and help inmigrants have not been discussed. Data here are very thin, but a few suggestions may perhaps be made. At one level, of course, this willingness to assist was probably normatively influenced, and this was surely strengthened by the clustering and the close relationships between kin in the towns which made it easier for the kinship system to enforce compliance on potential miscreants. In part also status may have been gained by demonstrating an ability to help others.[142] Many, too, particularly those who were short of money, probably found the influx of additional incomes to share the household expenses beneficial to them, and certainly few of the migrants would actually have been a charge on the household for long.

At the structural, as well as at the phenomenal level, some form of indirect reciprocation may also have been involved.[143] Those who had once migrated, realising how important kin had been to them and just how perilous their own migration would have been without this kind of assistance, might well have reciprocated *to the system as a whole* by providing such services to those who followed them. This would have been fairly viable even in a situation of relatively weak norms because the costs involved were fairly small.[144] No phenomenal level data on this topic, however, emerged in the course of the research.

Two other sets of factors which may also have been important here, and which would have involved a direct return to the individual providing the assistance also merit brief comment. Firstly, no one could ever have been sure that the time would not come within a very few years when he might have to move again, and might want from kin elsewhere a similar service, which might not be forthcoming to those who were known to have refused to provide it for others.

A second aspect also seems important. So far, migration has largely been portrayed as a *one-way* affair, with inmigrants coming to join the *urban* kinship network. In practice, however, town and country were often *united* into *one* kinship network with *reciprocal* exchange of services, and, indeed, reciprocal transfer of members. Indeed, the relatively short distance which many migrants had come made the maintenance of this kind of system a relatively easy affair. Sooner or later, of course, contacts with the country would have become more tenuous, as members of the original migrant nuclear family and their children died out, but if the London evidence is anything to go on this was a rather gradual process.[145]

Systematic evidence on this kind of topic is rather difficult to collect in a study of this kind, but it does seem that exchanges of this kind between migrants and their home villages were by no means infrequent. In times of distress some migrants sought assistance from their families back home and sometimes returned home for a while, this being the parallel for them of assistance to the Preston born from kin in the town.[146] There are a small number of cases in the sample where, while most of the children of a migrant couple were born in Preston, suddenly a child or two, in a known depression period, had been born in the village of birth of one or other of their parents. Adshead notes a Manchester bricklayer, who, when his wife was ill, 'was obliged to go into the country to some friends to beg something from them for his wife'.[147] A sick Irish widow 'went over to Ireland to be with her own friends'.[148] One of the poets whose lives are recounted by Hull[149] migrated to Blackburn in 1858, but returned to his village for a while in 1864, probably because of distress due to the cotton famine. Arrangements were made for Bamford, when sick as a child, to go to the country to stay with one of his cousins for a time.[150] Paupers removed to Ireland, the unemployed, and those who were unable to settle down in the towns are also noted variously as returning specifically to their native villages.[151] One source notes that in London 'a great many young children are sent over (to Ireland) to the parents' relatives to be reared'.[152]

There is also evidence to suggest that contact was typically maintained with home, that visiting occurred, and that addresses of relatives were known from whom help could be sought if necessary, a prerequisite of the kind of practices outlined above. It may be noted that on census night no fewer than 9% of adult migrant households had visitors, including many who were specifically referred to as kin, and most of whom came from the home village. Visiting of a social nature seems to have been quite common. References appear fairly frequently in the literature to persons going off to see kin at holiday times or weekends.[153] One case was noted of a man actually being given several days off work to go and see kin in the country.[154]

Contact by letter probably also occurred not infrequently among those who were either themselves literate or had friends who could write and decipher letters on their behalf. Extracts from a letter from a Manchester hand-loom weaver who had emigrated to Australia are reproduced below, as an example of what such letters may well have been like. Note how one letter sent good wishes to many people, a further suggestion of contact between urban kin: 'Please Mr. Winstanley to be so kind as to shew this letter to my wife's relations, also mine as well, and we will write to them shortly, not forgetting our kind love to them all ... Mr. Winstanley, let me intrude on your kindness to impress on all our relations that is our dear Sisters and Brothers that we often talk and think of them and repeatedly shed tears for them and they may depend upon hearing from us the next opportunity. George Margaret and Mary send their kind love to their companions and schoolfellows and little Henry many times speaks of Robert Fielding and his cousin William Lomas ...'[155]

There is, nevertheless, no doubt that migration did somewhat disrupt the functioning at a high level of efficiency of the kinship network as a service agency. Migrants were less often able to live with kin in the towns than were townsmen, and migration did sometimes lead to contact being lost with kin for some periods of time. It will be recalled from Chapter 5 how Ward on two occasions temporarily became ignorant of the address of his brother Dan.[156] If he too had been forced to move during his periods of ignorance so that Dan had lost his address also, then it seems likely that only by pure chance would contact have ever been re-established, though this may well do less than justice to the information grapevine which operated within and between these communities. How typical this was it is impossible to say, but it does suggest very strongly the rather precarious nature of the kinship bonds under these highly fluid conditions.

It may be concluded then that, to a considerable extent, urban and rural kin, or at least some representatives of each and at least in the first generation of migrants, formed *one* kinship system at a functional level. Migrants moved along kinship channels into slots prepared for them by kin, and advice and assistance flowed along these channels in both directions.[157] These services, and the need for them, plus the absence of any other immediately available source of assistance except for co-villagers seem, at the structural level, to be the main factors encouraging the considerable attempt made by migrants to maintain relationships with kin.

Conclusion

In sum, I am suggesting that the frequency of critical life situations and the almost complete absence of viable alternatives to the kinship system (and to some extent to neighbours) as sources of help in solving the problems which ensued from these crises, were, at the structural level, and to a very considerable extent at the phenomenal level also, key factors encouraging members of the Lancashire Victorian working class to make such great efforts to maintain relationships with kin. Although they were largely free from the economic and normative constraints which, in the rural areas, made terminating relationships with family and kin such a precarious and consequently rare business, yet, because they faced other problems of social welfare and, for migrants, of accommodation and information, they could not exist for long at an optimum level of satisfactions without some kind of assistance from others. Kin were the major source of assistance. I shall suggest in the next chapter that this was so because they were, in the longer run, the only source of assistance which even began to promise an adequate (if qualified) predictability of response at a cost which could be met with the resources available.

11. Poverty, and the time span and quality of relationships

In this chapter I try to reach conclusions, some rather hypothetical, some more certain, on a number of topics which have cropped up at a number of points earlier in the book but have not been fully discussed there. In particular three areas seem to merit brief comment.

Firstly, why did so many of the Lancashire proletariat consciously confine even their relational bargains with family and kin to those which offered fairly immediate instrumental returns, when other bargains offering longer run returns appear logically, at first glance, to have been more beneficial?

Secondly, why should kin have been particularly preferred as the source of assistance, rather than neighbours or friends? Everyone always has neighbours near them, but kin are few in number and not, in such a fluid society, always on the spot when required. Why, therefore, did not patterns of close functional exchange develop with neighbours, thus rendering the kinship system largely redundant?

Finally, how might one explain the substantial hint provided by the quantitative data presented in Chapter 5, and somewhat supported by some later discussion, to the effect that there was a tendency for men to have particularly strong links with male kin, and women with female kin?

The bases of calculative short-run instrumentalism

I suggested in the last chapter that, at the structural level, a potent force encouraging the population under study to seek to maintain close relationships with kin was the high frequency of critical life situations which they were forced somehow to face. This, I suggested, meant that they needed help from others because they lacked adequate resources to enable them to meet these problems in any other way. It was above all through their relationships with kin that actors were able to maximise their satisfactions in the face of these contingencies.

This being the case, however, why was it that some actors, notably when in their teens, deliberately broke off relationships with their parents and kin, and why did many others who maintained relationships yet tend to behave towards kin in a manner calculated to maximise short-run satisfactions, but at the expense of possible longer-run rewards? It might seem logical that it was in the long-run interests of all actors to maintain close relationships with kin, and to make every effort to help kin in every possible way, in all the contingencies in which they might find themselves, for they themselves would almost certainly need reciprocal assistance in a whole range of contingencies in the future. Would it not have been logical, then, for actors not only to help to the utmost, but also to try to establish by their example values which would encourage others to maintain family and kinship relationships?

The reasons why, even at the structural level, this was not altogether the optimum course of action for many members of the society are here considered in the light of the heuristic framework outlined in Chapter 2. The last section of that chapter is particularly relevant here and readers who omitted it first time may find it useful to look at it at this point. In particular, both the certainty necessary for the taking of such a long-run view, and the resources necessary to make the following of its precepts possible, were absent in the early factory towns.

A number of pieces of evidence under both of these headings have been discussed in earlier chapters and need be rehearsed only briefly here. In Chapter 9 I noted the very limited extent to which persons breaking off relationships with family and kin would severely disadvantage themselves economically at least in the short run. Though there were some small advantages to be gained from assistance from kin in the economic sphere, these could rather easily be outweighed by associated dissatisfactions. Moreover, as I showed in Chapter 8 even in non-economic matters, so frequent and so pressing were the needs of many of the population, so fluid the society, and so large the numbers with no family or kin group to assist them, that some other servicing agencies had evolved. The neighbourhood community would provide services, at least to some degree. Other basic necessities of life – a roof over one's head and the provision of food and domestic assistance in particular – could be purchased by those who could afford to pay for them: – and even quite young men and women could afford to do this. Thus, most members of the society, in the short run at least, could terminate relationships with kin without major disruptions to life chances should the disadvantages of maintaining kinship relationships become too great. In addition, the loosely structured nets, fluid population and weak hold of ideologies minimised normative control.

Thus the general weakness of structural constraints on the one hand directly reduced the dependency of actors on others, and thus others' ability to control their response, and, on the other, allowed the establishment of groups supporting variant subcultures, which further increased uncertainty. In this situation the trust necessary for long-run reciprocation to emerge was lacking. Moreover, the very fluidity of the population, the high death rates and the unpredictability of sudden depression periods and, for the older men, of continued employment even in good times, made the future highly uncertain. This must have further reduced the certainty that reciprocation in a long-run bargain would be obtained.[1]

However, in spite of the uncertainty of the environment many and probably most actors did in fact choose to enter relationships with kin. Even so, many appear to have done this with only a rather short-run and calculative orientation, so that if a reasonable level of reciprocation was not forthcoming within a comparatively short time span, attempts were either made to alter the terms of the bargain or to terminate the relationship altogether. I noted in Chapter 10 that considerable advantages could ensue from relationships with kin. However, crucial to my interpretation is the fact that, in most of the cases noted, the relationships, and particularly the costly relationships, which *were* maintained were *mutually advantageous within a rather short time period*. It is clear, moreover, that contemporaries were phenomenally very aware of the fact that, and the extent to which, the relationships which were maintained were mutually advantageous, and some evidence was produced to suggest that they deliberately organised their relationships to ensure that the maximum of mutual advantage ensued in the short run.

Thus, the general lack of certainty of reciprocation (including the lack of trust) may be seen as one explanation of the short-run calculative orientation which, I have argued, was to be found.[2] A second factor, however, also seems important and is necessary to account for the widespread and even normative nature of this calculative instrumentalism. I noted in Chapter 4 that many of these people were very poor, and in various later chapters the effects of this poverty on family and kinship patterns have been discussed. In particular, the poverty of their nuclear families was noted as one factor which seemed to be at work in encouraging some, but only some, teenagers to terminate their relationships with their nuclear families.

I want to suggest here as a second factor underlying this short-run calculative orientation that those near the poverty line quite simply were unable to give assistance to others if it required the expenditure of cash resources, unless they and those already dependent upon them starved.[3] Thus even had they felt that they had a more or less absolute duty to contribute to assistance to kin, to have provided such assistance would have meant severe suffering for other claimants on their resources, and, as I noted in Chapter 9, where part of the family resources were dependent on the contribution of others, the possibility that these others might in their turn seek to terminate the relationship.

This point is explored further in Table 44 which suggests, as this argument would predict, that poverty did not greatly affect one's relationships with those of one's kin who were able to support themselves. For those not able to support themselves, however, a very different picture emerges. While one family in nine of those well above the poverty line had these dependent kin in their households, only about one in forty (2.4%) of the poorest group did so.

Moreover, at the phenomenal level, again and again poverty is appealed to in the literature by those who were not assisting their relatives. Thus, for example,

TABLE 44 *Proportion of households containing kin able and unable to support themselves, by standards of living of the primary family: married couples for whom data were adequate, Preston sample, 1851*

Amount by which weekly family standard of living exceeded the poverty line	Households containing: kin, but none self-supporting[a,b] %	kin, including some self-supporting %	All households with kin %	All N(100%)
Less than 4s.	2	9	11	122
4s.–19s. 11d.	7	10	17	211
20s. and over	11	12	23	57

[a] The difference between the three groups in this column is significant $p < 0.05$ (one-tailed test) by the one sample Smirnov test (chi^2 at 2 d.f. = 5.104), if randomness were assumed.
[b] No occupation given in the census schedule.

'Aw've three brothers, colliers – they've done their best to poo us through. But they're nobbut wortchin four days a week, now; beside, they'n enough to do for their own.'[4] Or, again, it was noted that a girl come recently from Blackburn 'contrives to *exist*, as a married brother gives her a home, but can do no more, as he has a wife and three young children dependent on him'.[5] Another source observed very significantly that weavers 'are so impoverished, that if they give a halfpenny out of their pockets, they must work for it again, and they will not give any aid to other men'.[6]

If, on the other hand, the person could make some useful immediate reciprocation either directly as with for example child care, or indirectly, by the Poor Law being willing to assist, then help was much more likely to be given to kin in need. Thus 'Children as were left orphans, ... had frequently been provided for, by being put out, at a weekly allowance, to some needy relations or others, who took care of them merely for the sake of the parish allowance.'[7] The insistence that children or supported kin should maximise their earnings, however arduous the employment, is but one further example of the effects of extreme poverty on attitudes to relatives.[8] It may also be suggested that those who supported or assisted relatives in good times willingly enough (because, for example, they were useful around the house when the mother worked), put them on poor relief in crises. Between 1839 and 1846, as unemployment rose and fell, so did the numbers of old and invalid persons described as completely unable to work who appeared in the relief lists. Some at least of this fluctuation must reflect changes in the willingness of kin to support those in need.[9]

In sum, then, I would argue that an additional potent force encouraging actors to adopt a fairly calculative and short-run orientation in their relationships with kin was the extreme poverty which prevailed. The development of a similar orientation in rural Ireland, as poverty increased, was noted in Chapter 7. In the next chapter, I shall present some comparative cross-cultural data and data on other areas and periods in Britain, all of which show similar reactions to similar situations.

One other interpretation of the relationship between poverty and kinship co-residence must also be mentioned here. Foster[10] has suggested that the most feasible explanation of his finding that households containing kin were significantly commoner in Oldham than in Northampton and South Shields, is that this 'huddling' provided in Oldham but not in the other towns a partial solution to the problems of poverty. The major cause of poverty in Oldham as in Preston was large families and low incomes. Most families could expect to go through a period of poverty, but, because work was readily available for wives and children, this spell of poverty would, in Oldham, last only for a few years. Foster, basing his case on aggregate household composition data only, suggests that by sharing with parents and other kin families with young children could avoid this period of poverty by obtaining support from younger siblings and parents. When, in their turn, the parents grew old, they would be given assistance by a family now out of the poverty period of its life-cycle. In Northampton and South Shields the cycle of poverty was different and so the advantages of co-residence were less.

This is obviously a very elegant argument which, if borne out by the facts, would somewhat further support the arguments being advanced here, though it would suggest a rather longer time span of reciprocation than has seemed general from data produced in this study. There was indeed almost certainly some tendency for small scale transfer of resources between families in different stages of the poverty cycle, particularly with regard to things like cast off clothing and, occasionally, the taking of an odd child or two into one's own household.[11] The data for Preston, however, lend no support to Foster's suggestion that this was a major cause of the prevalence of families with co-residing kin in Oldham.

It is true that almost the whole of the excess of co-residing kin in Oldham over Foster's other two industrial towns[12] results from there having been in Oldham a larger number of stem families and a smaller number of single person and married couple households.[13] However, I noted in Chapter 5 that in Preston the peak period in the life-cycle for sharing with kin was not, as Foster's analysis would suggest, in LCS 3 when family poverty was greatest, but in LCSs 1 and 2, when families had few children and were unlikely to be in poverty. In all, 61% of all married couples living in their parents' homes were in the short (and relatively affluent) period of the life-cycle between marriage and the first birthday of their only surviving child. Only just over one-third were in the next, poorer, *and much longer* period until the first child began to work.

Besides the fact that it meant that reciprocation would be received only in a rather long period of time, there seem a number of other reasons which probably explain why the logically mutually advantageous pattern of behaviour suggested by Foster was not, in fact, generally followed.

Firstly, the average child spacing was only two years. Even allowing for mortality and assuming that couples always preferred to live with, say, the wife's parents,[14] then there would only have been, at most, eight years between the occasions on which children would have entered the state of needing to co-reside. This might just about have been enough had newly married couples been able to move straight out into homes of their own. In practice, however, most had few savings and no possessions with which to do so.[15] It was thus necessary for these children to co-reside, and this meant that, on purely demographic grounds, the arrangement described by Foster would normally have been impossible.

Secondly, however, and probably more crucially, there was the problem of the overcrowding which would have resulted. After five years of marriage the average couple might have expected to have had two surviving children and to be in some poverty. Seven years later, the earliest time when the first child might be beginning to work and beginning rather slowly to bring the family income back into balance with necessary expenditure, this figure might well have risen to five. This would have meant a secondary nuclear family (including the parents) of up to seven. Added, for the earlier children of a marriage, to a primary family which might still contain four or five persons at least, this would have resulted in considerable overcrowding of the tiny cottages, little privacy for anyone, and an open invitation to some of the younger sons and daughters of the primary family to seek to maximise their satisfactions by moving out to live elsewhere, thus rendering the whole exercise fruitless. The considerable relationship between family size and co-residence was noted in Chapter 5.

Kinship and neighbourhood

The second question which I want briefly to discuss here is why the society under study should not have organised its main channels of assistance through neighbours rather than through kin. One answer may of course be that, at the phenomenal level 'the idea didn't occur to them' since, traditionally, such functions had normally been provided by kin. There appear, however, to be good reasons also at the structural level in favour of kin as the normal source of aid in this society, and also some limited empirical data on their actual operation.

The first point is a very obvious one. Neighbours could not provide information for new migrants as to where to go, nor could they provide them with somewhere where they could automatically go on arrival, since, until they arrived, migrants had no neighbours. It is, of course, true that co-villagers provided these functions, and, indeed, much of the argument advanced here on the part of kin applies also to some extent to co-villagers, who seem to have stood somewhere in the middle of a neighbour–kin continuum.

Secondly, on his arrival the new migrant needed someone who was prepared to invest a certain amount fairly rapidly in the relationship. I argued in Chapter 2, however, that in societies where norms are weak functional relationships take time to develop between persons who have no previous history of relationships, and people are only gradually prepared to trust strangers as they become more certain that these alters define the rights and duties of the relationship in the same way as they do themselves. Thus, if new migrants were to get any assistance on arrival, it had to be from a relationship which they could bring with them and which involved someone who was under some generalised obligation to them based on ascribed characteristics. Only if this was the case would the relationship remain *immutable over time*. This immutability of the bond would introduce some degree of certainty into the relationship, and, of course, this certainty would be stronger to the extent that both parties to the relationship were part of the same larger network which could bring meaningful sanctions to bear on any who attempted to reject obligations.

This ascribed and enduring link between actors is important in a more general way also.[16] Given the very high population turnover of these communities, neighbours would frequently change. Thus, one might expect that people would have been less prepared to commit themselves to any great degree or for any long period of time to a neighbour, because, if that person moved, the dyadic relationship would break down and direct reciprocation would not ensue. This would not, of course, matter, if there existed in the community a strongly held norm to the effect that such assistance should always be given (in other words if a generalised exchange net developed), but I suggested in Chapter 8 that no such norm could be maintained in these communities. Thus actor A might on one occasion give up scarce resources to actor B, but when A was next in need, B might have moved and the new neighbour, C, having no experience of relationships with A, and no debt to him, might not be prepared to assist, so A has lost on the bargain. Assistance from kin, too, was also of course somewhat uncertain in these communities for similar reasons. However, the kinship system was much smaller and was by definition structurally close knit so that somewhat greater sanctions could be imposed. No sanctions of this kind were, however, likely to be forthcoming on to an ex-neighbour.

Data on a point such as this are obviously not plentiful, but there is some limited evidence which suggests that such factors did indeed operate in these communities to encourage relationships with persons in a fixed and ascribed relationship to ego. Perhaps this feeling comes out most clearly when the migration agent for Parish Assisted Migrants, noting that he had attempted to direct families from the same village to the same town and employer, goes on 'Families, so circumstanced, have stated to me the comfort and assistance they have derived from having a neighbour to whose habits and feelings their own are assimilated; and particularly in cases of sickness, or temporary distress from any cause, the advantage has been peculiarly felt, and very thankfully admitted.'[17] There is considerable evidence to suggest that when sickness struck, kin were sent for (often from a considerable distance) as rapidly as possible, to take over from the temporary assistance provided by neighbours,[18] and that, indeed, it was considered that where a person had kin within reach, they, rather than neighbours should provide the assistance needed as soon as possible.[19] In this context one may perhaps also compare Williams's observation that in Ashworthy kindred and close friends were the stable element in a society where neighbours came and went.[20]

Patrilaterality and matrilaterality

Finally, just a few words seem in order on the possible factors underlying a relationship suggested by the statistical data produced in Chapter 5 and hinted at from time to time in subsequent chapters. This is the apparent tendency for men to have particularly close bonds with male kin, and women with female kin. In present-day traditional working class communities, it is women who seem to bind together the kinship system,[21] and this seems to be because it is above all women in these communities who face the critical life situations and are therefore in need of kin assistance. In the nineteenth century the same was true, but men too were, particularly in the employment field, dependent on other men for the maximisation of their satisfactions. This being the case, a bifocal system might indeed be expected, since men needed above all help from male kin, and women help from female kin.[22]

This, then, concludes the presentation of data on family structure in nineteenth century Lancashire. In Part 4 which follows, some of the questions raised by these data are further discussed and an attempt is made to set them and the interpretation offered for them in a broader theoretical and substantive setting.

Part Four. Concluding discussion

12. The wider implications

In this chapter I shall briefly consider some of the substantive and theoretical implications of the present study, and some possible openings for future research in this field.

This kind of research demonstrates in its interpretations even more markedly than does most scientific work the basic principle that one can never positively say that one has proved anything. Rather, the most that one can claim is that, after reviewing all the available evidence, it has been possible to show that some interpretations are almost certainly wrong and that others seem most likely to be reasonably correct.[1] This is the kind of status I would claim for my findings. I stressed in Chapter 1 that it is a first attempt at this kind of research, in many ways a pilot study. I have, I hope, shown that fruitful research into family structure in Victorian England is possible, and that it can deepen our understanding of the workings of the family systems of our own present day and of other societies. I hope that, aided by what I have learnt by hard experience,[2] and by the new techniques that are now available,[3] others will follow along this path, and look at other Victorian urban areas with very different economies and also at the neglected subject of rural areas.

As far as theory is concerned, I have argued in this book that a fruitful approach to the interpretation of changes and differences in kinship structure is to concentrate on the interrelationships in any society of three structural elements:

(*a*) The social, material and affective problems which an actor must try to solve in order to attain his goals. (Not merely must economic problems be considered but problems of residence, social welfare, knowledge and information, protection, and many others including affect.)

(*b*) The social, material and affective resources that he has at his personal disposal.

(*c*) The supplies of resources under the control of others which can be made available for his use if he trades some of his own resources in return.

I have suggested that the highest probability that a kinship relationship of a functional kind will come into being between kinsman A and kinsman B will be when A has resources inadequate to solve one or more problems alone *and* when B also has or expects to have problems which A is or will be able to help him solve because he (A) has a surplus of the required resources, *and* when neither of them have open to them alternative suppliers of resources of which they are in need who will demand a lower expenditure of resources by them in reciprocation. Conversely, functional ongoing kinship relationships remain a possibility as long as both A and B each have even one major problem which they cannot solve simply with their own resources together with assistance from third parties. I have suggested that generalised or indirect reciprocation can arise under certain circumstances; in particular trust must be high. And I have suggested that if reciprocation must be delayed then trust must also be high even in a two-person situation and both parties must be able to do without the resources invested in the relationship for the period until reciprocation occurs. If the problem requires help from more than one person then numbers must be large enough so that the amount demanded by the person in need from each of the contributors in any time period is not greater than each is prepared to invest in this way; this I have suggested will be related partly to the extent to which each thinks he can rely on his own problems being met in turn when they arise, and partly to alternative demands on his resources.

Using this heuristic framework to study the Lancashire cotton towns I showed that economically, once they had found a job, men and women could be more or less independent of kin at an early age. For the young and healthy, day-to-day life could largely continue independently of any family or kinship relationship. However, for most of the population critical life situations of one kind or another were common and I pointed to a number of particular problems faced by the population of the Lancashire towns; I noted distress resulting from sickness, death, and unemployment, the problems of old age and those resulting from a housing shortage, the difficulties of finding good employment, and the special problems of working mothers and of inmigrants needing advice and shelter in a strange community.

Though neighbours did provide some help, and though there were certain bureaucratically organised assistance agencies, each had major drawbacks as a reliable and low cost source of aid. Neighbours lacked a firmly enough structured basis of reciprocation in a heterogeneous and mobile society. Kinship, by contrast, could provide this structured link and could thus form a basis for reciprocation. Kin did, indeed, probably provide the main source of aid. However, because this was a poor (and also a rapidly changing) society, this aid, quite logically in terms of the perspectives used here, was limited in cost, and family and kinship relationships tended to have strong short-run instrumental overtones of a calculative kind. The fact that they were nevertheless so frequently functional – probably more so than in most other areas of urban or rural Victorian England – could, I suggested, be attributed to the fact that the demands of the labour market for child and female employment and the frequency of the crises made most aid relatively low in cost and relatively rapid in reciprocation, and thus made a strongly functional aid system possible in spite of the other circumstances.

Concluding discussion

In Chapter 7 I applied this framework to rural Lancashire and rural Ireland. Here it enabled me to interpret the strong positive correlations between kinship co-residence and farm size, and also in rural Ireland the partial replacement as poverty became extreme of a normative traditional kinship orientation by a markedly calculative one.

Generalising from this analysis a number of more formalised suggestions can be made about the situations in which different degrees and kinds of relational involvements with any given class of kinsmen will emerge; also, and probably with a higher expectation of empirical verification, suggestions can be made about the situations in which they will change, and the directions of such changes.[4] Each of the following statements is to be seen as of a *ceteris paribus* kind.

1. Any hypothetical actor who could be completely self-reliant, in that he could attain his goals with no assistance from any other person, would tend not to maintain any given kinship relationship. Absence of self-reliance is therefore a necessary, but not a sufficient condition for kinship relationships to exist. Self-reliance is a function of goals, of resources available to the individual to assist him in reaching these goals, and of conditions impeding his ability to meet these goals. A principle task of research is to specify these for any given situation.
1.1 When faced with alters with equal resources, environmental conditions, and goals, an actor with greater resources or lower impediments has less motivation to maintain any given relationship than one with lower resources or greater impediments; kin are one possible form of assistance.
1.2. When faced with alters with equal resources, environmental conditions, and goals, any increase in resources or fall in impediments increases an actor's motivation to reduce involvement in any given relationship. Decreases in resources or rises in impediments should increase motivation to seek assistance; kin are one possible form of assistance.
2. Mutually satisfying social relationships involving ego with one or more alters are a possible but not a necessary consequence:
2.1. when ego has special skills or resources attractive to others but needs complementary assistance in the form of different skills or resources if he is to make use of his resources to attain his own goals.
2.1.1. similarly when this kind of complementarity is temporally separate, so that situations where ego has resources useful at one point in time but lacking in others can be complemented by situations where alter lacks resources at the first time but has them in the second (notably where dependency follows an active period where other forms of insurance (e.g. saving) are discouraged by institutional arrangements).
2.2. where critical situations are known to hit individual members of a population from time to time and are either:

2.2.1. costly to solve but relatively rare; or
2.2.2. of irregular occurrence so that resources, although adequate in the long run are not necessarily adequate in the short run.
3. Willingness to enter into relationships with any given alter will increase, the greater is the certainty that alter will in turn help one out in time of need. This in turn involves:
3.1. certainty about one's own future needs and about alter's future resources and other prior demands on them; such certainty is likely to be reduced in such situations as the following: situations of rapid social change; situations where major crises are frequent; situations where sizes of available resources fluctuate greatly; situations where actors are not in frequent interaction with each other and are therefore likely to be unsure of each other's resources and prior commitments.
3.2. certainty about alter's commitment to the relationship and his expectations of his obligations to it; such trust is likely to be reduced in such situations as the following: situations of normative change or heterogeneity, particularly where some actors in similar statuses are known to be failing to meet expectations of a similar kind; situations where alter's socialisation is outside one's own control or where his present relationships are not encapsulated by a close-knit network on which he is dependent and of which ego is a powerful member; situations where interaction with alter is infrequent and other reports on his activities are not regularly available to ego.
4. Actors will be increasingly unwilling to enter relationships where the return is only in the long run:
4.1. the lower the trust and certainty,
4.2. the more pressing are alternative uses for their resources. In particular this means that there must be some surplus of resources above other present demands on resources with higher personal priority due to the higher costs of not applying them to that use.
4.3. If trust and certainty are not high, then willingness depends on there being no other alternative offering a somewhat smaller reward but in the less distant future.
5. As a corollary, the lower the certainty and trust, the shorter the preferred time span which must pass before reciprocation.
5.1. If certainty is low but trust is high, then there is a pressure towards the development of normative prescriptions which demand both stress on short time span relationships and a calculative orientation towards longer span relationships.
5.2. If certainty is low and trust is also low, then there will be a pressure towards calculativeness in all relationships and towards the termination or non-establishment of some relationships.
6. In situations where calculativeness is a dominant orientation, whether

normatively prescribed or not, there will tend to be wide variability in behaviour and in role maintenance even among those in similar statuses.

7. The lower the certainty, the greater will be the emphasis on low cost behaviour even if this involves lower long-run returns.

8. The more alternative sources of assistance there are to individuals in the form of assistance by bureaucracies, the greater is the possibility though not the necessity that emphasis on kinship as a source of assistance will be reduced. Any movement towards complete or major termination of kinship relationships is, however, only possible if all the individual's major problems of goal attainment can be met through non-kinship sources, i.e. at least, in the usual case, if he can obtain alternative sources of employment and income, accommodation, protection, social welfare, and also of knowledge necessary to obtain these.

8.1. When a considerable number of people in any given status take up the opportunities offered by the bureaucratised sources of assistance, certainty becomes reduced for the remainder.

8.2. Given equal exposure to the new influences, and subject to the qualifications noted in proposition 8 above, alternatives of this kind will prove most attractive to those whose kin have least to offer in return for expenditure of the required resources or who make greatest demands on resources.

8.3. Again subject to the qualifications noted under 8, any increase in the resources demanded by the kinsman will lead to a reduction of attraction to the kinship relationship.

8.3.1. As a special case of 8.3, an increase in longevity will tend to reduce the attractions of long-run support of kin in old age unless counterbalancing increases in rewards can be obtained.

9. Because relationships with bureaucratised sources of assistance are contractual they will tend to increase in attractiveness the lower the degree of trust.

10. Because sanctions are more easily applicable to them over long time periods through the structured networks of the kinship system, in situations of equal trust, resources, and conditions (notably frequency of contact), relationships with kin will usually be preferred to other primary relationships.

11. Where certain conditions are met, in situations of the kind described in 2.1.1 2.2.1, and 2.2.2 generalised exchange networks of kin and/or of others in primary relationships with ego will tend to become important functional assistance nets.[5] It is unnecessary here to give a full exposition of all these conditions, but the main points are summarised in 12 and 13 below.

11.1. As a corollary of 11 note that changes in the numbers of available kin will, in the conditions discussed under 12 and 13 below be one important factor tending to change the extent of involvement in non-kin net activity.

12. Aid nets will not occur where costly events occur very frequently or in very poor populations unless occurrence of crises is very infrequent and aid nets can be very large.[6]

13. The necessary minimum size of aid nets (assuming trust is high) is increased:
13.0.1. the greater the degree to which actors wish to be certain that the net will be able to solve their problems.
13.0.2. the higher the mean frequency of occurrence of events and the greater the variations between net members in the incidence of events.
13.0.3. the larger the cost of crises or the smaller the surpluses available to meet them and also the greater the variation between net members in costs or surpluses.[7]
13.1. Other things being equal, the larger the net, the more difficult it is to maintain trust. Thus there is pressure in large nets to build subnets where trust can more easily be enforced.

Subnets became viable in situations where there is heterogeneity of surpluses or of incidence of crises and particularly in poor and crisis smitten populations.[8]
13.2. Where trust is weak, nets are only viable where individual contributions can be very small relative to an individual's total available surplus.[9]
13.3. Diachronically, an increase in poverty, and increase in the incidence of crises and a rise in fluctuations in either of these will exert pressures to increase net size. However, at a certain point this leads to a total breakdown of nets.[10] Also, nets can only increase to the size at which adequate trust is maintained so there is again some point where total breakdown will ensue.

This outline conceptual approach obviously still requires much further development. In particular, the specification of important resource and problem areas and of boundary conditions is necessary. Nevertheless, by starting from this approach one can set the findings of this study in a broader cross-cultural setting with reference both to traditional societies and to industrialisation in the twentieth century. One can also make further interpretative guesses about the patterns of development of kinship structure in Britain over the past 300 years. In turn, each of these exercises seems to give further support to the kind of interpretations offered in this book for nineteenth century Lancashire. Some also seem to point to fruitful lines for future research.

For example, as far as traditional societies are concerned Nimkoff and Middleton[11] have demonstrated on the basis of an examination of some 550 societies that hunting and gathering societies (where not merely can the individual solve his life problems independently of kin but often is compelled to given a sparse food supply) have predominantly a nuclear family pattern; by contrast, societies such as agricultural societies whose economy depends on scarce property (notably land) and where consequently individual independence is difficult, tend to have family systems of an extended type. Similarly, Simmons in a cross-cultural study of the social relationships of the old[12] finds a correlation of +0.92 between old men having property rights in a society and their being supported by their families in old age. Since in most cases this property is necessary for the child's long-run economic viability a similar mechanism seems to be in operation.[13] Moreover, Simmons later shows[14] that control of information by the old is also a major source of power and prestige important in ensuring support in old age. So too is an ability to continue to exercise any other important socially useful work.

Within Western cultures many analogous situations are reported in the literature. Petersen[15] has noted that land reclamation in Holland always led to a situation where many children who had previously been working on family farms instead took advantage of the independence offered by this situation to set up on their own. Bicanic[16] has shown how the replacement of oxen by horses as ploughing animals in Yugoslavia made it possible to form viable one-man ploughing units instead of ploughing needing four or five men, and how this made possible a more nucleated family system. Gadourek[17] has noted that while self-employed bulb growers are able to keep their children in subordinate positions in the family system even after marriage because both father and son have a common long-run interest in increasing the value of their business,[18] working class parents who have nothing to offer in return are rebelled against.

The development of a short-run instrumental orientation to kinship analogous to that found in Lancashire and rural Ireland has also been noted elsewhere in similar circumstances. Generally speaking, in traditional societies, the poorer the society and the more irregular the food supply, the more likely it is that food sharing among the community as a whole will be found.[19] In these societies trust is likely to be high enough for aid nets of considerable size to develop, and the very fact that such a society has survived means that such a procedure has usually proved over time to be a viable way of covering the continuing crises if the aid net is large enough. However, in most of the societies where food supply is most irregular, this food sharing does not in crisis times include the old, who are highly likely to be deserted or killed.[20] Simmons notes, as one would predict in a traditional and thus phenomenally normatively oriented society, that this manner of treating the old is part of the normative system of these societies. However, there is some evidence that very extreme conditions can lead to normative collapse even in traditional societies. Sahlins has suggested that it appears that 'every primitive society has its breaking point, or at least its turning point. Everyone might see the time when co-operation is overwhelmed by the scale of disaster ... The range of assistance contracts progressively to the family level; perhaps even these bonds dissolve and, washed away, reveal an inhuman, yet most human, self-interest.'[21]

Among the studies of contemporary Western societies Banfield's village of 'Montegrano'[22] seems to show a classic case of the operation of a similar mechanism to that posited here, though, given the long-run stability of the situation, the fact that the calculative orientation has become normative is to be expected.

The uncertainty of life in Banfield's village, together with extreme poverty, has led to a situation where any service rendered even to close kin is mentally recorded and reciprocation demanded, and where no long-run obligations are entered into; normatively prescribed short-run instrumentalism of a calculative kind is the rule. Note also that a number of studies of the impact of the unemployment of the father on the father-son relationship have shown how the father rapidly loses authority and how this is recognised phenomenally as resulting from the changed balance of earning power.[23]

Studies of the impact of urban-industrial life on the family in currently developing countries show further parallels with the situation in Victorian Lancashire. Indeed the problems faced by the people involved in these changes are very similar indeed, and the resources at their disposal, and even the available bureaucratised sources of aid, are equally meagre.[24] Thus, many students draw attention to the impact of the individual wage as a crucial source of change, giving as it does an independent source of support to the young and an ability to purchase for themselves many things (even including brides) previously under the elders' control.[25] But, secondly, almost all studies of these same peoples in the urban industrial situation point to the uses made of kinship bonds as a way of meeting the problems of adaptation and of migration to the towns.[26]

Finally, I should like to use the same heuristic framework to state what in the present state of knowledge amounts to little more than a series of hunches or hypotheses for future research about the factors involved in the changes in patterns of relationships between working class married children and their parents in Britain over the past 300 years.[27]

Compared with the Lancashire situation I outlined above the co-residence of parents and married children was probably rare in pre-industrial England.[28] At the same time there are scraps of evidence to suggest that a short-run instrumental orientation to kin was not uncommon,[29] and certainly in the early nineteenth century a number of cases of this kind were noted by the 1834 Poor Law Commissioners.[30] In interpretation I suggest that the critical life situations faced by these populations were almost as great as, while their resources were in general considerably less than, those of the Lancashire operatives (and this would apply particularly to the potential contribution of those below or above working age). In addition, the alternative of the Poor Law was available, relatively lenient of administration, and indeed believed to give to the old a better standard of living than their children could provide.[31] In these circumstances a calculative orientation of this kind and a relatively low functionality of the kinship system is only to be expected. Since even sociability might be taken to imply other assistance which could not be forthcoming, even sociability as a kinship function may well have been quite low.

In many ways the polar opposite case is to be found in 'traditional' working class communities of the 1930s as described by Hoggart from his own memory,[32] by Young and Willmott from the memories of their informants,[33] and very picturesquely by Rosser and Harris through the mouth of 'Mr. Hughes of Morriston'.[34] It remains for future research to establish just when these solidary collectivistic communities with their frequent exchange of services (costly in time but *not* usually costly in cash) through a strongly affective and close-knit kinship system really began to flourish to the full.[35] The replies on kinship aid to the old made to Booth's inquiries in the 1890s[36] were very variable. In addition Thompson, on the basis of preliminary data from interviews with old people about conditions before 1914, has recently stressed the limitations placed by poverty on kinship and neighbourhood activities and the sudden rejection by kin which occurred when one's family fell into serious difficulties.[37] Certainly the heuristic framework outlined here would lead one to predict that as working class affluence slowly increased towards the end of the nineteenth century (thus increasing both individual resources and those of kin), as the death rate fell so that the burden of dependence fell on the shoulders of more married children, and as communities began to stabilise and a new normative system could be built up so that the time span of reciprocity could be somewhat increased, then and only then could a more functional and less calculative orientation to kinship begin to develop. However, I would suggest that it was probably only after the introduction of the old age pension transferred much of the economic burden of old age from kin, and above all in the interwar period when economic problems caused by other critical life situations began to be eased by the beginnings of that bureaucratised system that we now call the Welfare State to the point where kinship aid was not very costly per capita in cash terms (though still costly in time which was not so scarce, at least for women), that a really strong affective and non-calculative commitment to the kinship net could develop and 'traditional' community solidarity become possible.[38]

Since the Second World War, by contrast, we have apparently seen further changes leading to some eclipse of the most solidary and normative kinship bonds. In terms of this analysis I should attribute this change on the one hand to some decline in the frequency of critical life situations as health improved, family size declined, and the scourge of unemployment was reduced, and on the other to an increase in people's ability to meet these crises for themselves through increased wages and increased benefits and services from the Welfare State.[39] Relationships with kin can now and only now become a matter of choice within the working class, one of a multiplicity of possible viable sources of assistance instead of the only one, something to be taken advantage of selectively and seldom as a matter of absolute dependence. Note finally that in this interpretation the population movements and the subsequent decrease in the homogeneity of populations and in the degree of superimposition of different relationships, on which some have laid so much stress as factors in the decline in traditional communities, are not themselves to be seen as direct causes of this decline but rather as made possible by the very independence from kin which is now open to those who move in this way. Thus the working class have come, at least at present, something of a full circle, from pre-industrial kinship weakened because the problems were so great and the resources so small, through a functional 'traditional' kinship system, to a situation where kinship is again weakened but now, by contrast, because the problems are reduced, resources are so much increased, and ready alternatives are open to all.[40]

Appendix
Collection and analysis of descriptive data

Data collection began with reading of the principal social and economic secondary sources. In turn almost all the sources of information cited there which appeared possibly to be even remotely relevant were looked into. Information was recorded with one item on each piece of paper for subsequent sorting.

In the initial stages all statements on any aspect of family life (except conjugal relationships) and on relationships with friends and neighbours were recorded. So, as far as possible, was any information on relationships with other collectivities which could possibly be conceived of as providing a functional alternative to kinship, together with any information which suggested that a function (such as assistance in sickness) which one might have expected to be a kinship function was not being performed by a kinsman. Background information on migration, poor relief, social and work life, and economic and industrial matters was also collected. The date, place, and any biographical details on the person in question were also noted. As time went by, on a very small number of topics of marginal interest to this research (such as certain aspects of child neglect or family employment in mills) on which a mass of data almost all pointing in the same direction could be found, some selectivity was employed, and only a few cases, plus any contrary or interesting additional cases were collected from each piece of work. No serious analysis was attempted until virtually all the available data sources had been worked. Then a complete list of hypotheses, indicators, and points on which data were required was drawn up and all the sheets of data were looked at in turn. On each sheet a note was made of any topic for which the information recorded might be relevant. The sheets were then sorted into order and analysis and preliminary drafting proceeded by examining all the data on any one topic and then resorting relevant items for later use. Thus all the scraps of descriptive data were considered at the analysis stage in terms of the indicators required by the theoretical rationales of the study. In this way at least some attempt was made to avoid purely deductive or impressionistic analysis.

List of works cited in the text

(Dates of first editions or of writing in the case of originally unpublished works, where different from those cited, and where known, are given in second brackets.)

I BOOKS, PAMPHLETS, ARTICLES, ETC.

Abram, W. A. (1868). 'Social condition and political prospects of the Lancashire workmen'. *Fortnightly R.*, new series, vol. 4, 426–41.

Adams, B. N. (1967). 'Interaction theory and the social network'. *Sociometry*, vol. 30, 64–78.

(1968a). *Kinship in an urban setting*. Markham, Chicago.

(1968b). 'The middle class adult and his widowed or still married mother'. *Social Problems*, vol 16, 50–9.

Adshead, J. (1842). *Distress in Manchester. Evidence ... of the state of the labouring classes in 1840–42.* Henry Hooper, London.

Aikin, J. (1795). *A description of the country from thirty to forty miles around Manchester.* John Stockdale, London.

Alexander, J. (1861). *Memoirs of the Rev. William Alexander, by his son.* Fletcher and Alexander, Norwich.

Anderson, M. (1969). *Family structure in nineteenth century Lancashire.* Ph.D. dissertation, University of Cambridge.

(1970a). 'Urban migration in nineteenth century Lancashire; some insights into two competing hypotheses'. mimeo.

(1970b). 'Smelser revisited: problems of inference in historical sociology'. mimeo.

(forthcoming a). 'Household structure and the industrial revolution: mid-nineteenth century Preston in comparative perspective'. in Laslett, T. P. R. (ed), *The comparative history of family and household.* Cambridge University Press, Cambridge.

(forthcoming b). 'The study of family structure'. in Wrigley, E. A. (ed), *The study of nineteenth century society.* Cambridge University Press.

(forthcoming c). 'Standard tabulation procedures for the census enumerators' books 1851 to 1891'. in Wrigley, E. A. (ed), *The study of nineteenth century society.* Cambridge University Press.

Anderson, N. (1960). *The urban community. A world perspective.* Routledge and Kegan Paul, London.

Arensberg, C. M. and Kimball, S. T. (1961) (1940). *Family and community in Ireland.* Peter Smith, Gloucester, Mass.

Armstrong, W. A. (1966). 'Social structure from the early census returns'. in Wrigley, E. A. (ed), *An introduction to English historical demography*, Weidenfeld and Nicolson, London.

(1968). 'The interpretation of the census books for Victorian towns'. in Dyos, H. J. (ed), *The study of urban history.* Edward Arnold, London.

(1969). 'Some further comparisons between Mr. Laslett's 100 pre-industrial communities, and York in 1851'. Paper read at the International Conference on the Comparative History of Household and Family, Cambridge.

Arnold, R. A. (1864). *The history of the cotton famine ...* Saunders, Otley, and Co., London.

List of works cited in the text

Ashworth, H. (1842). 'Statistics of the present depression of trade at Bolton'. *J. statist. Soc.*, vol 5, 74–81.

Avonson, H. (1912). 'Liberalism in the village'. *Nation*, 18 May 1912.

Back, K. W. (1965). 'A social psychologist looks at kinship structure'. in Shanas, E. and Streib, G. F. (eds), *Social structure and the family: generational relations*. Prentice-Hall, New Jersey.

Baines, M. A. (1862). 'Summary of a paper on infant mortality'. *Trans. natn. Ass. Promotion soc. Sci.*, 1862, 678.

Bakke, E. W. (1960) (1940). 'The cycle of adjustment to unemployment'. in Bell, N. W. and Vogel, E. F., *A modern introduction to the family*. Free Press, New York.

Bamford, S. (1844). *Walks in South Lancashire and on its borders* ... published by the author, Blackley, Manchester.

(1893a) (1841). *Early days*. Fisher Unwin, London.

(1893b) (1843). *Passages in the life of a radical*. Fisher Unwin, London.

Banfield, E. C. (1958). *The moral basis of a backward society*. Free Press, New York.

Banks, J. A. (1954). *Prosperity and parenthood*. Routledge and Kegan Paul, London.

Barlee, E. (1863). *A visit to Lancashire in December 1862*. Seeley, Lackson and Halliday, London.

Beckett, J. R. (1965). 'Kinship, mobility and community among part-aboriginees in rural Australia'. *Int. J. comp. Sociol.*, vol 6, 7–23.

Beesley, G. (1849). *A report on the state of agriculture in Lancashire* ... Dobson and Son, Preston.

Bell, C. (1968). *Middle class families*. Routledge and Kegan Paul, London.

(1970). 'Occupational career, family cycle, and extended family relations'. Paper read at the 11th International Family Research Seminar, London, mimeo.

Bell, Lady F. (1907). *At the works*. Edward Arnold, London.

Bicanic, R. (1956). 'Occupational heterogeneity of peasant families in the period of rapid industrialisation'. *Trans. third Wld. Congr. Sociol.*, vol 4, 80–96.

Binns, J. (1851). *Notes on the agriculture of Lancashire with suggestions for its improvement*. Dobson and Son, Preston.

Blalock, H. M. (1960). *Social statistics*. McGraw-Hill, New York.

Blau, P. M. (1964). *Exchange and power in social life*. Wiley, New York.

Booth, C. (ed) (1892). *Life and labour of the people in London*, vol 3. Macmillan, London.

(1894). *The aged poor in England and Wales*. Macmillan, London.

Bosanquet, H. (1899). *Rich and poor*. Macmillan, London.

Bott, E. (1957). *Family and social network*. Tavistock, London.

Bremner, J. A. (1866). 'By what means can the impediments to the education of the children of the manual-labour class ... be most effectually removed?' *Trans. natn. Ass. Promotion soc. Sci.*, 1866, 307–17.

Brierley, B. (*c*1886). *Home memories and recollections of a life*. Heywood, Manchester.

Brown, J. S., Schwartzweller, H. K., and Mangalam, J. J. (1963). 'Kentucky mountain migration and the stem family'. *Rur. Sociol.*, vol 28, 48–69.

Caird, J. (1852). *English agriculture in 1850–1*. Longman, Brown, Green and Longmans, London.

Calman, A. L. (1875). *Life and labours of John Ashworth*. Tubbs and Brook, Manchester.

Chadwick, D. (1860). 'On the rate of wages in Manchester and Salford, and the manufacturing districts of Lancashire, 1839–59'. *J. statist. Soc.*, vol 23, 1–36.

Chadwick, W. (*c* 1900). *Reminiscences of a Chief Constable*. Heywood, Manchester.

Clay, J. (1853). *Burial clubs and infanticide in England*. Dobson and Son, Preston.

(1861). *The Prison Chaplain*. Macmillan, Cambridge.

Clegg, J. (1877). *A chronological history of Bolton* ... Daily Chronicle, Bolton.

Cobden, J. (1881) (1862). Speech to a meeting of gentlemen residents of Manchester, 29 April, 1862. in Waugh, E., *Works*, vol 2. Heywood, Manchester.

Collier, F. (1965) (1921). *The family economy of the working classes in the cotton industry 1784–1833*. Chetham Society, Manchester.

Comhaire, J. L. (1956). 'Economic change and the extended family'. *A. Amer. Acad. polit. soc. Sci.*, vol 305, 45–52.

Connell, K. H. (1950a). *The population of Ireland. 1750–1845*. Oxford University Press, Oxford.

(1950b). 'The colonization of the wasteland in Ireland'. *Econ. Hist. R.*, second series, vol 3, 44–71.

(1962). 'Peasant marriage in Ireland: its structure and development since the famine'. *Econ. Hist. R.*, second series, vol 14, 502–23.

Corbridge, S. L. (1964). *It's an old Lancashire custom*. Guardian Press, Preston.

Crozier, D. (1965). 'Kinship and occupational succession'. *Sociol. R.*, new series, vol 13, 15–43.

Cumming, E. and Schneider, D. M. (1966) (1961). 'Sibling solidarity: a property of American kinship'. in Farber, B. (ed), *Kinship and family organisation*. Wiley, New York.

Dager, E. Z. (1964). 'Socialisation and personality development in the child'. in Christensen, H. T. (ed), *Handbook of marriage and the family*. Rand NcNally, Chicago.

Davies, C. S. (1963). *North country bred*. Routledge and Kegan Paul, London.

Davies, J. B. (1964). 'Una teoria general de los determinantes de la edad de casarse'. *R. Mexic. Sociol.*, vol 26, 191–219.

Dennis, N., Henriques, F., and Slaughter, C. (1956). *Coal is our life*. Eyre and Spottiswoode, London.

Derby, Earl of (1881) (1863). Speech to a county meeting on the cotton famine on 2 Dec 1863. in Waugh, E., *Works*, vol 2. Heywood, Manchester.

Dodd, W. (1968) (1842). *The factory system illustrated in a series of letters to Lord Ashley*. Frank Cass, London.

Drake, M. (1963). 'Marriage and population growth in Ireland'. *Econ. Hist. R.*, second series, vol 16, 301–13.

Dunlop, J. (1839). *The philosophy of artificial and compulsory drinking usages in Great Britain and Ireland*. Houlston and Staleman, London.

Dunlop, J. and Denman, R. D. (1912). *English apprenticeship and child labour. A history*. Fisher Unwin, London.

Dunning, E. G. and Hopper, E. I. (1966). 'Industrialisation and the problem of convergence: a critical note'. *Sociol R.*, new series, vol 14, 163–86.

Dupaquier, J. (1969). 'Les recensements de la Corse à la fin de l'ancien régime'. Paper read at the International Conference on the Comparative History of Household and Family, Cambridge.

Durkheim, E. (1933) (1897). *The division of labour in society*. translated and edited by Simpson, G. Free Press, New York.

Dyos, H. J. and Baker, A. M. B. (1968). 'The possibilities of computerising census data'. in Dyos, H. J. (ed), *The study of urban history*. Edward Arnold, London.

Engels, F. (1958) (1844). *The condition of the working class in England*. translated and edited by Henderson, W. O. and Chaloner, W. H. Blackwell, Oxford.

Etzioni, A. (1965). *A comparative study of complex organisations*. Free Press, New York.

Farr, W. (1864). *English life tables*. Longmans, Green, London.

Faucher, L. (1845). *Études sur Angleterre*. Guillaumin, Paris.

Ferriar, J. (1795). *Medical histories and reflexions*, vol 2. Caddell, Warrington.

(1798). ibid, vol 3.

Firth, R. (ed) (1956). *Two studies of kinship in London*. University of London, London.

(1964). 'Family and kinship in industrial society'. in Halmos, P. (ed), *The development of industrial societies. Sociol. R. Monograph* no 8, Keele.

Firth, R., Hubert, J., and Forge, A. (1970). *Families and their relatives*. Routledge and Kegan Paul, London.

Fitton, R. S. and Wadsworth, A. P. (1958). *The Strutts and the Arkwrights 1758–1830*. Manchester University Press, Manchester.
Flinn, M. W. (1965). Introduction to Chadwick, E., *Report on the sanitary condition of the labouring population of Great Britain*. Edinburgh University Press, Edinburgh.
Foster, G. M. (1961). 'The dyadic contract: a model for the social structure of a Mexican peasant village'. *Amer. Anthropol.*, vol 63, 1173–92.
Foster, J. O. (1967). *Capitalism and class consciousness in earlier nineteenth century Oldham*. Ph.D. dissertation, University of Cambridge.
(1968). 'Nineteenth-century towns – a class dimension'. in Dyos, H. J. (ed), *The study of urban history*. Edward Arnold, London.
Freeman, T. W., Rodgers, H. B., and Kinvig, R. H. (1966). *Lancashire, Cheshire, and the Isle of Man*. Nelson, London.
Gadourek, I. (1956). *A Dutch community*. Stenfert Kroese, Leiden.
Garnett, W. J. (1849). 'Farming of Lancashire'. *J. roy. agric. Soc. Engl.*, vol 10, 1–51.
Gaskell, E. C. (1897) (1848). *Mary Barton*. Bliss Sands and Co., London.
(1906a) (1847). *Libbie Marsh's three eras*. in *Works*, vol 1. Smith, Elder and Co., London.
(1906b) (1850). *Lissie Leigh*. in *Works*, vol 2.
(1906c) (1850). *The heart of John Middleton*. in *Works*, vol 2.
(1906d) (1855). *Bessy's troubles at home*. in *Works*, vol 3.
(1906e) (1854–5). *North and south*. in *Works*, vol 3.
(1906f) (1855). *Hand and heart*. in *Works*, vol. 3.
(1906g) (1855). *Half a lifetime ago*. in *Works*, vol 5.
(1906h) (1858). *The half brothers*. in *Works*, vol 5.
(1906i) (1863–4). *Cousin Phillis*. in *Works*, vol 7.
(1906j) (1857). *The crooked branch*. in *Works*, vol 7.
Gaskell, P. (1833). *The manufacturing population of England*. Baldwin and Cradock, London.
Gaulter, E. (1833). *The origin and progress of the malignant cholera in Manchester*. Longman, Rees, London.
Gavron, H. (1966). *The captive wife*. Routledge and Kegan Paul, London.
Geiger, K. (1960). 'The family and social change'. in Black, C. E., *The transformation of Russian society*. Harvard University Press, Cambridge, Mass.
General Register Office (1968). *Sample census, 1966, Household composition tables*. HMSO, London.
George, M. D. (1953). *England in transition*. Penguin, Harmondsworth.
Gilbert, B. B. (1966). *The evolution of National Insurance in Great Britain*. Michael Joseph, London.
Goldthorpe, J. H. (1964). 'Social stratification in industrial society'. in Halmos, P. (ed), *The development of industrial societies. Sociol. R. Monograph* no 8, Keele.
(1966). 'Reply to Dunning and Hopper'. *Sociol. R.*, new series, vol 14, 187–95.
Goldthorpe, J. H., Lockwood, D., Bechhofer, F., and Platt, J. (1969). *The affluent worker in the class structure*. Cambridge University Press, Cambridge.
Goode, W. J. (1959). 'The theoretical importance of love'. *Amer. sociol. R.*, vol 24, 38–47.
(1960). 'A theory of role strain'. *Amer. sociol. R.*, vol 25, 483–96.
(1963). *World revolution and family patterns*. Free Press of Glencoe, New York.
(1963–4). 'The process of role bargaining in the impact of urbanization and industrialization'. *Current Sociol.*, vol 12, 1–13.
(1964). *The family*. Prentice-Hall, New Jersey.
Gosden, P. H. J. H. (1961). *The Friendly Societies in England, 1815–1875*. Manchester University Press, Manchester.
Gouldner, A. W. (1959). 'Reciprocity and autonomy in functional theory'. in Gross, L., *Symposium on sociological theory*. Row, Peterson and Co., Evanston, Illinois.
(1960). 'The norm of reciprocity: a preliminary statement'. *Amer. sociol. R.*, vol 25, 161–78.

Greenfield, S. M. (1961). 'Industrialization and the family in sociological theory'. *Amer. J. Sociol.*, vol 67, 312–22.

Greg, W. R. (1831). *An enquiry into the state of the manufacturing population* . . . Ridgway, London.

Grime, B. (1887). *Memory sketches Part 1.* Hirst and Rennie, Oldham.

Gross, J. (1965). 'Mrs. Gaskell'. in *The novelist as innovator*. BBC, London.

Gutkind, P. C. W. (1965). 'African urbanism, mobility, and the social network'. *Int. J. comp. Sociol.*, vol 6, 48–60.

Habakkuk, H. J. (1955). 'Family structure and economic change in nineteenth-century Europe'. *J. econ. Hist.*, vol 15, 1–12.

Hajnal, J. (1965). 'European marriage patterns in perspective'. in Glass, D. V. and Eversley, D. E. C. (eds), *Population in history. Essays in historical demography.* Edward Arnold, London.

Hall, W. (1826). *William Hall's vindication of the Chorley spinners.* Leigh, Manchester.

Hammond, B. (1928). 'Urban death rates in the early nineteenth century'. *Econ. Hist. R.*, vol 1, 419–28.

Hammond, J. L. and Hammond, B. (1917). *The town labourer 1760–1832.* Longmans, Green, London.

Hardwick, C. (1857). *History of the borough of Preston and its environs in the county of Lancashire.* Worthington, Preston.

Hardy, T. (1925) (1891). *Tess of the d'Urbervilles.* Macmillan, London.

Hatton, J. (1854). *A lecture on the sanitary conditions of Chorlton-upon Medlock* ... Beresford and Galt, Manchester.

Hertz, F. (1859). 'Mechanics institutes for working women ...'. *Trans. natn. Ass. Promotion soc. Sci.*, 1859, 347–54.

Hewitt, M. (1953). *The effect of married women's employment in the cotton textile districts on the home in Lancashire, 1840–1880.* Ph.D. dissertation, University of London.

(1958). *Wives and mothers in Victorian industry.* Rockliff, London.

Hill, R. (1965). 'Decision making and the family life cycle', in Shanas, E. and Streib, G. F., *Social structure and the family: generational relations.* Prentice-Hall, New Jersey.

Hobsbawm, E. J. (1964). *Labouring men.* Weidenfeld and Nicolson, London.

Hoggart, R. (1957). *The uses of literacy.* Chatto and Windus, London.

Homans, G. C. (1961). *Social behaviour. Its elementary forms.* Routledge and Kegan Paul, London.

Howitt, W. (1838a). *The rural life of England*, vol 1. Longman, Orme, Brown, Green and Longmans, London.

(1838b). ibid, vol 2.

de Hoyos, A. and de Hoyos, G. (1966). 'The amigo system and alienation of the wife in the conjugal Mexican family'. in Farber, B. (ed), *Kinship and family organisation.* Wiley, New York.

Hubert, J. (1965). 'Kinship and geographical mobility in a sample from a London middle class area'. *Int. J. comp. Sociol.*, vol 6, 61–80.

Hull, G. (1902). *The poets and poetry of Blackburn (1793–1902).* Toulmin, Blackburn.

Humphreys, A. J. (1966). *New Dubliners.* Routledge and Kegan Paul, London.

Husband, W. D. (1864). 'Infant mortality'. *Trans. natn. Ass. Promotion soc. Sci.*, 1864, 498–508.

Hutton, W. (1841). *The life of William Hutton* ... Knight, London.

Inglis, K. S. (1960). 'Patterns of religious worship in 1851'. *J. ecclesiastical Hist.*, vol 11, 74–86.

Inkeles, A. (1963). 'Sociology and psychology'. in Koch, S. (ed), *Psychology: a study of a science.* McGraw-Hill, New York.

Kahl, J. A. (1959). 'Some social concomitants of industrialization and urbanization'. *Human Org.*, vol 18, 53–74.

Kay, J. P. (1832). *The moral and physical condition of the working classes* ... Ridgway, London.
Kelly (1858). *Post Office directory of Lancashire, 1858*. Kelly, London.
Kelly, E. and Kelly, T. (eds) (1957) (1835–48). *A schoolmaster's notebook*. Chetham Society, Manchester.
Kelly, T. (1806). *Thoughts on the marriages of the labouring poor* ... Kearsley and Hat, London.
Kennedy, J. P. (1847). *Digest of evidence taken before Her Majesty's Commissioners of Inquiry into the state of the law and practice in respect to the occupation of land in Ireland*. Dublin.
Kerr, M. (1958). *The people of Ship Street*. Routledge and Kegan Paul, London.
Klein, J. (1965). *Samples from English cultures* (2 vols). Routledge and Kegan Paul, London.
Knight, J. (ed) (1818a). *Important extracts from ... letters, written by Englishmen in the United States of America, to their friends in England*, first series. Manchester.
(ed) (1818b). ibid, second series.
Komarovsky, M. (1940). *The unemployed man and his family*. Dryden, New York.
Lancaster, L. (1961). 'Some conceptual problems in the study of family and kin ties in the British Isles'. *Brit. J. Sociol.*, vol 12, 317–33.
Lansing, J. B. and Kish, L. (1957). 'Family life cycle as an independent variable'. *Amer. sociol. R.*, vol 22, 512–19.
Laslett, T. P. R. (1965). *The world we have lost*. Methuen, London.
(1969). 'Size and structure of the household in England over three centuries; Part 1 – Mean household size in England since the sixteenth century', *Population studies*, vol 23, 199–223.
Laslett, T. P. R. and Harrison, J. (1963). 'Clayworth and Cogenhoe'. in Bell, H. E. and Ollard, R. L. (eds), *Historical essays 1600–1750 presented to David Ogg*. Black, London.
Lawton, R. (1955). 'The population of Liverpool in the mid-nineteenth century'. *Trans. hist. Soc. Lancashire and Cheshire*, vol 107, 89–120.
Leigh, W. (1833). *An authentic account of the melancholy occurrences at Bilston ... during the awful visitation ... by cholera* ... Parke, Wolverhampton.
Lenski, G. E. (1966). *Power and privilege. A theory of social stratification*. McGraw-Hill, New York.
LePlay, P. G. F. (1855). *Les ouvriers européens* ... L'imprimerie impériale, Paris.
Levy, M. J. (1949). *The family revolution in modern China*. Harvard University Press, Cambridge, Mass.
(1955). 'Contrasting factors in the modernization of China and Japan'. in Kuznets, S. S., Moore, W. E. and Spengler, J. J., *Economic growth: Brazil, India, Japan*. Duke University Press, Durham.
Linton, R. (1959). 'The natural history of the family'. in Anshen, R. N. (ed), *The family, its function and destiny*. Harper, New York.
Litwak, E. (1960a). 'Occupational mobility and extended family cohesion'. *Amer. sociol. R.*, vol 25, 9–21.
(1960b). 'Geographic mobility and extended family cohesion'. *Amer. sociol. R.*, vol 25, 385–94.
(1965). 'Extended kin relations in an industrial democratic society'. in Shanas, E. and Streib, G. F., *Social structure and the family: generational relations*. Prentice-Hall, New Jersey.
Litwak, E. and Szelenyi, I. (1969). 'Primary group structures and their functions: kin, neighbours and friends'. *Amer. sociol. R.*, vol 34, 465–81.
Livesey, J. (*c* 1885). *Autobiography*. National Temperance League, London.
Loudon, J. B. (1961). 'Kinship and crisis in South Wales'. *Brit. J. Sociol.*, vol 12, 333–50.
MacFarlane, A. (1970). *The family life of Ralph Josselin*. Cambridge University Press, Cambridge.
MacIntyre, A. (1967). Review of Blau (1964). *Sociology*, vol 1, 199–201.
McKenzie, J. C. (1962). 'The composition and nutritional value of diets in Manchester and Dukinfield'. *Trans. Lancashire and Cheshire antiquarian Soc.*, vol 72.

Manchester Statistical Society (1836). *Report of a committee of the Manchester Statistical Society, on the state of education in the Borough of Salford in 1835.* Ridgway, London.
(1864). *Inquiry into the educational and other conditions of a district of Deansgate.* Manchester.
Mantoux, P. (1928). *The industrial revolution in the eighteenth century.* Jonathan Cape, London.
Marshall, D. (1926). *The English poor in the eighteenth century.* Routledge, London.
Marshall, J. D. (1961). 'The Lancashire rural labourer in the early nineteenth century'. *Trans. Lancashire and Cheshire antiquarian Soc.*, vol 71, 90–128.
(1968). 'Colonisation as a factor in the planting of industrial towns in north-west England'. in Dyos, H. J. (ed), *The study of urban history.* Edward Arnold, London.
Mayer, P. (1961). *Townsmen or tribesmen.* Oxford University Press, Cape Town.
Mayhew, H. (1851a). *London labour and the London poor*, vol 1. London.
(1851b). ibid, vol 2.
Mitchell, B. R. and Deane, P. (1962). *Abstract of British historical statistics.* Cambridge University Press, Cambridge.
Mitchell, J. C. (1969). 'The concept and use of social networks'. in Mitchell, J. C. (ed), *Social networks in urban situations.* Manchester University Press, Manchester.
Mogey, J. (1962). Introduction to issue on Changes in the family. *Int. soc. sci. J.* vol. 24, 411–24.
Moore, W. E. (1965). *The impact of industry.* Prentice-Hall, New Jersey.
Moore, W. T. (1889). *The life of Timothy Coop.* Christian Commonwealth Publishing Co., London.
Musson, A. E. and Robinson, E. (1960). 'The origins of engineering in Lancashire'. *J. econ. Hist.*, vol 20, 200–33.
Neale, W. B. (1840). *Juvenile delinquency in Manchester.* Gavin Hamilton, Manchester.
Neild, W. (1841). 'Comparative statement of the income and expenditure of certain families of the working classes in Manchester and Dukinfield in the years 1836 and 1841'. *J. statist. Soc.*, vol 4, 320–34.
Nimkoff, M. F. and Middleton, R. (1960). 'Types of family and types of economy'. *Amer. J. Sociol.*, vol 66, 215–25.
Nunns, T. (1842). *A letter ... on the condition of the working classes in Birmingham ...* Langbridge, Birmingham.
O'Brien, G. (1921). *The economic history of Ireland from the Union to the famine.* Longmans, Green, London.
Ogburn, W. F. (1956). 'Why the family is changing'. in Anderson, N. (ed), *Recherches sur la famille*, vol 1. Mohr, Tübingen.
Parkinson, R. (1841). *On the present condition of the labouring poor in Manchester ...* Simkin and Marshall, London.
(1844). *The old church clock.* Rivington, London.
Parnell, E. A. (1886). *The life and labours of John Mercer.* Longmans, Green, London.
Parsons, T. (1949) (1937). *The structure of social action.* Free Press, Illinois.
(1952). *The social system.* Tavistock, London.
(1959). 'The social structure of the family'. in Anshen, R. (ed), *The family. Its function and destiny.* Harper, New York.
(1963) (1943). 'The kinship system of the contemporary United States'. in *Essays in sociological theory.* Free Press, Illinois.
(1965). 'The normal American family'. in Farber, S. M., Mustachi, P. and Wilson, R. H. L., *The family's search for survival.* McGraw-Hill, New York.
Parsons, T. and Bales, R. F. (1956). *Family, socialization and interaction process.* Routledge and Kegan Paul, London.
Petersen, W. (1965). *The politics of population.* Anchor Books, New York.
Pickering, W. S. F. (1967). 'The 1851 religious census – a useless experiment?' *Brit. J. Sociol.*, vol 18, 382–407.
Pinchbeck, I. (1930). *Women workers and the industrial revolution.* Routledge, London.

Pizzorno, A. (1966). 'Amoral familism and historical marginality'. *Int. R. Community Dev.* nos 15–16, 55–66.

Pollard, A. (1965). *Mrs. Gaskell, novelist and biographer.* Manchester University Press, Manchester.

Procter, W. (1966). 'Poor law administration in Preston Union, 1838–48'. *Trans. hist. Soc. Lancashire and Cheshire*, vol 117, 145–66.

Quarantelli, E. L. (1960). 'A note on the protective function of the family in disasters'. *Mar. Fam. Living*, vol 22, 263–4.

Ransome, A. and Royston, W. (1866). 'Report upon the health of Manchester and Salford during the last fifteen years'. *Trans. natn. Ass. Promotion soc. Sci.*, 1866, 454–72.

Rathbone, H. R. (ed) (1927). *Memoir of Kitty Wilkinson of Liverpool 1786–1860.* Young, Liverpool.

Reader, D. H. (1964). 'Models in social change, with special reference to Southern Africa'. *African studies*, vol 23, 11–33.

Redford, A. (1926). *Labour migration in England, 1800–50.* Manchester University Press, Manchester.

Robins, L. N. and Tomanec, M. (1966) (1962). 'Closeness to blood relatives outside the immediate family'. in Farber, B. (ed), *Kinship and family organisation.* Wiley, New York.

Rodman, H. (ed) (1965). *Marriage, family, and society: a reader.* Random House, New York.

Rosenfeld, H. (1958). 'Processes of structural change within the Arab village extended family'. *Amer. Anthropol.*, vol 60, 1127–39.

Rosser, C. and Harris, C. C. (1965). *The family and social change.* Routledge and Kegan Paul, London.

Rothwell, W. (1850). *Report of the agriculture of the County of Lancaster* ... Groombridge and Sons, London.

Rowe, G. P. (1966). 'The developmental conceptual framework to the study of the family'. in Nye, F. I. and Berardo, F. M. (eds), *Emerging conceptual frameworks in family analysis.* Macmillan, New York.

Rowntree, B. S. (1901). *Poverty. A study of town life.* Macmillan, London.

Rowntree, J. and Sherwell, A. (1900). *The temperance problem and social reform.* Hodder and Stoughton, London.

Rundblad, B. G. (1956). 'Family and urbanisation'. in Anderson, N. (ed), *Recherches sur la famille*, vol 1. Mohr, Tübingen.

Rushton, A. (1909). *My life, as farmer's boy, factory lad, teacher and preacher.* Clarke, Manchester.

Sahlins, M. D. (1965). 'On the sociology of primitive exchange'. in Banton, M. (ed), *The relevance of models for social anthropology.* Tavistock, London.

Sanderson, J. M. (1966). *The basic education of labour in Lancashire 1780–1839.* Ph.D. dissertation, University of Cambridge.

Secord, P. F. and Backman, C. W. (1964). *Social psychology.* McGraw-Hill, New York.

Shaw, J. G. (1889). *History and tradition of Darwen and its people.* Toulmin, Blackburn.

Shaw, S. (1843). *Replies of Sir Charles Shaw ... regarding the education and moral and physical condition of the labouring classes.* Oliver, London.

Shuttleworth, J. (1843). 'On the vital statistics of the spinners and piecers employed in the fine cotton mills of Manchester'. *Report of the twelfth meeting of the British Association for the Advancement of Science; transactions of the statistical section*, 93–4.

Simmons, G. (1849). *The working classes; their moral, social and intellectual condition* ... Partridge and Oakley, London.

Simmons, L. W. (1945). *The role of the aged in primitive society.* Yale University Press, New Haven.

Slater, E. and Woodside, M. (1951). *Patterns of marriage.* Cassell, London.

Smelser, N. J. (1959). *Social change in the industrial revolution.* Routledge and Kegan Paul, London.

Smith, R. (1970). 'Early Victorian household structure'. *Internat. R. soc. Hist.*, vol 15, 69–84.

Smith, T. C. (1888). *A history of Longridge and district.* Whitehead, Preston.

Smout, T. C. (1971). *Sexual behaviour and class distinction in the nineteenth century.* typescript.

Southall, A. W. (1961). Introductory summary to Southall, A. W. (ed), *Social change in modern Africa.* Oxford University Press, Oxford.

Stehouwer, J. (1965). 'Relations between generations and the three generation household in Denmark'. in Shanas, E. and Streib, G. F., *Social structure and the family: generational relations.* Prentice-Hall, New Jersey.

Stryker, S. (1966) (1959). 'Symbolic interaction as an approach to family research'. in Farber, B. (ed), *Kinship and family organisation.* Wiley, New York.

Sussman, M. B. (1953a). 'The help patterns in the middle class family'. *Amer. sociol. R.*, vol 18, 22–8.

(1953b). 'Parental participation in mate selection and its effect on family continuity'. *Soc. Forces*, vol 32, 76–81.

(1965). 'Relationship of adult children with their parents in the United States'. in Shanas, E., and Streib, G. F., *Social structure and the family: generational relations.* Prentice-Hall. New Jersey.

Sweetser, D. A. (1968). 'Intergenerational ties in Finnish urban families'. *Amer. sociol. R.*, vol 33, 236–46.

Talmon-Garber, Y. (1966) (1962). 'Social change and family structure'. in Farber, B. (ed), *Kinship and family organisation.* Wiley, New York.

Taylor, W. C. (1842). *Notes of a tour in the manufacturing districts of Lancashire* . . . Duncan and Malcolm, London.

Thernstrom, S. (1964). *Poverty and progress. Social mobility in a nineteenth century city.* Harvard University Press, Cambridge, Mass.

Thibaut, J. W. and Kelley, H. H. (1959). *The social psychology of groups.* Wiley, New York.

Thomas, W. I. and Znaniecki, F. (1958) (1919–20). *The Polish peasant in Europe and America.* Dover Publications, New York.

Thompson, D. M. (1967). 'The 1851 religious census: problems and possibilities'. *Victorian Studies*, vol 11, 87–97.

Thompson, P. (1969). 'Memory and history'. *Social Science Research Council Newsletter* no. 6, 17.

Tillott, P. M. (forthcoming). 'Sources of inaccuracy in the 1851 and 1861 censuses'. in Wrigley, E. A. (ed), *The study of nineteenth century society.* Cambridge University Press.

Tonna, C. (1841). *Helen Fleetwood.* Seeley and Burnside, London.

Touraine, A. (1965). *Sociologie de l'action.* Editions du Seuil, Paris.

Townsend, P. (1957). *The family life of old people.* Routledge and Kegan Paul, London.

(1965). 'The effects of family structure on the likelihood of admission to an institution in old age'. in Shanas, E. and Streib, G. F. (eds), *Social structure and the family: generational relations.* Prentice-Hall, New Jersey.

UNESCO (1956). *Social implications of industrialisation and urbanisation in Africa south of the Sahara.* Unesco, London.

(1957). *Urbanisation in Asia and the Far East.* Unesco, Calcutta.

(1961). *Urbanisation in Latin America.* Unesco, Paris.

(1965). *Handbook for social research in urban areas.* Unesco, London.

Unwin, G., Hulme, A., and Taylor, G. (1924). *Samuel Oldknow and the Arkwrights.* Ma chester University Press, Manchester.

Wadsworth, A. P. and Mann, L. de L. (1931). *The cotton trade and industrial Lancashire 1600–1780.* Manchester University Press, Manchester.

Ward, J. (1953) (1860–64). 'The diary of John Ward of Clitheroe, Weaver, 1860–1864' (transcribed by R. S. France). in *Trans. hist. Soc. Lancashire and Cheshire*, vol 105.
Watts, J. (1866). *The facts of the Cotton Famine*. Simpkin, Marshall, London.
Waugh, E. (1881a) (1857). *Lancashire Sketches*. in *Works*, vol 1. Heywood, Manchester.
(1881b) (1862). *Factory folk during the Cotton Famine*. in *Works*, vol 2.
(1882) (various). *Tufts of heather*. in *Works*, vol 4.
(1883) (various). *The chimney corner*. in *Works*, vol 8.
Wheeler, J. (1836). *Manchester: its political, social and commercial history* ... Whittaker, Manchester.
Whyte, W. H. (1957). *The organisation man*. Jonathan Cape, London.
Williams, W. M. (1956). *The sociology of an English village: Gosforth*. Routledge and Kegan Paul, London.
(1963). *A West Country village: family, kinship and land*. Routledge and Kegan Paul, London.
Willmott, P. (1963). *The evolution of a community*. Routledge and Kegan Paul, London.
Willmott, P. and Young, M. (1960). *Family and class in a London suburb*. Routledge and Kegan Paul, London.
Wirth, L. (1938). 'Urbanism as a way of life'. *Amer. J. Sociol.*, vol 44, 1–24.
Wood, E. E. (1936). *Is this theosophy?* Rider, London.
Wrong, D. M. (1961). 'The over-socialised conception of man in modern sociology'. *Amer. sociol. R.*, vol 26, 184–93.
Young, M. (1954). 'The role of the extended family in a disaster'. *Hum. Relats.*, vol 7, 383–91.
Young, M. and Willmott, P. (1957). *Family and kinship in East London*. Routledge and Kegan Paul, London.
Zelditch, M. (1964). 'Family, marriage and kinship', in Faris, R. E. L., (ed), *Handbook oj modern sociology*. Rand McNally, Chicago.

2 PARLIAMENTARY PAPERS

1803–4 XIII. Abstract of the answers and returns ... relative to the expense and maintenance of the poor in England.
1816 III. Minutes of evidence taken before the Select Committee on the state of the children employed in the manufactories of the United Kingdom.
1830 VII. First, second, and third reports of evidence from the Select Committee on the state of the poor in Ireland.
1831–2 XV. Report from the Committee on the 'Bill to regulate the labour of children in the mills and factories of the United Kingdom', with minutes of evidence ...
1833 V. Report from the Select Committee on agriculture, with minutes of evidence.
1833 VI. Report from the Select Committee on manufactures ..., with minutes of evidence.
1833 XX. First report of the ... Commissioners ... [on] ... the employment of children in factories ..., with minutes of evidence ...
1833 XXI. ibid, second report.
1833 XXXVI. Abstract of answers and returns ... [on] ... the population of Great Britain ... Enumeration Abstract vol I.
1834 X. Report from the Select Committee on hand-loom weavers' petitions, with minutes of evidence.
1834 XIX. Supplementary report of ... Commissioners ... [on] ... the employment of children in factories ... Part I.
1834 XX. ibid, Part II.
1834 XXVII. Report from his Majesty's Commissioners for inquiring into the administration and practical operation of the Poor Laws.
1834 XXVIII. ibid, Appendix A. Reports of Assistant Commissioners, Part I.
1834 XXX. ibid, Appendix B(i). Answer to rural queries, Part I.
1834 XXXV. ibid, Appendix B(ii). Answers to urban queries, Part I.

1834 XXXVI. ibid, Part II.
1835 VII. Minutes of evidence taken before the Select Committee on education.
1835 XIII. Report from the Select Committee on hand-loom weavers' petitions, with minutes of evidence ...
1835 XXXII. Poor inquiry, Ireland; Appendix A.
1835 XXXV. First annual report of the Poor Law Commissioners ...
1836 VIII. Third report from the Select Committee ... [on] ... the state of agriculture, with minutes of evidence ...
1836 XXIX. Second annual report of the Poor Law Commissioners ...
1836 XXXIII. Poor inquiry, Ireland; Appendix F.
1836 XXXIV. Poor inquiry, Ireland; Appendix G. Report on the state of the Irish poor in Great Britain.
1837 XVII. First report from the Select Committee on the Poor Law Amendment Act, with minutes of evidence.
1837–8 VII. Report from the Select Committee on the education of the poorer classes in England and Wales, ... with minutes of evidence ...
1837–8 XVIIIa. Eighth report from the Select Committee on the Poor Law Amendment Act, with minutes of evidence.
1837–8 XVIIIb. ibid, ninth report.
1837–8 XIX. Report by the Select Committee of the House of Lords ... [on] ... several cases ... [arising from] ... the operation of the Poor Law Amendment Act ..., with minutes of evidence ...
1840 X. Sixth report from the Select Committee on the Act for the Regulation of Mills and Factories ..., with minutes of evidence ...
1840 XXIVa. Reports from Assistant Hand-loom Weavers' Commissioners; Part V ...
1840 XXIVb. Copy of report by Mr. Hickson on the condition of the hand-loom weavers.
1841 X. Report from the Commissioners for inquiring into the condition of the unemployed hand-loom weavers in the United Kingdom.
1841 XI. Seventh annual report of the Poor Law Commissioners ...
1842 XVII. Children's Employment Commission. Appendix to first report of the Commissioners; Mines; Part II, Reports and evidence from Sub-commissioners.
1842 XIX. Eighth annual report of the Poor Law Commissioners ...
1842 XXXVa. ... Report made by Mr. Tufnell ..., in October 1841, as to the state of the poor in the Borough of Rochdale.
1842 XXXVb. ... Evidence taken, and report made, by the Assistant Poor Law Commissioners sent to inquire into the state of the population of Stockport.
1842 XXXVc. Distress (Bolton). Copies of communications ... [and] reports ...
1843 XIIa. Reports of Special Assistant Poor Law Commissioners on the employment of women and children in agriculture.
1843 XIIb. A report on the ... practice of interment in towns [by] Edwin Chadwick ...
1843 XIV. Children's employment Commission. Appendix to the second report ... Trades and manufactories; Part I, Reports and evidence from Sub-commissioners.
1843 XV. ibid, Part II.
1843 XXI. Ninth annual report of the Poor Law Commissioners ...
1843 XXIV. Report of the Commissioner appointed to take the census of Ireland for the year 1841.
1844 XVIII. First report of the Commissioners for inquiring into the state of large towns and populous districts. With minutes of evidence ...
1844 XIX. Tenth annual report of the Poor Law Commissioners ...
1845 XV. Report of the Commissioner appointed to inquire into the condition of the framework knitters ...
1845 XVIII. Second report of the Commissioners for inquiring into the state of large towns and populous districts. Appendix (minutes of evidence etc.), Part II.

1845 XIXa. Report from Her Majesty's Commissioners of Inquiry into the state of the law and practice in respect to the occupation of land in Ireland.
1845 XIXb. Evidence to ibid, Part I.
1845 XX. Evidence to ibid, Part II.
1845 XXI. Evidence to ibid, Part III.
1845 XXIIa. Appendix to minutes of evidence to ibid.
1845 XXIIb. Index to minutes of evidence to ibid.
1845 XXV. Reports of the Inspectors of Factories for the quarter ending 30th Sept 1844.
1845 XXVII. Eleventh annual report of the Poor Law Commissioners ...
1846 XIX. Twelfth annual report of the Poor Law Commissioners ...
1846 XXXVIa. Return specifying the number of families and persons removed ... to their places of settlement, from each manufacturing town in Lancashire ... during the years 1841, 1842, and 1843 ...
1846 XXXVIb. Further return ... (as PP1846 XXXVIa).
1846 XXXVIc. A copy of reports received by the Poor Law Commissioners in 1841 on the state of the Macclesfield and Bolton Unions.
1847 XIa. Fourth report from the Select Committee on settlement and poor removal ..., with minutes of evidence ...
1847 XIb. ibid, sixth report ...
1847 XVa. Reports of the Inspectors of Factories for the half year ending 31st Oct 1846.
1847 XVb. ibid, for the half year ending 30th April 1847.
1847 XXVIII. Thirteenth annual report of the Poor Law Commissioners ...
1847 LVII. Returns of agricultural produce in Ireland in the year 1847. Part II, Stock.
1847–8 XXVI. Reports of the Inspectors of Factories for the half year ending 31st Oct 1847.
1847–8 XXXIII. Fourteenth report of the Poor Law Commissioners ...
1847–8 LIII. Return showing the population, the annual value of the property rated to the poor's rate, expenditure for the relief of the poor ...
1849 XXI. Appendix to the ninth annual report of the Registrar-General of Births, Deaths and Marriages in England and Wales.
1849 XXII. Reports of the Inspectors of Factories for the half year ending 31st Oct 1848.
1849 XLVII. Return of the number of children in the workhouses of the several Unions and parishes in England and Wales ...
1850 XIX. Report from the Select Committee on investments for the savings of the middle and working classes; ... with ... minutes of evidence ...
1850 XLII. Returns of the number of cotton, woollen, worsted, flax, and silk factories ...
1852 VII. Report from the Select Committee on criminal and destitute juveniles; ... with ... minutes of evidence ...
1852 XI. Report from the Select Committee on Manchester and Salford education; ... with ... minutes of evidence ...
1852–3 XXIV. ibid (a further report).
1852–3 LXXXV. Census of Great Britain, 1851. Population tables I, vol I.
1852–3 LXXXVI. ibid, vol II.
1852–3 LXXXVIIIa. ibid, Population tables II, vol I.
1852–3 LXXXVIIIb. ibid, vol II.
1852–3 LXXXIX. ibid, Religious worship ...
1852–3 XC. ibid, Education.
1854 XIV. Report from the Select Committee on public houses, with minutes of evidence.
1854 LXIII. ... Reports and tables ... on the subject of sickness and mortality among the members of friendly societies.
1854–5 XIII. Report from the Select Committee on poor removal ... [with] ... minutes of evidence ...
1859 Ses 2 VII. Minutes of evidence taken before the Select Committee on irremoveable poor..

1860 XVII. Report from the Select Committee on irremoveable poor ... with ... minutes of evidence ...

1861 XVIII. Twenty-second annual report of the Registrar-General of Births, Deaths, and Marriages in England.

1862 XXII. Fourth report of the Medical Officer of the Privy Council ...

1862 XLIX. Copy of Mr. Farnall's reports to the Poor Law Commissioners on the distress in the cotton manufacturing districts.

1862 L. Census of England and Wales, 1861. Population tables, vol I.

1863 XVIII. Children's Employment Commission (1862). Second report of the Commissioners with appendix.

1863 XXV. Fifth report of the Medical Officer to the Privy Council ...

1863 LIII. Census of England and Wales for the year 1861. Population Tables, vol II.

1864 XXIIa. Children's Employment Commission (1862). Second report of the Commissioners, with appendix.

1864 XXIIb. ibid, third report ...

1864 XXIIc. Reports of the Inspectors of Factories ... for the half year ending 31st Oct 1863.

1864 LII. Report ... on distress in the cotton manufacturing districts.

1865 XIII. Supplement to the twenty-fifth annual report of the Registrar-General of Births, Deaths, and Marriages in England.

1865 XX. Children's Employment Commission (1862). Fourth report of the Commissioners, with appendix.

1865 XXVI. Seventh report of the Medical Officer of the Privy Council ...

1866 XXIV. Children's Employment Commission (1862). Fifth report of the Commissioners, with appendix.

1868–9 XIII. Commission on the Employment of Children, Young Persons, and Women in Agriculture (1867). Second report of the Commissioners, with appendices.

1871 VII. Report from the Select Committee on protection of infant life; ... with ... minutes of evidence ...

1872 XXVI. Second report of the Commissioners ... into friendly and benefit building societies. Part II, evidence.

1873 XXIII Pt I. Fourth report of the Commissioners ... into friendly and benefit building societies ... with appendix.

1873 XXIII Pt II. Friendly and benefit building societies Commission. Reports of the Assistant Commissioners: Cheshire, Derbyshire, Lancashire ...

1873 LV. Report ... on proposed changes in hours and ages of employment in textile factories ...

1887 LXXXIX. Return relating to wages ... paid to different classes of workers in various industries ... during many years prior to 1850, in 1855, and in subsequent years.

1890 LVII. Report of the Committee ... to inquire into ... the taking of the census, with minutes of evidence ...

1898 XXXVI. Third report of the Royal Commission on liquor licensing laws, with minutes of evidence.

1904 XXXII. Minutes of evidence taken before the inter-departmental committee on physical deterioration; vol I.

3 LORDS SESSIONAL PAPERS

1818 CXVI. Minutes of evidence taken before the Lords Committees ... [on] ... the Bill ... [on] ... cotton ... factories.

1819 CX. Minutes of evidence taken before the Lords Committees ... [on] ... the state and conditions of the children employed in the cotton manufactories of the United Kingdom...

1842 XV. Return of ... reports ... upon the state of the Burnley Union during the months of May and June 1842 ...

4 PARLIAMENTARY DEBATES

Hansard. Third series, vol 73.

5 CONTEMPORARY NEWSPAPER AND PERIODICAL LITERATURE

The Lion (1828–9).

Reports addressed to the Committee of the Liverpool Domestic Missionary Society, by their ministers to the poor ... (1859, 1860).

The Liverpool Health of Towns Advocate (1845–6).

The Morning Chronicle (1849–50) (and *Supplements*, being a series of letters from special correspondents on *Life and labour of the poor*).

Chaplain's reports on the Preston House of Correction presented to the Magistrates of Lancashire (1845, 1848, 1851, 1855).

The Preston Pilot (1851).

Reports of the Society for Bettering the Condition and Increasing the Comforts of the Poor (vol 1, 1798; vol 3, 1802).

6 ACTS

4 & 5 William IV c. 76. An Act for the Amendment and better administration of the Laws relating to the Poor in England and Wales (1834).

7 & 8 Vict c. 15. An Act to amend the Laws relating to Labour in Factories (1844).

13 & 14 Vict c. 54. An Act to amend the Acts relating to Labour in Factories (1850).

7 COLLECTIONS

Letters (1837). Letters from John Barnes, William Courtnage, and others who emigrated under the management of the Petworth Committee; written 1837 and bound in British Museum, Tracts 1821–44, C.T. 240.9.4.

Webb MSS., being the Webb Trade Union Collection. Library of the London School of Economic and Political Science.

Section A, vol VII: General history etc.

vol XXXIV: Cotton spinners, history 1700–1896.

8 MANUSCRIPT SOURCES

Public Record Office:

H.O. 107. Census papers – population returns 1841 and 1851. Enumerators' schedules.

RG/9. ibid for 1861.

Notes

1. THE ORIGINS OF THE STUDY

1 cf e.g. Wirth (1938); Ogburn (1956); Parsons (1959); Parsons and Bales (1956); Litwak (1960a) (1960b); Goode (1963) (1963–4).
2 Admirably summarised in the then just published Goode (1963).
3 e.g. Unesco (1956) (1957) (1961) passim; Rundblad (1956); Brown et al (1963); Sussman (1965) esp 65; Back (1965) esp 332–3.
4 e.g. Nimkoff and Middleton (1960); Greenfield (1961).
5 e.g. Young and Willmott (1957); Kerr (1958); Willmott and Young (1960); Willmott (1963). Note also Rosser and Harris (1965); Bell (1968); Firth et al (1970); and the mass of American studies summarised in e.g. Sussman (1965) and Adams (1968a).
6 e.g. Rosser and Harris (1965) esp 14–17.
7 cf Adams (1967); Firth (1956); also Parsons (1963).
8 cf Rosser and Harris (1965) esp 228. Southall, discussing the impact of modernisation on kinship in developing countries makes a similar point in a different way when he says that the share of kinship as a determinant of action has fallen (Southall (1961) 31).
9 For perceptions cf e.g. Young and Willmott (1957) esp chap 9, and Willmott and Young (1960) esp chap 5. For ingenious demonstrations of the reality of these deprivations see Townsend (1965) and Bell (1968) chap 4.
10 Laslett and Harrison (1963); Laslett (1965).
11 Laslett (1969).
12 Anderson (forthcoming a).
13 For example, some 40% of childless married couples where the wife was under 45 years of age were in Swansea in 1960 living with the parents of one or other spouse. But the overall proportion of households with co-residing kin was only slightly above the national average.
14 and cf here for example the discussion in MacFarlane (1970) chaps 7–10.
15 Laslett (1965) 94–5; cf also the case cited in MacFarlane (1970) 129.
16 esp PP1834 XXVII 54**.
17 LePlay (1855).
18 e.g. Gaskell (1833).
19 Mayhew, for example, was mainly concerned with costermongers and street traders, an unusual group if only because only some 10% of the men cohabiting with a woman were legally married to her (Mayhew (1851a) 20).
20 One other partial exception to this is the *Morning Chronicle* reports on *Life and labour of the poor*.
21 Collier (1965).
22 Smelser (1959) esp chaps 9–13.
23 Hewitt (1953) (1958).
24 Pinchbeck (1930).
25 Redford (1926).
26 Williams (1963).
27 Preliminary reports in Armstrong (1968); Dyos and Baker (1968); Smith (1970).
28 Crozier (1965).
29 Firth (1964); Firth et al (1970).
30 Foster (1967).

2. HEURISTIC PERSPECTIVES

1 In the recent literature, this perhaps is shown most clearly in Goldthorpe et al (1969). It is, however, unfortunately true that this kind of data, on attitudes and on strengths of feelings of deprivations, seldom survives in any great detail or quantity from a historical context.
2 One major problem of phenomenal level interpretations in any comparative study, be it synchronic or diachronic, is that we do not have, at present at least, any conceptual categories at a higher level of

generality by reference to which, while remaining at a cultural or phenomenal level, we can classify and order the idiosyncratic subcultural images and explanations offered by individual populations into a set of more general causal inferences. This we can only do by reference to properties of various structural elements in the environment and of changes in them.

3 In particular, there is the problem that the economists have always had with their analogous concepts of 'welfare', of knowing what to do in a situation where a person is manifestly better off on most parameters as a result of maintaining a particular relationship, but worse off on one or two. This inevitably means that no quantitative or minutely precise comparisons are possible with this approach. But nor is this possible with any other line of attack. One is nevertheless often able to make rough comparative estimates of the significance of goals, rewards, and deprivations of a more or less, great or small kind. This is all that I (or any other exchange theorist) am claiming to do.

4 In the discussion so far I have sometimes implied that the kinship system is in some sense homogeneous, but this, of course, is far from being the case. Rather, there are marked variations within the same society in both the pattern and content of relationships with kin, not only as between different classes of kinsmen, but also over the life-cycle. It is with exploring differences in these patterns that comparative family research is concerned. It seems to me that it is only by confining one's analysis to each in turn of the different dyadic relationships at different points of the life-cycle that direct and meaningful comparisons become possible. This to some extent circumvents the problem that one meets when one tries to aggregate these relationships into different family 'types' (extended, stem, joint etc.), for, unfortunately, family types do not vary along a single dimension. Even the simple 'extended'/'stem'/'nuclear' trichotomy which is often used can conceal within the classes as much variation in some kinship dyads as it reveals in others. I have in this study then taken as my basic unit of analysis individual kinship dyads at different points in the life-cycle.

There is one further implication of this position. Such an approach implies that there is no logical reason for treating the relationships of parents with married children in any different way from those of parents with unmarried children. It is, indeed, notable that many of the most insightful studies (e.g. Arensberg and Kimball (1961) and Dennis *et al* (1956)) have been those which considered the relationships of married children with their parents in the light not only of their present situation but also by reference to earlier interactions between them when the children were young and adolescent. The impact of marriage is a variable phenomenon which requires empirical research, rather than something the consequences of which can implicitly be assumed by one's theory to have a major impact and which suddenly terminates one of an individual's roles and replaces it by another. In some societies the married son continues to be completely subordinate to the father until the latter dies, while in others, independence and the restructuring of relationships begin in adolescence at the latest. Note also, as a number of writers have correctly pointed out (e.g. Rodman (1965) 266n; Mogey (1962) 504–11), that industrialisation has usually had a great impact on adolescents' relationships with their parents, and that, in the controversy over the survival or non-survival of the 'extended family', this has been almost entirely overlooked.

5 Since the concept of false consciousness when used to imply that actors pursue objectively erroneous goals (as opposed to meaning the employment of inefficient means to maximise achievement of stated goals) seems to me to be both philosophically dubious and heuristically useless, I have taken it as axiomatic that actors' own definitions of what constitutes rewards or deprivations are the only set of definitional orientations worthy of serious sociological study.

6 Touraine (1965) esp 5 is very good on this point.

7 For useful contributions to the debate over 'convergence' see esp Goldthorpe (1964) (1966); Dunning and Hopper (1966); Moore (1965).

8 In support of this notion see esp the literature on the independent role of the family in industrialisation, e.g. Habakkuk (1955); Levy (1955); also the theoretical comments of Greenfield (1961). Contrast the following statement by Parsons which seems to have served as a model for many: 'It is an essential feature of our family system that sons on maturity must be emancipated from their families of orientation and must make their own way in the world, rather than fit into a going concern organised around kinship. Determination of occupational status by family connection threatens the universalistic standards so important to the system as a whole' (Parsons (1959) 254–5).

9 In one sense this analysis of the mutual interaction of different subsystems is what structure-functionalist writers on this topic claim to be about. In fact, however, the consensus underpinning of their analysis is not really capable of handling the exploration of these dynamic relationships, for the consensus element of structure-functionalism and its holistic or closed-system approach to social organisations make it ill-fitted to handle the study of the mechanisms by which in different

situations different compromises emerge between family and other organisations. A quite different approach is therefore necessary, to replace what has been the dominant heuristic perspective until recently.

10 It may perhaps be noted that one of the most important points for the future which emerged from the 11th International Family Research Seminar which I attended just as this book was going to press was the need for emphasis on mechanisms of interaction between systems (in this case work and family), the disadvantages of closed system thinking, and the advantages of taking the individual as the focus of one's analysis for such an emphasis. Contrast structure-functionalist thinking which must, by its very logic, take as axiomatic that all members of a system are equally committed to its continuance (cf Gouldner (1959)).

11 There is a useful discussion of the advantages and limitations of a number of actor-based approaches in Reader (1964). In his terms my analysis is a network analysis heuristically focusing in particular on the determinants of choices between different alternative relationship patterns.

12 The kind of perspective I have developed here is not of course wholly new even in the family field. What I have rather tried to do is to link together, systematise, and provide a coherent underlying rationale for, a large number of exchange perspective-based ideas which other writers have put forward, more often than not as *post hoc* rationalisations when faced with the problem of explaining particular differences in and changes in kinship relationships. I have then extended the resulting analysis in certain directions in order to meet the particular problems raised by this study.

Among the writers on kinship relationships who have used exchange formulations fairly explicitly are Adams (1968b); Geiger (1960); Rosser and Harris (1965) 280–2. Analyses implicitly not very different from those used here may be found in Litwak (1965), ideas in Secord and Backman (1964); Banfield (1958) esp 121; Rosenfeld (1958); Greenfield (1961); Linton (1959) 45–6; Sussman (1953a) 23–4; Levy (1949) 154–5; Thomas and Znaniecki (1958) 91; LePlay (1855) 188, 289–90; Klein (1965) 1, passim. Not unrelated theoretical approaches are advocated in e.g. Lancaster (1961); Stryker (1966); Back (1965).

However, only Goode (1963–4) has made any considerable attempt to develop and apply exchange perspective notions in this area, and even his applications are somewhat unsystematic (e.g. Goode (1963) 170ff). My analysis obviously owes much to his but is more oriented to interpretation of changes in kinship values instead of concentrating mainly on adaptations taking place within a given value structure. As developed here it also enables me to offer some interesting insights into the quality of the relationships which are maintained, through the introduction of the certainty and time span elements.

Exchange perspectives can never, of course, provide the sort of precise quantitative predictive power found in some natural science subjects, because choices made are only balanced at and integrated at the cathectic level where quantification is not possible. (For the cognitive, cathectic, evaluative framework cf Parsons (1952) 7.) Thus, like any other perspective in sociology, exchange-based perspectives can never be more than conceptual frameworks pointing the way to hypotheses and providing a logical framework in terms of which disparate ideas can be ordered. They do not claim to be logically any different from any others, even though their basis is somewhat different. But under certain circumstances they may well prove to have a greater utility, as long as it is possible to rank in some rough way goals and evaluations in terms of more or less, strong or weak.

On a different point, I realise that the social action elements that I have used here are more deterministic than many. While I agree with the advocates of a 'weaker' line when they argue that a change (particularly a reduction) in the constraints imposed upon an actor does not necessarily lead to automatic changes in his behaviour, I believe that ideally at least this should then lead us on to an examination of the structural conditions which allow existing reference groups and ideologies to retain a hold over behaviour. This point is further elaborated below.

13 This distinction, although there is an excellent discussion of it in Parsons (1952), seems frequently to have been overlooked by those who adopt a structural social action or exchange perspective. Behaviour may vary not only because of differences in the structural constraints operating on actors but also because of differences in their goals and in the hierarchy in which they rank these goals. These differences in goals and in rankings will in turn affect their evaluations of rewards and sanctions. Although changes in structural constraints may frequently be associated with goal changes there seems to be no logical reason why the two should necessarily co-vary. Thus a continuing source of variation in behaviour patterns between populations will be variations in goals and evaluations, and changes in goals and evaluations may lead to changes in behaviour patterns independently of changes in structural environmental constraints. Economists have, of course, long

distinguished structural constraints from goals and goal hierarchies, with their distinction between supply and demand forces on the one hand and utility on the other.

14 I do not propose to attempt to elaborate here the factors involved in goal change. Not only is this topic rather underdeveloped in sociological theory, but also, with certain exceptions noted in Chapter 8, I shall not in this study be greatly concerned with goal change as a source of change in behaviour. The populations which I am considering were broadly members of one culture. Moreover, since they operated at a low standard of living, it seems not unreasonable to assume (and evidence presented later tends to support this assumption) that the goals to which the greater primacy was given were anyway fairly similar across the populations, being primarily those associated with survival, health, and basic creature comforts. It would, however, be foolhardy to assume that some changes and differences in goals and in the relative priority given to goals did not occur, and specific instances will be hinted at from time to time. Today, moreover, it is quite possible that changes in goals may be as or even more important than changes in structural constraints in leading to changes in family patterns.

15 The analysis is obviously deeply indebted to Blau (1964); Goode (1963–4); Thibaut and Kelly (1959). Important ideas are also derived from Homans (1961); Sahlins (1965); Parsons (1949) 731–48; Parsons (1952) chap 1; Etzioni (1965); Lenski (1966); Humphreys (1966) esp 20–2 and 225–33.

16 Note that members of the actor's family are but some of a number of these possible sources of assistance, and are conceptualised as in no fundamental way different from them.

17 The formulation I have adopted here is broader than most exchange theory as hitherto formulated, which, probably largely because of its basis in experimental social psychology, has tended to consider in detail only one or two of three parameters which in fact appear to me to determine an actor's choice among the theoretically available alternative sources of assistance. Factor C, certainty of reciprocation, is discussed to some extent by Thibaut and Kelly (1959), but receives only very limited attention from e.g. Blau (1964).

18 Or, cast in Homans's terms, which maximised his psychic profit.

19 N.B. that, at the phenomenal level, even in a situation where decisions are largely culturally determined and where norms prescribe the priority to be given to different relationships, where the actor is faced with conflicting demands there is often considerable room for this kind of bargaining. Most decisions an actor makes are not of an either/or nature, but are over the allocation of *marginal units* of outgoings, so that the very vagueness of norms leaves considerable scope for bargaining (and cf Goode (1960)).

20 and cf Greenfield (1961) 31–2; Anderson (1960) chap 11; Thomas and Znaniecki (1958) esp 102; Levy (1949) 5; Litwak (1965) 310. Note also Mitchell's ((1969) 23) discussion of the way in which multi-item relationships with a network make breakaway more difficult.

21 Durkheim (1933): cf Parsons (1949) 311–14; Parsons (1952) 11–12. MacIntyre (1967) has pointed to the same feature in his review of Blau (1964).

22 Note that Parsons ((1965) esp 36) and also Klein (1965) point to the importance of socialisation in the nuclear family in the development of the ability to experience this sense of trust. Klein's discussion is especially important here as she suggests that different environments and different socialisation techniques greatly affect this ability (cf also the discussion in Dager (1964) 753).

23 cf Blau (1964) 94, 98–9.

24 cf Thibaut and Kelly (1959) 132–3.

25 ibid 20; Blau (1964) esp 94.

26 and cf Thibaut and Kelly (1959) 127–8, 140–1; Blau (1964) esp 155.

27 On norms as a crucial basis of exchange cf also Gouldner (1960) esp 176–7.

28 To adopt this position does not mean, of course, that one has to assume that actors continuously calculate and overtly bargain in their relationships with each other nor that they actually attain maximal positions. Such bargaining and such calculation and indeed change itself all involve costs. To calculate carefully the advantages and disadvantages of every single piece of interaction that one entered in any one day even in a situation of perfect knowledge would take several months or even years. Normally actors follow their past practices and these in turn are more or less closely influenced by those of other members of the society. Nevertheless, consciously or unconsciously, variant patterns of relationships are always being tentatively explored. If they were not, negative sanctions would never need to be applied. It thus seems not unrealistic to take as a working assumption that, over time, changes in sanctioning power and in the effects of sanctions due to changes in

alternative sources of the satisfactions which the sanctions withdraw, will lead to changes in preferred relational patterns. So too will changes which open up new alternatives.

Moreover, because each member of a society has anyway to attain a socially sanctioned increase in independence in a situation where his interests and those of his parents seldom coincide exactly so that some conflict is probable, it is by no means unrealistic to make this set of assumptions even in an area like the family which has conventionally been seen as based on consensus and socialisation. Even in traditional societies where strict institutional controls usually cover this increase in independence in adolescence or later, conflicts, notably over love marriages, do arise (Goode (1959)).

Similarly, though ideologies (notably religion) undoubtedly structure and constrain perceptions of a situation at a point in time, it is by no means clear that their long run effect is any other than to slow down changes which result from changes in structural forces. Moreover, while political and economic ideologies are providing an interpretation of a highly complex situation about which no one individual can ever feel even remotely competent to form a secure opinion, kinship values are much more susceptible to testing against the immediate constraints of the situation.

29 Not a simple function, of course, but rather following the principle of decreasing marginal utility.

30 Similar arguments may be applied to any other scarce resource, e.g. time, effort, houseroom etc.

31 Also, the more difficult it is to be sure about alter's ability, the greater, presumably, is the risk. Geographical separation is but one factor which may increase this kind of ignorance.

32 For more extended theoretical discussions of these points cf Bott (1957) chap 4 and Mitchell (1969) p. 6; for empirical case material cf e.g. the refs cited in Mitchell (1969) 6.

3. THE DESIGN OF THE RESEARCH

1 I have discussed this point, and its justifications, at greater length in Anderson (forthcoming b).

2 These calculations are based on PP1852–3 LXXXVIII, tables of occupations. In the absence of an agreed definition of what constituted an industrial occupation at this period, all those engaged in trades typically based on a place geographically separate from the home, where some form of manufacture was undertaken, and in which at least 50% of the employers who made returns to the census authorities claimed to employ 10 or more men, are included in this category. The mean number of employees in these concerns would thus have been well over 30. Besides textiles, a number of engineering and metal-making trades were included. The census figures include some handicraft workers, entrepreneurs, and white-collar workers employed in these industries. The same trades are treated as industrial in data taken from the samples, but only factory manual occupations are there included in the industrial working class.

3 See Chapter 4 below.

4 Smelser (1959).

5 See Chapter 4 below.

6 ibid pp. 25–9.

7 cf Bremner (1866) 310; PP1852–3 XXIV 58; PP1837–8 VII 2, 102.

8 Adshead (1842) 1.

9 ibid 33; Bamford (1844) 68; Cobden (1881) 191–2, etc.

10 cf PP1890 LVII 97.

11 Anderson (forthcoming b) (forthcoming c).

12 PRO H.O. 107 and RG/9. For a description and discussion of these data, and of their reliability, see Armstrong (1966); also Tillott (forthcoming) and Anderson (forthcoming b) (forthcoming c).

13 For a discussion of the meaning of this term in the mid-century census context see Anderson (forthcoming c). All references to 'households' are to 'co-residing groups' as defined there. The definition of household here is thus not quite identical to the modern census definition, which is based on commensality.

14 cf e.g. PP1852 VII 182 and Chapter 4 below. A comparison of the age, sex, occupational and birth place characteristics of the population of Preston with other large cotton towns supports this view.

15 cf MCS 1 Jan 50 14.

16 Including quasi-institutions. In addition, the residents of institutions were sampled on the basis of one inmate in ten for use on those occasions when data for the whole population were required.

17 In all, the occupants of some 1,700 houses were examined in this way in each of the three censuses, making 5,000 in all. This analysis would have been considerably improved had vital registration data been incorporated, though the high rates of population turnover would have raised some difficulties. Unfortunately time considerations precluded any such attempt in this piece of research.

Future researchers should, however, seriously consider attempts at reconstitution of this kind; the work of Michael Drake and Carol Pearce on Ashford is an important pioneer effort here.

18 For full details see Chapter 4 below. There is, of course, no certainty that those who moved away and were lost to sight were necessarily similar in their family patterns to those who remained.

19 On Mrs Gaskell cf Gross (1965); Pollard (1965).

4. THE SOCIAL AND ECONOMIC BACKGROUND

1 For these changes, their incidence and effects see e.g. Freeman et al (1966) 3, 67; Mantoux (1928) 227–32, 244–5, 253, 342; Redford (1926) 35–7; Smelser (1959) 55, 117–28, 147–50; Wadsworth and Mann (1931) 316–8; Watts (1866) 53; PP1834 X; 1835 XIII; 1840 XXIV a and b passim; PP1852–3 LXXXVI div VIII 47n–57n; PP1862 L 567n–81n; PP1862 XLIX 10; and census enumerators' books.

2 cf Sanderson (1966) 429.

3 These figures, and those for women given below, are derived from PP1852–3 LXXXVIIIa ccxl-cclxiii.

4 by 7 & 8 Vict c. 15.

5 From PP1850 XLII 2–3.

6 Figures for wages are only approximate and are derived, *inter alia*, from Chadwick (1860); PP1834 XX 21; PP1849 XXII; PP1887 LXXXIX.

7 PP1850 XLII.

8 Chadwick (1860).

9 Freeman et al (1966) 4; Musson and Robinson (1960).

10 by 13 and 14 Vict c. 54.

11 cf MCS 4 Jan 50 19.

12 Arnold (1864); for the details of the depressions see e.g. Annual Reports of Poor Law Commissioners; for descriptions of the distress and of those affected Adshead (1842); Arnold (1864); Bamford (1844); Watts (1866); PP1842 XXXV a and b; LSP1842 XV etc.

13 PHoC (1855) 42; and cf Clegg (1877) 27, for Bolton; this is particularly advantageous from the point of view of this study because it makes it possible to assume near full employment when discussing census data for that year.

14 Mayhew guessed that as few as one-third of all labourers were permanently employed. Even artisans were usually employed for less than twelve months a year. For a discussion of this whole topic see Hobsbawm (1964) 72–82.

15 PP1833 VI 286.

16 LSP1819 CX 244; PP1833 VI 105, 107, 287, 289, 608.

17 cf e.g. Watts (1866) 340.

18 For a fuller analysis of the employment of women in the nineteenth century see Pinchbeck (1930).

19 cf PP1864 XXIIa 11–25.

20 cf Waugh (1881b) 22; PP1863 XXV 305.

21 PP1852–3 LXXXVIIIb 648–53.

22 The town had also, besides its other small textile industries, a small but growing machinery industry. (From the occupations found in the sample; PP1833 VI 623; Kelly's directory (1858) 288.) In all, 36% of the adult male population was recorded as engaged in factory industries as defined by this study. Among the town's non-factory occupations the most important were shoemakers (of whom there were 586 aged 20 and over (3½% of the group)), carpenters and joiners (511), tailors (408), blacksmiths (242), masons and paviors (226), and railway employees (224). There were also 1,266 general labourers. About 7½% of adult women were in domestic service, and there were large numbers of milliners, chars, and washerwomen, and also women shopkeepers. (from PP1852–3 LXXXVIIIb 648–53).

23 I have considerable reservations about the validity of Armstrong's approach to this problem, which involves the use of the present day Registrar General's classification. It is anyway too imprecise for the purposes of this study. Further details of the schema used here can be obtained on request.

24 Employer, self-employed, employed.

25 This group, SEG IX, contains: (*a*) those persons whose stated occupations were insufficiently precise to be allocated to another SEG, notably 'weavers'; (*b*) a small number of occupations which did not readily fit into any of the other groups; these were mainly tertiary occupations of a working class kind, notably in transport (particularly railways) and in trade and commerce.

26 SEGs IX and X are not shown. SEG X includes 55% of age group 10–14 and 31% of age group 65 and over (56% of those aged 75 and over). In addition, unfortunately, many of the 65 and over age

group recorded as employed in other SEGs were, in fact, totally or mainly non-employed, this group frequently recording themselves as engaged in their old occupation. (cf Hewitt (1958) 190–1).

27 The marked rise in the numbers of hand-loom weavers in the older age groups is partly due to these factors, but also to a secular decline in the number of young men recruited to the trade (cf PP1834 XXVIII 910A; PP1834 XIX D1 169).

28 cf in particular Ashley in *Hansard* vol 73 cols 1085–6.

29 There has in fact been almost no research in any depth into social mobility in Victorian Britain. Contrast Thernstrom (1964) for the USA. The main drawback of these data is that almost 50% of all persons found in the first census are not traceable in the second. This loss is particularly severe in the younger age groups.

30 PP1864 XXIIb 187, 168; PP1842 XVII 206–7; MCS 4 Jan 50 19; and the interesting table in PP1833 XX D1 88. For the pattern of incomes in cotton over the life-cycle see PP1834 XX 21. Peak earnings for men were reached by the mid-twenties at the latest. Women's earnings rose little after the early twenties.

31 cf PP1834 XIX D1 passim.

32 PP1833 VI 245; PP1834 XXVIII 909A; Gaskell (1833) 187.

33 PP1833 VI 629, 632; PP1835 XXXV 187–8; PP1835 XIII 151.

34 Webb MSS vol VII, 170.

35 e.g. PP1834 XXVIII 920A; PP1833 XXI D3 4, D1 41; LSP1819 CX passim.

36 Bamford (1844) 70; LSP1819 CX 63; Gaskell (1833) 187.

37 and cf LSP1819 CX 117, 235.

38 Booth (1892); Rowntree (1901). The most important mid-Victorian surveys (e.g. Ashworth (1842); MSS (1864), and those cited by Faucher (1845) I 263) are all taken in depression periods, and so while their conclusions are important as indicating the appalling situation in badtimes, they are less relevant in the present context.

39 Average money wages rose by 67–79% between 1851 and 1897–1900, but Wood estimated a fall in retail prices over the period of 8–10%. Two other indexes based on wholesale prices and on the unit value of imports suggest broadly similar price movements. There had, however, been some increase in coal prices. (Mitchell and Deane (1962) 343–4, 474–5, 472–3, 483).

40 Foster (1967) esp 334–42.

41 Foster (1968) 284.

42 Further details and a worked example are given in Anderson (forthcoming b). Wages figures were rough averages taken from the sources cited in note 21 above.

43 But see Chapter 9 for some qualifications arising from data on income sharing.

44 *The Rowntree scale of primary poverty expenditure*

Family composition	Weekly expenditure							
	Food		Rent[a] (approx.)		Household[b] sundries		Total	
	s.	*d.*	*s.*	*d.*	*s.*	*d.*	*s.*	*d.*
1 man or 1 woman	3	0	1	6	2	6	7	0
1 man and 1 woman	6	0	2	6	3	2	11	8
1 man and 1 woman and 1 child[c]	8	3	2	6	3	9	14	6
1 man and 1 woman and 2 children	10	6	4	0	4	4	18	10
1 man and 1 woman and 3 children	12	9	4	0	4	11	21	8
1 man and 1 woman and 4 children	15	0	5	6	5	6	26	0
increasing thereafter at the rate of 2*s.* 10*d.* per child.								

Source: Rowntree (1901) 110.

[a] Rowntree in his study actually used rents as paid. This is clearly not possible here. Rowntree's estimates are probably slightly higher than the rents actually paid by those in poverty in mid-nineteenth century Lancashire towns, possibly because building costs were 11–21% higher at the end of the century (Mitchell and Deane (1962) 240). They are not, however, wildly erroneous, and true rents undoubtedly varied widely. For rents in the 1840s in Manchester see e.g. Kelly and Kelly (1957) 9 and Neild (1841); for the 1850s MCS 24 Dec 49 5; and for the 1860s PP1863 XXV 312.

[b] heat, light, clothes, bedding etc.

[c] Boys over 14 were counted as additional adults for food purposes.

45 For sources see note 39 above.

46 This variable was preferred for most analysis to the alternative, grouping by the age of one or other spouse, on the grounds that couples married at widely differing ages and had their children at different ages. It was expected that the number of children and number of working children would be key variables influencing family behaviour patterns. Life-cycle stage proved indeed to have a considerably greater predictive power than did age grouping (and cf also Anderson (forthcoming a)). The stages distinguished, for married couples only, were the following:

1. Wife under 45, no children at home.
2. Wife under 45, one child under 1 year old at home.
3. Children at home, but none in employment.
4. Children at home, and some, but under half, in employment.
5. Children at home, and half, or over half, in employment.
6. Wife 45 and over, no children, or one only aged over 20, at home.

For life-cycle stage analysis in general cf. e.g. Hill (1965); Rowe (1966); Lansing and Kish (1957). It may be noted that the more usual system, based on all children ever born, cannot be used here, because there is no record of children who had died or left home. Given the purposes in view, a method based on co-residing children only is anyway probably to be preferred.

47 For contemporary comment cf Engels (1958) 90; PP1841 X 44; Neild (1841); McKenzie (1962).

48 Watts (1866) 99.

49 and cf for hand-loom weavers PP1834 XXVII 917A, 920A; PP1837–8 XVIIIa 6 etc.

50 On this point cf McKenzie (1962) 140.

51 Ward (1953) for 10 May 64.

52 Foster (1968).

53 and cf Kay (1832) 26–7; Engels (1958) 85; Barlee (1863) 14; PP1842 XXXVb 6; PP1863 XXV 325.

54 From Hardwick (1857) 457.

55 cf also Watts (1866) 338–9; Arnold (1864) 138; Smelser (1959) 374; Rowntree (1901) 23; PP1834 XXXVI 64h–77h.

56 cf on working class home ownership e.g. PP1833 VI 237, 288; PP1834 X 382; PP1850 XIX 507; Arnold (1864) 637; MCS 24 Dec 49 5; Marshall (1968) 10; Rowntree (1901) 166; and for the small number of persons in working class occupations who made wills compare PP1861 XVIII 173–81 with PP1865 XIII 439–49.

57 PP1852–3 LXXXV xlvi.

58 From PP1852–3 LXXXVI div VIII 65–6. There were also two such towns in the manufacturing parts of Cheshire (Stockport and Staleybridge) with a combined population of 39,453.

59 The Manchester and Liverpool complexes were, of course, exceptional, and considerably larger.

60 Freeman et al (1966) 115.

61 The figures for the population of Preston (Metropolitan Borough Area) for the censuses 1801–1861 are as follows:

Census of	*Population*	*Intercensal growth* %
1801	12,174	
		43
1811	17,360	
		43
1821	24,859	
		36
1831	33,871	
		50
1841	50,887	
		37
1851	69,542	
		19
1861	82,985	

Sources: PP1852–3 LXXXV cxxvi; PP1862 L 59.

62 There are many detailed descriptions of these communities in other sources (e.g. Gaskell (1897) 54; Engels (1958) 51–73; Arnold (1864) 437–43; Kay (1832) 17–25; PP1844 XVIII etc.) so it is unnecessary here to outline more than one or two of the more salient points. For a caution on applying the worst descriptions generally cf Hammond (1928) 421.

63 PP1863 XXV 314; Engels (1958) 51.

64 cf particularly here the comments of a Preston enumerator in PRO RG/9 3131/3 enumeration district 2; and e.g. PP1833 XX D1 23.

65 The detailed distribution was as follows:

Number of persons per household	1	2	3–4	5–6	7–8	9–11	12 and over	All	*N*
Percentage of households	1.4	9.6	32.7	26.1	17.7	10.2	2.3	100.0	1,241

66 For further descriptions of the states of the interiors of these cottages cf e.g. Bamford (1844) 68–9; Waugh (1881b) 29; Abram (1868) 429; MCS 24 Dec 49 5. For a different view, probably applicable to a minority of houses, see Gaskell (1833) 115, 133.

67 Data on causes of death are very inaccurate due both to bad diagnosis and bad reporting. These come from PP1865 XIII 340–1. See also Flinn (1965) for a useful discussion of causes of mortality.

68 PP1834 XX 59; Ransome and Royston (1866) 467–8; PP1854 LXIII 20; Shuttleworth (1843) 93–4; PP1844 XVIII App, 52.

69 cf Procter (1966) 154.

70 PP1844 XVIII; PP1845 XVIII.

71 Full details of the calculation of this life table are given in Anderson (forthcoming b). Since there exist no tables of annual mortality rates for any Lancashire town, but only for England and Wales as a whole (Farr (1864)) it is necessary to construct a life table on the basis of estimates from known data. In brief the procedure used was as follows. In 1849 the Registrar General published tables showing the mortality rates for each registration district in England and Wales for decennial periods of life, except that for the first five years of life annual figures and for the next ten quinquennial figures are given (PP1849 XXI). These figures can be compared with those for the same period of life for England and Wales as a whole and a measure of the proportional excess or short fall in mortality in the registration district under study can be obtained. This proportional excess or shortfall was used to adjust upwards or downwards the national annual mortality for the years in question and a local life table was then constructed on the basis of these adjusted figures. Because the Preston registration district contained a considerable rural area, Manchester mortality rates were used.

72 I have further explored some aspects of migration to Preston in Anderson (1970a).

73 cf esp Redford (1926) 16 for a general discussion of migration in Victorian England.

74 53% of the population as a whole.

75 A small number of birthplaces (some 2% in all) were not traceable. Many of these were more or less completely illegible.

76 The census tables suggest that, except for a slight over-representation of Irish born, Preston's pattern of migration was not very different from that of the other cotton towns (cf PP1846 XXXVIC 2; PP1852–3 LXXXVIIIb 664; also cf PP1846 XXXVI a and b).

77 Redford (1926); Lawton (1955).

78 cf e.g. Moore (1889) 29; Livesey (c1885) 10–15*; Ward (1953) passim** etc.

79 PP1833 XXXVI. The censuses after 1831 do not give occupational breakdowns for the populations of individual villages. I considered, however, that any changes in the occupational structures of these villages from 1831 to the date when the migrants left were unlikely to have been very great, and this was confirmed by the occupational compositions of the samples drawn from these villages.

80 Most of these towns had some industry.

81 Many of this group were, of course, and in some ways unfortunately, hand-loom weaving villages.

82 cf e.g. Young and Willmott (1957) chap 7; Rosser and Harris (1965) esp p. 15; etc.

83 cf e.g. Arnold (1864) 105; Redford (1926) 104–5; PP1864 XXIIC 16–32; PP1835 XXXV 187–8.

84 Wadsworth and Mann (1931) 313.

85 Redford (1926) describes this process in some detail.

86 and cf PP1847 XXVIII App A no 8.

87 PP1843 XXIV lxxxix.

88 PP1852–3 LXXXVIIIb 659.

89 PP1843 XXIV lxxxviii; PP1852–3 LXXXVIIIb 664.

90 Age structure figures calculated from PP1852–3 LXXXVIIIb 616.

91 cf e.g. Laslett (1965) 14; MacFarlane (1970) esp App B.

92 PP1868–9 XIII App, 560; and cf PP1862 L 567n, 570n, 579n; Davies (1963) 24–5*; Marshall (1961) 114–15. 80% of Booth's migrants to London in the last half of the century were aged 15–24. Only 5% were aged 30 or over (Booth (1892) 139 and 139n). cf also for comparable American data Thernstrom (1964) 106, 112.

93 PP1836 XXXIV 81; and cf PP1854–5 XIII 17.
94 For the relevant data see Table 16, p. 54 below.
95 This would not be true if substantial proportions had returned to their native communities for their confinements (N.B. the incidence of such a practice in pre-industrial England as suggested by MacFarlane (1970) 114). Analysis, however, revealed that hardly any children under one year of age had been born outside Preston, so this can hardly have affected these figures to any significant degree.
96 cf e.g. Marshall (1961) 114–15 on the reluctance of older and more established farm labourers to leave their homes.
97 cf PP1834 X 494; LSP1819 CX 63*.
98 e.g. PP1836 XXXIV 81.
99 e.g. PP1834 X 440, 494; PP1852–3 LXXXVI div VIII 47n–57n passim.
100 cf also Watts (1866) 139.
101 It would be interesting to know the proportion for the whole town. Because the house numbering is not always entirely consistent from census to census a complete and detailed study of a street and of surrounding streets is often necessary even to locate individual houses and this therefore precludes the use of a random sample for this purpose. A check with other areas, and general impressions, seem to suggest that the intensive survey area was not untypical of the town as a whole in this respect. It should be noted also that these figures do not represent all the moves made in a ten-year period. Reference to the directories suggest that several members of the local population lived at a third address or even more in the intervening years.
102 PP1847 XIa 51–2.
103 and cf Booth (1892) 61 on London; Gaskell (1897) 100; Wood (1936) 21–2*.
104 and cf Booth (1892) 81 on London.
105 It is not possible to say with any accuracy what proportion of women lived nearby, because the method used could not take account of women whose surnames had changed due to marriage. This would require laborious searches through marriage registers, and the additional effort was not considered worthwhile here, though it is recommended to future researchers.
106 The intensive survey data suggest as might be expected that lodgers, young persons including young married couples, and those in less regular occupations, were particularly likely to disappear from their old homes. There was some very slight suggestion also, that inmigrants were also somewhat more likely to move than the rest of the population. Further details are given in Anderson (1969) 90–2.

5. URBAN HOUSEHOLD AND FAMILY STRUCTURE

1 This calculation excludes those in institutions. See also note 2 below.
2 Relationships between lodgers are not usually given in the schedules. Parent–child relationships are, however, normally entered and where they are not specifically given they can usually be deduced from the schedule entries. Sibling and other kinship relationships present greater problems and no attempt was made to guess at them. However, nearly one in five of all single lodgers and servants did have the same name as someone else in the household. If these were all related they would add a further 2% to the overall proportion living with relatives.
3 However, I shall show below that a very considerable proportion of couples probably lived in a 'stem' family at some stage in the life-cycle. For the misleading nature in this respect of census type data taken alone cf Goode (1963) 2, 123–4, 239–44.
4 cf Armstrong's 22% for York (Armstrong (1968)), Crozier's 30% for a middle class sample in Highgate (Crozier (1965) 17) (though only 16% for the population as a whole (Firth (1964) 76)), Foster's 15% for Northampton, 14% for South Shields, and 21% for Oldham (Foster (1967) 314), and Smith's 17% for Nottingham and 15% for Radford (Smith (1970)).
5 Figures for England and Wales calculated from General Register Office (1968); for Swansea and Bethnal Green from Rosser and Harris (1965) 148. All these figures are subject to a margin of error. Firstly, the definition of 'household' in the Preston data is not quite identical to the modern one (see p. 199). Secondly, not all the 1966 sample census categories are sufficiently detailed, though the doubtful categories contain relatively few cases. Thirdly, the original Swansea and Bethnal Green data are from a sample of *individuals* from the electoral register and therefore show the *proportion of adults* living in any given household type. Full details of the adjustments made in order to estimate the *proportions of households* are given in Anderson (forthcoming a) note 2.
6 For a tentative essay in interpretation of this kind of pattern, see Anderson (forthcoming a).

7 1% of all households, 14% of all stem families.
8 For the fair see Kelly (1858) 288.
9 Evidence for this suggestion comes mainly from the intensive study where there were a number of individuals listed in one census as visitors but present as resident in the same or nearby households in the next, and also from observations to this effect in the enumerators' comments at the beginning of the enumerators' books.
10 See below, p. 53.
11 Enumerators are not consistent enough in differentiating between lodgers and boarders to make it possible to make use of this distinction in analysis.
12 cf 22% for York, 22% for Nottingham, and 14% for Radford in 1851 (Armstrong (1968)).
13 Defined here as married couple with or without children, or widow or widower with children.
14 cf e.g. PP1844 XVIII App, 84; PP1845 XVIII App, 25; MC 15 Dec 49; MCS 4 Jan 50 17.
15 This figure seems rather low. The Manchester Statistical Society found that the average sum paid by those lodgers who paid rent in Deansgate in 1864 was 1*s*. 7*d*. (MSS (1864) 12).
16 PP1863 XXV 312, 316–17, 339.
17 note 64 to Chapter 4.
18 PRO RG/9 3131 p. 54; cf also for London MCS 1 Jan 50 15.
19 e.g. Gaskell (1906a) 462, 465**; Bell (1907) 40 (for Yorkshire).
20 Shaw (1843) 28.
21 Hatton (1854) 115; and cf PP1865 XXVI 479, 489.
22 Inspection of the intensive survey data showed that the patterns revealed by cross-sectional data at a point in time did in fact show a pattern that was also true over time.
23 The change between LCS 4 and LCS 6 is significant $p < 0.05$ ($chi^2 = 5.506$).
24 The fact that family size is also important for widowed persons and that it is also important for lodgers helps to support the notion that it was increasing size and not any partially correlated changes in the availability of kin over the life-cycle which was at work here.
25 The proportion adopting this pattern is increased, however, by an operational procedure adopted in this study. Married men and women who were not co-residing with their spouses on census night were classified as widowed. Because the objective position of the separated was similar to the widowed it seemed that they should be classified together and this had the additional advantage of avoiding excessive subdivision of the data. It did mean, however, that itinerant artisans and men on tramp and living in lodgings would inflate the totals for widowers to some small degree.
26 cf Banks (1954).
27 The differences between the proportion of higher factory and artisan families sharing and both the professional, white collar and trade group and the lower factory, labourer and H. L. Weaver group are significant $p < 0.01$ (chi^2 being 11.269 and 8.298 respectively).
28 This difference is significant $p < 0.02$ ($chi^2 = 6.251$).
29 This group includes all couples where both spouses were born outside Preston, and whose eldest cohabiting child was also born outside Preston. All other couples where one or other or both spouses were not born in Preston are classed as 'intermediate'. Many of these would have come to Preston as children. On the average, therefore, the more immediate kinship patterns of the members of this group would not have been as greatly disrupted by the move.
30 See note 29 for elaboration.
31 This relationship is not significant at $p < 0.05$.
32 This relationship is significant $p < 0.05$ (chi^2 (one tailed) $= 3.091$).
33 Contrast the situation in Swansea where, while 57% of couples in LCS 1 (compared with 58% in Preston) were living in a home of their own, almost all the rest (a further 40%) in Swansea were living with parents, compared with only 15% in Preston.
34 The mean age of husbands and wives in LCS 1 was 27. If the spouses had been born when their parents were 33, then my mortality table suggests that 9% of couples would have had none of their four parents still alive on their wedding day. For those in later LCSs the figure would of course have been markedly higher.
35 See below, p. 53 and Chapter 9.
36 See Chapter 9.
37 Boys: aged 15–19 $p < 0.001$ ($chi^2 = 11.737$); aged 20–24 $p < 0.001$ ($chi^2 = 13.214$). Girls: aged 10–14 $p < 0.01$ ($chi^2 = 8.641$); aged 15–19 $p < 0.001$ ($chi^2 = 23.336$); aged 20–24 $p < 0.01$ ($chi^2 = 8.474$); aged 25–34 $p < 0.01$ ($chi^2 = 7.939$).

38 Boys: aged 15–19 $p < 0.05$ ($chi^2 = 4.181$). Girls: aged 15–19 $p < 0.05$ (chi^2 (one tailed) = 3.464).

39 The differences between migrant and non-migrant lodgers are not significant; differences between migrant and non-migrant servants are significant for girls: aged 15–19 $p < 0.05$ (chi^2 (one tailed) = 3.018); aged 20–24 $p < 0.05$ (chi^2 (one tailed) = 3.070); aged 25–34 $p < 0.05$ (chi^2: = 4.869).

40 It may be noted however that migrants were significantly more likely to live in the larger lodging houses (which can legitimately be considered as an inferior situation). When Preston born and migrant lodgers are compared in terms of number of lodgers in the households of which they are members, the inmigrants lived in larger groups ($p < 0.01$; chi^2 by the Smirnov test at 2 d.f. = 11.885 ($D = 0.32$; $N^1 = 88$; $N^2 = 203$)).

41 These figures are based on an assumption that the mean age of their parents when these children were born was 33, that the children had lived 17 and 22 years respectively, and that the probabilities of mortality were independent for each parent so that the square of the probability for one parent gives the probability for both. Not merely is there some error in these assumptions but the figures in Table 15 with which they are being compared are also subject to a margin of error. For boys, at the 95% level, this error is about 5% in the 15–19 age group, and 7% in the 20–24 group. In fact, however, the figure given here is probably very much of the right order. Young and Willmott found that 29% of those in their sample who had been born before 1891 had had their homes broken by the death of at least one parent *before they were 15*. On an assumption of independence this would suggest that both parents would have been dead in 8% of cases (from figures in Young and Willmott (1957) 7). The Preston survival tables on the assumptions made here suggest that 28% of the population of Preston would have lost one parent by the age of 15, a comparable figure.

42 $p < 0.001$ ($chi^2 = 19.491$).

43 The difference between childless widowers and childless widows is significant $p < 0.05$ (chi^2 = 4.164).

44 e.g. Young and Willmott (1957); Rosser and Harris (1965); Firth (1956); Cumming and Schneider (1966); Robins and Tomanec (1966); etc.

45 Compare Young and Willmott's married sample, 71% of whom lived with the wife's parents (Young and Willmott (1957) 16).

46 Contrast the opposite trend in Crozier's middle class sample, probably reflecting the importance of the economic links through the male line (Crozier (1965) 18, 40).

47 Young and Willmott (1957) 20.

48 and cf Lancaster (1961); Rosser and Harris (1965) 30–1; etc.

49 This is suggested by, for example, Kahl ((1959) 67).

50 Davies (1963) 35; cf also Dodd (1968) 90.

51 The quantitative analysis of propinquity in a historical context poses more or less insuperable problems. Construction of life histories from the enumerators' books by the location of the same family in successive censuses obviously allows one to determine an absolute lower limit. Further information of a less certain nature can be obtained by a review of the residence patterns of persons with the same surname. Both these analyses, however, understate the true situation, because some families are missed and, more importantly, women tend to disappear almost without trace on marrriage, with the result that affinal relationships are grossly under-recorded; reconstitution techniques using vital registration data are strongly recommended to future researchers in order that the maximum use be obtained from intensive survey analysis. Nevertheless even this relatively crude method gives some idea of the extent of kinship propinquity. For the exact criteria used in allocating doubtful individuals to families see Anderson (forthcoming b).

52 The difference between these two figures alone is probably some indication of the extent to which this method understates affinal relationships.

53 The assumptions used were age 5–9 becoming 15–19: 2.5% marrying; 10–14 becoming 20–24: 20%; 15–19 becoming 25–9: 65%; 20 and over becoming 30 and over: 65%. The marriage rates are computed from the distributions of the population married at the 1861 census, no data on ages at marriage being available. They are thus obviously subject to considerable error (and see the discussion in Anderson forthcoming b).

54 The fact that some areas of the town were predominantly middle class renders this assumption a slightly generous one, but no alternative suggests itself.

55 A Smirnov test applied to these data gives a chi^2 value at 2 d.f. of 15.101, which, if the assumptions were met, would give $p < 0.001$. In fact, since the data from the intensive survey are not

based on a random sample, statistical tests of this kind provide only a rough indication of significance.

56 It should be remembered of course that where kin moved further away they will frequently have moved right outside the searched area and thus will have disappeared from view. Thus cases where kin are noted as moving nearer together can only be seen as illustrations.

57 Thus, in the 'other villages sample' only 2 out of 51 household heads in a one in five sample of Longton had the surname Wignall, and none out of 51 in a one in five sample of Penwortham were called Eastham.

58 Had the assumptions necessary for the Smirnov test been met, chi^2 at 2 d.f. of 5.294 would be not quite significant $p < 0.05$. See note 55 above.

59 and cf generally e.g. Hubert (1965) 77–9; Humphreys (1966) 110; Rosser and Harris (1965) 30–1.

60 Note, however, in the light of later discussion, that most of the examples cited here did not cost much in money, though some were quite time consuming.

61 The references given here are only illustrations selected largely at random. Almost every work discussing the social life of the working classes contains some references to interaction with kin.

62 Gaskell (1833) 18; Ward (1953) for 13 Apr 62*; *Preston Pilot* 5 Apr 51*; MCS 1 Jan 50 14; Davies (1963) 35.

63 Censuses and intensive study; on visiting: Davies (1963) 36–7 and passim**; Bamford (1893a) 182*; Gaskell (1897) e.g. 13, 14, 18; PP1836 XXXIV 74.

64 Gaskell (1906a) 469*, 473*; Ward (1953) for Good Friday 1860, Whit 1861 etc.**

65 e.g. Clegg (1877); Corbridge (1964) 89.

66 MCS 4 Jan 59 19; Brierley (*c* 1886) 23*; Rushton (1909) 246–50*.

67 e.g. Clay (1853) 5**; Chadwick (*c* 1900) 12, 43**; Waugh (1881b) 167, 171*.

68 See Chapter 10.

69 PP1833 XX D1 48* 98**; PP1843 XV e.g. m26*, m27*; PP1844 XVIII App., 48n*; Ferriar (1798) 53*; Waugh (1881b) 67–9**; Gaskell (1897) 90*; etc. See also Chapter 10.

70 Ward (1953).

71 6 Apr 60; 23 Oct 64.

72 9 Jul 61.

73 10 Apr 64 (my italics; and cf also his automatic use of Dan's house for lodging on a number of occasions – 27 Feb 61, Apr 61 etc.)

74 cf 19–21 May 61.

75 27 Feb 61.

76 Gaulter (1833).

77 p. 171.

78 p. 178.

79 It may not be without significance that in all these cases this assistance was given to persons who had no recorded contact with kin; if kin had assisted, but not become infected, however, there is a much lower likelihood that Gaulter would have mentioned them, so this should not be considered more than an interesting hint at a possible situation on which more will, however, be said in later chapters. Similar patterns of assistance are also found between lodgers, again, except in one case, only among those who have no recorded interaction with kin.

80 p. 189.

81 p. 191.

82 cf e.g. the 'Kinsfolk are kinsfolk' of Gaskell (1897) 226*, and cf 206*; also Gaskell (1906i) 7, 9**.

83 Gaulter (1933) 190.

84 ibid 183 and see e.g. the letters from migrants discussed in Chapter 10.

85 Hardy (1925) 40.

86 PP1833 XX D1 1*, 11*, 34* etc.**; and see Chapters 9 and 10. These practices may partly, however, reflect the fact that kin may, because they were more easily sanctioned, have been considered more reliable. See also Chapter 9.

87 Bamford (1893a) 30*; cf also the sentiments felt by Mary in Gaskell (1897) 204*.

88 See Chapter 10; and cf e.g. the letters from overseas and internal migrants cited there, and also the underlying sentiments in LDM (1860) 25, and the disapproving remarks of Ward (1953) for 23 Oct 64, 6 Apr 60 and 24 May 60**.

89 Though the extreme mobility of the population would create considerable problems and would lead to some under-recording.

90 cf Chapter 9; and cf PP1833 XX D2 112*; Gaskell (1906f) 547*.

91 See esp James Ramsbottom, *The operative's lament*, stanzas 4–6, cited Arnold (1864) 148–9; cf Taylor (1842) 143–4*.
92 MC 29 Oct 49.

6. ASPECTS OF RELATIONSHIPS WITHIN THE URBAN NUCLEAR FAMILY

1 Among the more extreme examples are, for example, Gaskell (1833); Clay (esp 1853); Ashley in *Hansard* vol 73 esp cols 1073–173; Kay (1832); Tonna (1841); and others summarised by e.g. Hewitt (1958).
2 On the use of abortion and contraception by the Lancashire working class see e.g. Hewitt (1958) 93–7; also Gaskell (1833) 85n.
3 PP1836 XXXIV 18; and cf e.g. PP1871 VII 105–6; PP1862 XXII 192.
4 and cf e.g. PP1842 XVII 857.
5 cf Brierley (*c* 1886) 2*; Simmons (1849) 22.
6 e.g. LDM (1860) 48**.
7 ibid 47.
8 Gaulter (1833) 184*.
9 cf also for affect on death Kelly and Kelly (1957) 111*; PP1843 XIIb passim; and, among the novelists, e.g. Gaskell (1897) 22–3*.
10 I discuss this further in Chapter 9.
11 PP1843 XIV b8*, b19*.
12 Hewitt (1953) 171–2; Husband (1864) 504; PP1871 VII 98, 101, 106, 153; Baines (1862) 678.
13 PP1852 VII 428*.
14 PHoC (1855) 20*.
15 ibid 20–1**. These cases are further examples of the instrumental attitude among the older sections of the population which I discussed in Chapter 5.
16 LDM (1860) 65*.
17 cf also LDM (1859) 18*, 20**.
18 PP1842 XVII 202–3*, 236 etc; PP1865 XX 272; PP1863 XVIII 161*.
19 PHoC (1848) Narr, 60*; cf PP1852 VII 431*.
20 LDM (1859) 43; PP1871 VII 100.
21 Clay (1861) 511.
22 Rowntree (1901) 143; data on prices from Rowntree and Sherwell (1900) and from PP1898 XXXVI 307, 309. I am grateful to D. C. Paton of the Edinburgh Economic History Department for helping me with references on this topic.
23 PHoC (1855) 59; data on prices from Rowntree and Sherwell (1900) and from PP1854 XIV 261, etc.
24 e.g. PP1833 VI 632; *The Lion* 283; PP1833 XX D1 73; Barlee (1863) 33. The survey by Rowntree and Sherwell ((1900) 616) supports this idea for the end of the century. Cotton workers in this survey spent half the mean figure and averaged only 12 pints of beer equivalent per week. Artisans and heavy engineering workers averaged two or three times this amount. Their survey also revealed that 50% of adult men consumed only 10% of all alcohol, consuming less than 10 pints of beer equivalent each per week with a mean of 5 pints. The lowest 80% of consumers drank 25 pints or less with a mean of 9 pints. By contrast, the top 10% consumed 30% of the alcohol, all consuming over 50 pints of beer equivalent with a mean of 70 pints. The top 2% averaged 100 pints per week. (from Rowntree and Sherwell (1900) 15.)
25 And see below, p. 127, for limited evidence here; also, for modern communities cf e.g. Kerr (1958) 40. For data on affective bonds between siblings cf e.g. Bamford (1893a) 91*; Barlee (1863) 136**; Hull (1902) 361*.
26 Hewitt (1953) (1958).
27 Pinchbeck (1930) esp 84, 238; Hewitt (1953) 91–2.
28 PP1852–3 LXXXVIIIa lxxxviii.
29 Intensive study; PHoC (1855) 64n*; Waugh (1881b) 41–2; Watts (1866) 340*.
30 The actual percentages are: factory occupations 52%, non-factory occupations 33%, 'weaver' 14% ($N = 278$).
31 Though N.B. for an exception the Warrington pin makers (PP1843 XV m passim).
32 Hewitt found that 30% of married women and 53% of widows were in employment in 'industrial occupations' in seven Lancashire registration districts (Hewitt (1953) 271). Her figures for working wives will include some separated wives classified in this study with widows (see above, note 25 to Chapter 5).

33 e.g. PP1833 XX D2 108*.
34 Hewitt ((1953) 271, 275) found that for her seven registration districts only 1.5% of all married women had 3 children under 10 and were yet working in the cotton industry. Similarly, only 3.6% of those with a child under one year of age were working in cotton, though 12% of those with at least one child at home were. At any one time, therefore, the social problem aspect of this issue can be overstressed.
35 e.g. PP1866 XXIV 100*.
36 Hewitt (1958) 126–7; LSP1819 CX 412, 398, 385; PP1844 XVIII App, 77; Greg (1831) 16; PP1862 XXII 191; PP1833 XXI D3 13.
37 See Hewitt (1958) esp 191–3, 126–7, 178–80; cf also esp PP1871 VII 156.
38 less than 4*s*. per week above subsistence.
39 The difference, in the number of wives employed as a percentage of all wives, between those otherwise in difficulties and those not, by the criterion used above is significant $p < 0.001$ ($chi^2 = 15.841$).
40 The difference, in the number of working wives employed in factories as a percentage of all working wives, between those otherwise in difficulties and those not, by the criterion used above is significant $p < 0.05$ ($chi^2 = 4.538$).
41 For an expression of this role conflict cf PP1834 X 496*.
42 See also Chapter 10 for a discussion of the implications of this fact.
43 cf on co-residing and non-co-residing kin as nurses PP1871 VII esp 98; also 105; PP1873 LV 55–6; PP1849 XXII 48*, 54*; MCS 1 Jan 50 16*; cf Hewitt (1958) 129; Waugh (1881b) 121*; Bamford (1893b) 324*; contrast, however, PP1871 VII 112.
44 This figure is half of the 3.4% which can be calculated from Hewitt (1953) 271, 275.
45 Kay (1832) 39–40; and cf PP1833 XX D2 54; and, more generally, allegations on the early employment of children in e.g. PP1864 XXIIb 183**, 188*; Grime (1887) 20; Wheeler (1836) 187; PP1833 XXI D2 and D3 passim; PP1833 VI 302; PP1845 XXV 3; LSP1819 CX 81; etc.
46 PP1833 XX D1 47 and cf e.g. 53, 90, 102 etc.; also a similar orientation of a grandfather who put his orphan granddaughter into unpleasant work, in order to maximise her income (PP1833 XX d1 34*); note once again the instrumental overtones in these actions and attitudes.
47 See Chapter 9 for further discussion of this point.
48 and cf e.g. PP1833 XX d1 41. It should also be remembered that children had always worked in England from an early age in domestic industry (cf Pinchbeck (1930) 232–4; Dunlop and Denman (1912) 262–8).
49 PP1843 XV M2, M6; PP1863 XVIII 85–90; PP1865 XX App, 88.
50 PP1863 XVIII 161; PP1864 XXIIb 174; PP1842 XVII 149; PP1843 XIV B4.
51 *Reports of Factory Inspectors*, passim.
52 The possibility should not be overlooked that these children may have sometimes received satisfactions in the form of gratitude and status in the eyes of the family and, in particular, of younger siblings, which may have gone some way to compensate them for the deprivations of work.
53 LSP1819 CX 242*.
54 ibid 179*.
55 PP1837–8 VII 63; and cf more generally Hall (1826) 4; PP1816 III 152–3; LSP1818 CXVI 144; PP1833 XX D1 42, 91*, 128–9; PP1833 XXI D2 and passim; D3 10*, 26* etc.; PP1866 XXIV 34; Kelly and Kelly (1957) 44.
56 LSP1819 CX 235–6*.
57 For the contribution such children might make to family incomes, see Chapter 4 above.
58 And see Hewitt (1958) 190–1; and N.B. PP1833 XX D2 47, and the discussion in Chapter 4, pp. 25–9 above.
59 Adshead (1842) 38.
60 PP1836 XXXIV 15; and cf a Scottish priest on Irish parents, ibid 139–40.
61 MC 29 Oct 49.
62 Though some of these comments may have been 'translated' into more sensitive language by the middle class persons who recorded them.
63 PP1849 XXII 28*.
64 ibid 47*; cf 48*, 75* etc; also MCS 8 Jan 50 22.
65 PP1849 XXII 69*; cf 28*, 33*, 29*, 74*; cf also PP1834 XX D1 173*.
66 ibid 39*; cf 34*.
67 e.g. PP1865 XX 78*; 1866 XXIV 33*; note also LSP1819 CX 235–6*.

68 For a classic symptom of this, the fact that wives seem often to have been ignorant of the amount of their husbands' wages may be noted (e.g. PP1833 XX DI 39*; MCS 4 Jan 50 20*). On the topic more generally see also Barlee (1863) 31. Sex segregated leisure time groups are noted by MCS 21 Dec 49 3.
69 Barlee (1863) 30–1.
70 LSP1819 CX 239*; Waugh (1881b) 68*; Gaskell (1897) 100*, 230*; MCS 1 Jan 50 14.
71 LDM (1859) 37; cf PHoC (1855) 44.
72 PP1863 XXV 301; and cf e.g. PP1843 XV M13*.
73 e.g. MCS 1 Jan 50 14*, 16*; PP1833 XX DI 82*; Gaulter (1833) 79*, 161*, 181*, 186*; Waugh (1881b) 146*; PP1852 VII 427*; etc.
74 MCS 4 Jan 50 20; cf also Waugh (1883) 195 (the callous indifference of the husband to his children is also to be noted in Waugh's example).
75 Simmons (1849) 23; cf Brierley (*c* 1886) 54; cf also e.g. Clay (1861) 524*; Waugh (1881b) 139*; also Gaskell (1897) e.g. 40, 80**.
76 cf also Ramsbottom, *The operative's lament*, cited Arnold (1864) 148–9, esp stanza 3.

7. FAMILY, SOCIETY, AND ECONOMY IN THE BIRTHPLACES OF THE RURAL BORN MIGRANTS

1 It should be noted that, because of the method of sampling, these data are in no way necessarily representative of the Lancashire rural population as a whole. They instead provide a fairly precise contrast between the family structure of the urban migrants and the family structure of the populations of the villages from which they had come.
2 esp PP1835 XXXII.
3 PP1843 XXIV 440.
4 Connell (1950a) 38–41, 58; PP1835 XXXII App, passim; etc.
5 O'Brien (1921) 93; PP1836 XXXIII 142–203 passim.
6 O'Brien (1921) chap 2.
7 Kennedy (1847) 474, cited by O'Brien (1921) 9.
8 O'Brien (1921) 9.
9 ibid 24.
10 For general descriptions of Lancashire agriculture at mid-century see e.g. Garnett (1849); Beesley (1849); Rothwell (1850); Binns (1851).
11 cf e.g. Waugh (1881a) 257; PP1835 VII 35; Gaskell (1906g) 280; Garnett (1849) 1, 18; Beesley (1849) 49, 18.
12 Only 14% of the farms were of 75 acres and over, and 45% were under 20 acres (PP1852–3 LXXXVIIIb 658; and cf Marshall (1961) 117; PP1834 XXX 269a–278a).
13 PP1836 VIII 319; Beesley (1849) 12; see also below. On farm servants see PP1868–9 XIII 138; Beesley (1849) 27.
14 LSP1842 XV 20; Waugh (1881a) 52–3. For a general description of the hand-loom weaver/farmer link see esp Davies (1963) 13.
15 Beesley (1849) 12. Many of those with farms of less than 20 acres were indeed probably as badly off as day labourers. For national evidence on this see MC 1 Jan 50 (and cf Young cited by George (1953) 87). But contrast Howitt (1838a) 145. For local evidence on the problems of small farmers see e.g. PP1833 V 175–6; PP1868–9 XIII 138–40 and App, 561; Gaskell (1906b) 209.
16 Binns (1851) 33; PP1868–9 XIII 154; cf MC 5 Jan 50.
17 Marshall (1961) 117; cf also Waugh (1881a) 51.
18 PP1834 XXX 269a–278a.
19 O'Brien (1921) 19.
20 Connell (1950a) 15; PP1835 XXXII passim; PP1845 XIXa, XIXb, XX, XXI, XXIIa, XXIIb, passim.
21 On these see Connell (1950a) 168; Connell (1950b); PP1843 XXIV xxvi–xxviii.
22 In some areas the eldest and youngest received larger shares (PP1835 XXXII 230); in other areas each son received half of what was left when he married.
23 PP1835 XXXII 187–284 passim; PP1845 XIX–XXI passim; Connell (1950a) 165.
24 PP1835 XXXII 229; and cf passim.
25 From PP1843 XXIV 438–9.
26 The female–male sex ratio in the 26–35 age group was 1.33 in Belfast, 1.30 in all towns over 2,000, and 0.87 in rural areas (PP1843 XXIV 438–9). With no hope of a dowry, there was nothing material to tie these girls to the parental land, and the considerable relative advantages of town life drew many

away from the family, though contact was probably usually maintained and financial assistance often sent to the parents (PP1835 XXXII 187–284 passim).

27 PP1843 XXIV 447.
28 PP1830 VII 408.
29 PP1835 XXXII 278.
30 PP1830 VII 479.
31 PP1835 XXXII 227.
32 PP1830 VII 240.
33 ibid 408.
34 e.g. PP1835 XXXII 208*, 277* etc.
35 e.g. ibid 288*.
36 ibid 197.
37 ibid 240, 261, 264 etc.
38 ibid 189, 208, 211 etc.
39 ibid 190, 221 etc.
40 ibid 204, 218.
41 ibid 268.
42 ibid 198.
43 ibid 267.
44 Gaskell (1906g) 280.
45 Garnett (1849) 18.
46 e.g. Hull (1902) 246*; Chadwick (*c* 1900) 10–11*; PP1834 XXX 275a; Brierley (*c* 1886) 1–4**; Moore (1889) 4*; Livesey (*c* 1885) 13*, 14*; Davies (1963) 23*; PP1868–9 XIII 139 and App, 551; 1833 V 326; Parnell (1886) 4*; and the works of Waugh and Gaskell on the rural areas, passim.
47 cf e.g. Chadwick (*c* 1900) 9*; Bamford (1893a) 32–3*; Shaw (1889).
48 Waugh (1881a) 162–5; cf also Waugh's work passim; also Howitt (1838a) 315 on Yorkshire.
49 Waugh (1881a) 66**; cf 67*; and Waugh (1883) 256. Other similar cases of kinship as the basis of reputation are in Waugh (1883) 187–8*, 304–7*; (1882) 249*; (1881a) 312.
50 e.g. Bamford (1893a) 174–5*; Calman (1875) 25–7* (where an interview between a young man and his prospective father-in-law is described) and the rural works of Gaskell and Waugh passim**; see also Chapter 9 below.
51 The difference is significant $p < 0.001$ ($chi^2 = 111.503$).
52 Though it should be noted that these farm servants were to some extent simply incorporated into the families of their masters as extra members (cf e.g. Gaskell (1906g) 281–2; cf also, on Devon, PP1843 XIIa 108; and on rural England Howitt (1838a) 150; also Laslett (1965) 2–3. The familistic basis of the society was thus less disrupted than it would otherwise have been.
53 and cf PP1868–9 XIII 138–9, 154. Note here also how at least two of the children of Parish Assisted Migrants who had previously been in service and separated from their nuclear families, came again to live with them when the family came to the manufacturing towns (PP1835 XXXV 196*, 198*). This pattern whereby even sons of the relatively well off left home to go into service in adolescence was a long-established feature of life in pre-industrial England. There is an excellent discussion of this topic and of its structural origins in MacFarlane (1970) App B. MacFarlane suggests that this pattern was a societal reaction to a situation of high death rates which would otherwise have left many teenagers helpless orphans. Compare propositions 4.1 and 9 in Chapter 12 (pp. 173 and 174 below) which suggest that high uncertainty leads to an emphasis on contractual rather than kinship relationships.
54 Arensberg and Kimball (1961); cf Connell (1962); and e.g. Williams (1956) chap. 2 on England.
55 For a discussion of succession practices see e.g. Caird (1852) 360 on Cumberland; Gaskell (1906b) 210–11; PP1868–9 XIII 553–4.
56 cf e.g. PP1868–9 XIII App, 555; and cf Pinchbeck (1930) 17.
57 cf e.g. PP1868–9 XIII App, 560.
58 cf Gaskell (1833) 101–2; Howitt (1838b) 245–8.
59 MC 9 Jan 50 5.
60 Gaskell (1906j) 231*.
61 ibid 253; and cf 192–3.
62 ibid 223, 244, 206.
63 ibid 226.
64 ibid 296.

65 ibid 207; and cf 192, 279.
66 See below, pp. 94–5.
67 PP1835 XXXII 215; and cf PP1835 XXXII 262, 266 etc.
68 For evidence on the extent to which this was the case see below, pp. 94–5.
69 e.g. PP1835 XXXII 210.
70 ibid 253. Significantly, perhaps, there is evidence that very strong pressures were brought even against those who used ill-treatment in childhood as a reason for not supporting their parents in old age (ibid 202* etc); contrast the Lancashire situation outlined in Chapter 9.
71 ibid 276*; and cf 202*, 206*, 219*, 277* etc.
72 ibid 187, and passim.
73 ibid 70 and 49–113 passim.
74 ibid 283, and cf 192, 279 etc.
75 Gaskell (1906h) 398; PP1843 XIIa e.g. 28–30 on Somerset.
76 Gaskell (1906h) 280, cited p. 83 above.
77 On religious census Sunday in 1851 attendances for the whole of the Garstang registration district (which covered much of the relevant area) were somewhere between 70% of the population (on the unreal assumption that no one attended more than once), and 40% (the numbers at the service most attended by the members of any given denomination in the registration district, but the true figure only if most people attended twice, which is an equally unreal assumption). Similar figures for the Fylde registration district (which covered another traditional rural area) were 60% and 33%.(PP1852–3 LXXXIX esp 97–8; see also Chapter 8, p. 215 below.)
78 Bamford (1844) 267–72.
79 MCS 15 Jan 50 29.
80 MCS 15 Jan 50 29.
81 Smith (1888) 75.
82 See also Chapter 8, pp. 99–100 below.
83 For a full discussion see Chapter 9 to 11 below.
84 PP1835 XXXII 59.
85 ibid 78; and cf PP1836 XXXIII 35–70 passim.
86 cf Connell (1950b).
87 On this point cf Binns (1851) 94.
88 cf PP1868–9 XIII 150, 159.
89 For Lancashire cf e.g. Bamford (1844) 45.
90 And cf LePlay (1855) 210–11. LePlay indeed argued on a similar reasoning to that employed here, that what he saw as much stronger family bonds among French than English farmers could be attributed directly to the fact that, in contrast to the situation prevailing in England, French farmers had no discretion as to whether or not a son was to get a share of the farm. The children were therefore able to break free from parental control at an early age, some apparently refusing to work on the farm at all, and squandering, in anticipation of receiving it, their small inheritances.
91 cf PP1835 XXXII 200, 207, 212 etc.
92 cf PP1835 XXXII 202, 217, 218, 228 etc.
93 The basis of this argument is, of course, derived from Connell (1950a) (see esp 55–6 and chap 5) and Connell (1962). Note, however, the criticisms of some parts of Connell's argument in Drake (1963). But see also the data on which is based note 94 which suggest that in richer single inheritance areas the proportion of any age group remaining unmarried was higher. Drake's data refer to the average age of marriage.
94 Data on subdivision by region taken from a content analysis of PP1845 XIXa and b, XX, XXI, XXIIa and b; data on wealth of landholdings from PP1847 LVII (in terms of average value of stock per farm); data on age of marriage from PP1843 XXIV (using proportion of the population unmarried in the age group 36–45, in the light of the comments of Drake (1963)). For contemporary comment cf PP1835 XXXII 392, 404, 406 and passim. Shortage of space precludes a fuller analysis here of this topic.
95 PP1835 XXXII 216.
96 ibid 232, 255–6; cf also 187.
97 For evidence on poverty as the crucial factor at work in most cases of non-support cf PP1835 XXXII 187–284 passim: PP1830 VII 254.
98 PP1835 XXXII 198, 229.
99 ibid 227; cf 229.

100 ibid 227; cf 229.
101 ibid 204, 218, 219, 228 etc.
102 ibid 238 and cf 198.
103 ibid 236 and cf 226.
104 ibid 215.
105 ibid 197.
106 ibid 218, 227.
107 ibid 197.
108 ibid 230 and cf 227, 257.
109 However a possible alternative explanation here is that relationships of affinity of the same degree were not subject to the same prescriptions as blood-ties. No further evidence emerged on this matter.
110 ibid 204–5.
111 ibid 200*, 276.
112 ibid 207, 210, 215, 232–3 etc.
113 It appears from a sentence in Gaskell (1906h) 226 that where nieces and nephews or other kin had co-resided and helped out on the farm, they too may have received in return some portion of the estate. If this was so, then this straight reciprocation is of considerable interest.
114 and cf on this relationship between size of farm and employment of sons Gaskell (1906h) 209; and on poverty and migration to the towns Marshall (1961); Waugh (1883) 168. And cf propositions 1.1 and 8.2 in Chapter 12, pp. 172 and 174 below.
115 cf e.g. Gaskell (1906g) esp 284; Gaskell (1906b) 210.
116 cf proposition 4.2 in Chapter 12, p. 173 below. The theoretical underpinnings of this discussion are to be found in the last section of Chapter 2.
117 and cf here e.g. Gadourek (1956) 174–5, 189–91 on similar differences between the willingness of labourers' and of farmers' children to support them in old age and remain at home, and for a similar explanation. Also Banfield's data on the relationship between stem families and farm size in Montegrano (Banfield (1958) 154). For England see also PP1834 XXVII esp 54; and Chapter 11 below.
118 And cf here PP1837–8 XVIIIb 21.
119 PP1834 XXVII 44–54 and see Chapter 11.
120 A number of witnesses to various inquiries into the state of the poor in Ireland are indeed noted as saying that they believed that establishment of a Poor Law system in Ireland would lead to a rapid decline in the willingness of the Irish to assist kin (e.g. PP1830 VII 340, 479; PP1835 XXXII 260).
121 cf PP1835 XXXII 187–284 passim.
122 cf e.g. Sahlins (1965).
123 and see also Chapter 11, and for an elaboration of the theory Chapter 12, esp propositions 13 through 13.3.

8. THE PHENOMENAL LEVEL: ENVIRONMENTAL SANCTIONS, IDEOLOGIES, AND SOCIALISATION

1 Formally, those discussed here are related to propositions 3.2, 4.1, 5.2, and 6 in Chapter 12, pp. 173–4, while those discussed in Chapter 11 are related to propositions 3.1, 4.2, and 7.
2 esp, perhaps, Wirth (1938).
3 For a discussion of the relevant theoretical considerations see especially Bott (1957) chap 3 and Mitchell (1969). For a particularly good example of networks in developing countries fulfilling such a role see Mayer (1961).
4 The precise degree of influence of ideologies and individuals on behaviour patterns is extraordinarily difficult to study even in a present day context with batteries of specially designed tests. When one has to rely on data which happen to have survived from a historical situation, the problems of interpretation, and, indeed, of finding data at all, become extremely great. I have discussed some of these problems in Anderson (1970b). In spite of all the well-known risks involved in such an enterprise I have at times been forced to assume or to argue on the basis of only weak data that the absence of any clearly coherent sanctioning force meant that normative pressures really were low, and also for example that low formal religious participation really did mean that the tenets of religion had a low hold on the population under study. The overall consistency of the findings seems to me to suggest that the picture I have drawn is broadly true. But I am aware that I have at times assumed that the links between structure and behaviour suggested in Chapter 2 and by general sociological theory did operate in this case in the way hypothesised there. In other words, I have at times been forced by weak data to place even more weight on my theory as an explanatory device

to fill in missing links between data and interpretation than would normally be considered desirable. I can only hope and believe that realisation of the dangers of this approach has allowed me to avoid gross exaggeration in favour of my interpretation. Certainly I have not suppressed any data which do not conform to the picture given here. Nevertheless, since, with only a few exceptions, it has proved impossible to locate any quantitative data on many of the topics covered by this chapter, and since there is a great shortage even of descriptive data, the conclusions of this chapter, on this topic of not inconsiderable importance in the framework of the study as a whole, must be considered somewhat tentative.

5 For a description of similar colonies in various African townships and of their importance see e.g. Unesco (1956) 266, 316; Mayer (1961) 107, 111, 125–33, 217.

6 See also Chapter 11.

7 cf e.g. Lawton (1955); MC 6 Jan 49 5; PP1836 XXXIV 10; Neale (1840) 8; PHoC (1848) 5.

8 The chances on a random distribution that three households out of eleven would be headed by people from a village which provided only 1% of the household heads are less than 0.0002. However, since possible kinship relationships are involved here, and because this is one case picked out and not selected at random, such an analysis is not applicable.

9 Households with more than ten lodgers where, significantly perhaps, this relationship did not emerge, were excluded from the analysis.

10 The difference is significant $p < 0.001$ ($chi^2 = 46.151$).

11 For contemporary comment to this effect cf Dunlop (1839); for modern parallel situations with similar consequences cf Dennis et al (1956) chap 5; de Hoyos and de Hoyos (1966); Young and Willmott (1957) chap 1.

12 cf on this topic e.g. MCS 4 Jan '50 17; also MC 15 Dec 49 5, and 22 Jan 50 5; Ferriar (1795) 203–4.

13 cf e.g. PHoC narratives passim**; also, on income as the enabling factor, see Chapter 9 below.

14 See below pp. 107–8.

15 cf LHoTA 1 Jan 46 37; for a modern parallel cf Rosser and Harris (1965) 76.

16 Parkinson (1841) 10–11.

17 Booth (1892) 81.

18 cf also Gaulter (1833)*, particularly perhaps on Allen's Court.

19 MCS 24 Dec 49 5.

20 cf PP1842 XVII 239; PP1836 XXXIV 63; Gaskell (1833) 123; Kelly (1806) 16; PP1873 LV 56; Rowntree (1901) 77; Gaskell (1906d) 515–17; Gaskell (1897) 40.

21 From the intensive study data. A complete study of this topic would be of some interest. cf also LDM 1860 15*.

22 Neild (1841) 322; Arnold (1864) 207–8.

23 Waugh (1881b) 159–61.

24 Bamford (1893b) 74–7*; the case is referred to on 69–70.

25 PHoC (1855) 109*. Both Davies ((1963) 36–7) and Mrs Gaskell (e.g. (1897) 13, 134, 221; (1906c) 592) note the power of gossip in these communities within communities.

26 See below, Chapter 10; also Bamford (1893a) 178*, 231*; Livesey (*c* 1885) 13*; and Gaskell (1897) passim; etc.

27 It is known, moreover, that networks of this kind develop very rapidly in the new towns of developing countries (e.g. Unesco (1956) 375). There is also evidence to suggest that some middle class sections of the population of modern industrial societies are also able to generate relationships of this kind in a very short period of time. cf e.g. Gavron (1966) 96–7; Whyte (1957) chap 25; Willmott and Young (1960) chap 9.

28 The extent to which they were a wholly viable alternative is considered in Chapters 10 and 11.

29 cf the discussion in Chapter 2.

30 p. 118.

31 For a fascinating paper on mill colonies and the paternalism of employers see Marshall (1968).

32 The latest statute being 4 & 5 William IV c. 76 ss. 56 and 78.

33 e.g. PP1834 XXXV 64g–77g; PP1834 XXVIII 921A; Bamford (1844) 139–40*.

34 PP1834 XXXV 64g–77g; Bamford (1844) 139–40; etc.

35 cf PP1834 XXVIII 729A: note also the discussion in Chapter 2.

36 esp Dunlop (1839). For more general information on friendly society organisation, membership, and customs see e.g. PP1873 XXIII Pts I and II; PP1872 XXVI Pt II; Gosden (1961); also Chapter 10 below.

37 Most statistical data on this topic come from the 1851 census of religious worship (PP1852–3 LXXXIX) on which see Inglis (1960); Pickering (1967); and Thompson (1967).

38 Attendance was not recorded at seven out of ten churches of the Established church and one out of four Roman Catholic churches. It may be deduced, however, that all of these established churches were very small (their total sittings were only 83), while the Roman Catholic church was almost certainly rather large (possibly about 600).

39 This figure of 18% is calculated on the basis of the aggregate numbers for each denomination present at the service most numerously attended by members of that denomination in Preston and is thus an underestimate. The Church of England churches for which figures are not given in the published figures are estimated on the basis of 100% attendance, and the missing Roman Catholic church on the basis of 80%. Both are probably generous assumptions. Contrast figures on this basis of over 50% of the population as a whole for parts of rural England and Wales.

40 Some 40% of whom would have been Sunday school attenders (from PP1852–3 XC ccii). The figure of 27% is based on the assumption that no one attended twice, which is undoubtedly untrue. Attendance at the missing churches is taken as proportional to the numbers for the denomination as a whole at the most attended service. Contrast figures on this basis of over 100% for some parts of Wales.

41 Sanderson (1966) 236–8.

42 LDM (1860) 32; cf also Clay (1861) 501–2; Gaskell (1833) 70–1n.

43 e.g. Simmons (1849) chap 5; PHoC (1845) 11.

44 PP1864 XXIIb 187, 198; PP1837–8 VII 8; PP1843 XV M13.

45 MSS (1836) 6; PP1835 VII App, 102.

46 PP1864 XXIIb 189, 196; PP1843 XV m27.

47 PP1837–8 VII 2–3, 120 and passim; PP1847 XVa 5; PP1836 XXXIV 58; MSS (1836) 8–9n, 20.

48 Sanderson (1966) 119–20; MSS (1836); Wheeler (1836) 390–1; PP1852–3 XC.

49 e.g. PP1837–8 VII 2.

50 Sanderson (1966) 100–4; MSS (1836).

51 and cf e.g. PP1833 XX DI 45.

52 Compare, in particular, a number of suggestions that the Irish often reacted favourably and automatically to requests for assistance even from kin they had never seen (Bell (1907) 111; PP1836 XXXIV App, 4, 81). These cases of course reflect to a considerable degree a cultural hangover from a differently structured society.

53 Inkeles (1963) 339–40.

54 Klein (1965) vol II.

55 cf Klein (1965) chap 1 and sec 3.

9. THE ECONOMIC INFLUENCES ON URBAN FAMILY STRUCTURE

1 Crozier (1965) esp 15, 20, 37–9.

2 cf e.g. PP1833 VI 675* and passim; also e.g. Livesey (*c* 1885) 58*; Davies (1963) 31*.

3 Gaskell (1833) 63–4; cf cases in PP1833 XX of spinners employed in cotton mills owned respectively by a father and uncle, and a brother-in-law (PP1833 XX DI, 1*, 2*, 11*; cf e.g. PP1847–8 XXVI 7, 15**.

4 Hull (1902) 164*.

5 Bamford (1893a) 253*.

6 PP1834 XX DI 176*.

7 e.g. PP1816 III 207; PP1843 XIV b42; MCS 1 Jan 50 14; PP1864 XXIIa 195, 203; PP1863 XVIII 160, 165; PP1865 XX 76–9; PP1845 XVIII App, 14.

8 cf e.g. Hammond and Hammond (1917) 18–19.

9 One quotation which throws some light on this point may, however, be cited here. A supporter of the factory system told PP1833 XX (DI 44): 'Where they (children) work at home they are shut up all day long with their parents, and scarce have any acquaintance with others and with the feelings of their neighbours. The whole of the feelings which they imbibe may be selfish, and as their mode of working does not throw them out of the circle of their own house, or lead them to form any connections with their neighbours, whatever connections they *do* form arise from other circumstances than those of work; but there is not half an hour passes in a factory, but what children are laying each other under obligations important to them. If one piecer finishes piecing up his ends before another, he runs to his neighbour to help him, and thus may save him a scolding or a

blow, and he may immediately after be indebted to his neighbour in return. This creates feelings of kindness ...' (and cf. 45).

10 Davies (1963) 33–4*.

11 Note, moreover, that he could do this without moving from the community or otherwise seriously disrupting his life and other patterns of relationships (and cf PP1863 XVIII 167); this obviously is a reflection of the relative weakness of sanctions – though it is possible that had he committed an even more serious breach of family duty rather more pressure (but never more than pressure) could have been brought.

12 Smelser (1959) chaps 9–11.

13 cf note 9 above; and also, on factories allowing children to learn values different from their parents', e.g. PP1833 XXI D3 18; and on the contrasts with the closed socialisation in hand-loom weaving families PP1833 XX D1 43; cf also PP1833 XX D1 57, D2 45; PP1843 XV M16; Ferriar (1795) 203–4.

14 PP1816 III 261.

15 PP1816 III 100, 261; LSP1819 CX 7, 16, 36, 41 and passim; Smelser (1959) esp 189.

16 PP1816 III 261.

17 See e.g. PP1833 XX D1, D2 passim; PP1833 XXI D2, D3 passim; PP1840 X 13; PP1849 XXII 62–4; etc.

18 PP1833 XX D1 51, 68; PP1834 XIX 136; PP1845 XXV 18; PP1849 XXII 63*; PHoC 1851 App, 16*; MCS 4 Jan 50 19.

19 Smelser probably underestimates the importance of recruitment by operatives in power-loom weaving (Smelser (1959) 200–1). The sample data show that many young persons became weavers in their own right in their mid-teens, while spinners often had to wait until their twenties; thus, figures giving the proportion of children and young persons employed by masters and by operatives will tend, regardless of the true case, to show a bias in favour of spinners (and cf e.g. PP1833 XX D1 36*).

20 From PP1834 XX 136.

21 cf e.g. PP1833 XX D1 passim; PP1849 XXIIa 62*, 63*, 64** and passim.

22 cf PP1833 XX D2 116*.

23 cf e.g. LSP1819 CX 235–6.

24 Shuttleworth (1843) 93–4.

25 cf also figures in PP1831–2 XV 452.

26 Few of the under 35s would have had any non-co-residing children either.

27 and cf PP1833 XX D2 53 and also the implication of the difference between the proportion of scavengers and of piecers employed by parents (PP1833 XX D2 8). This obviously throws some doubt on Smelser's analysis of the timing of cotton factory agitation in the early nineteenth century (cf Anderson 1970b).

28 cf Chapter 6 above, pp. 75–6.

29 PP1833 XX D2 9*.

30 cf LSP1819 CX 29 etc.

31 e.g. PP1849 XXII 55*; PHoC (1848) 73*.

32 PP1831–2 XV 450*; PP1833 XX D2 21; PP1845 XXV 3*; MCS 1 Jan 50 14*; etc.

33 PP1833 XX D1 33–4*.

34 PP1833 XX D1 102*.

35 PP1816 III 261. Smelser does not cite these figures, writing instead 'The exact proportion is a mystery in these early days' (Smelser (1959) 190; and see Anderson (1970b)).

36 From lists of employees in LSP1818 CXVI some other limited and approximate figures can be calculated. These suggest that a quarter at most of all piecers in these mills had the same surname as the spinners with whom they worked, though many piecers had the same surname as another piecer in the same work group. (From LSP1818 CXVI 46–62.)

37 Shuttleworth (1843) 93–4; the study dates from the early 1830s.

38 cf LSP1818 CXVI 177.

39 cf PP1849 XXII 55*; note also LSP1819 CX 111.

40 PP1863 XVIII 169.

41 PP1865 XX 266.

42 PP1863 XVIII 85–90.

43 Gaulter (1833) 181*.

44 PP1865 XX 93.

45 PP1843 XV M6.

46 PP1864 XXIIb 182–90.

47 ibid 180.
48 ibid 200.
49 ibid 167, 195–6.
50 PP1866 XXIV 51.
51 PP1842 XVII 177.
52 PP1842 XVII 181*.
53 ibid 223*, 227*.
54 ibid 232*.
55 ibid e.g. 215**.
56 Calculated from data in PP1842 XVII 197–9.
57 cf also e.g. PP1833 XX D1 42 where mothers are noted as receiving the whole of their children's wages.
58 See Fitton and Wadsworth (1958) 225; Redford (1926) 21; etc.
59 cf e.g. PP1835 XXXV 192–200. For a discussion of Parish Assisted Migrants see Redford (1926).
60 cf Unwin et al (1924) 166. The same problem has occurred in Japan and has been one factor in the decline in similar practices there, and with it of extended family control (Goode (1963)).
61 PP1835 XXXV 23.
62 PP1833 XX E 7; and cf PP1866 XXIV 99.
63 cf also PP1834 XX D1 169.
64 PP1842 XXXVb 77; cf also on this topic PHoC (1851) App, 19; PP1835 XXXV 203–4; *Hansard* vol 73 col 1146; PP1833 VI 647; MCS 1 Jan 50 14.
65 PP1833 VI 648.
66 PP1837 XVII 59.
67 Brierley (*c* 1886) 50–1.
68 Wood (1936) 50.
69 e.g. PHoC (1845) 10*; PP1836 XXXIV App, 5–6; PP1864 XXIIb App, 184; Parkinson (1844) xxxvii; MC 21 Dec 49 5; etc.
70 and cf Young and Willmott (1957) 73–5 on this practice in pre-war Bethnal Green.
71 And cf PP1864 XXIIb App, 184 on the advantages more generally.
72 Webb MSS vol XXXIV, 171; Smelser (1959) 189.
73 Webb MSS vol XXXIV, 31. Note here this emphasis on both the responsibility of men to orphan nephews, and to poorer kin more generally. This topic will be discussed further in Chapter 10.
74 Webb MSS vol XXXIV, 39.
75 ibid 170.
76 Smelser erroneously suggests (Smelser (1959) 189) that early trade union rules 'explicitly prohibited members from recruiting *assistants*' (my italics) outside these narrowly defined classes. In fact the restriction applied solely to the *training* of children to the skilled parts of the trade, which only a minority ever reached. Indeed as noted earlier, to have imposed these restrictions on recruitment would probably have been demographically impossible.
77 Webb MSS vol XXXIV, 182.
78 ibid 163.
79 ibid 168–9.
80 ibid 136–9.
81 ibid 127.
82 PP1843 XIV b35.
83 Webb MSS vol XXXIV 201–70.
84 One result of this was the fact that the parent seems usually to have been able to decide the occupation the child entered. Many children, indeed, may well have had no choice at all (cf e.g. PP1864 XXIIb 175*; PP1834 X 473; etc.).
85 For an example of such a contract written out in full see Moore (1889) 24–5.
86 PP1833 XXI 43; PP1843 XV M10–12; PP1863 XVIII 161–2; PP1864 XXIIb 167.
87 Waugh (1883) 298*.
88 PP1833 XX D1 5; cf also Dodd (1968) 161–2*.
89 LSP1819 CX 49; and cf on nuclear families PP1833 XX D1 102.
90 It may well be that men in many cases may have actually been *more* dependent in the towns on wider kin for the best employment opportunities, since it seems that most farms were worked by nuclear families only (with the possible addition of an odd orphan relative).
91 Contrast, for example, PP1833 XXI D2 49 with PP1833 XX D1 16.

92 Except, significantly, in harmful (PP1864 XXIIb 197) or declining (e.g. hand-loom weaving from Kelly and Kelly (1957) 73–4 etc.) trades.
93 PP1864 XXIIb 183*.
94 ibid 185*.
95 Listed in PP1843 XIV App IV B61–2.
96 and cf e.g. PP1834 XX D1 169; PP1834 X 460.
97 Compare proposition 1.1. in Chapter 12. The difference among the self-employed (SEGs III, V, and VIII) in the proportion of teenage sons in the same trade as their parents is significantly correlated with the affluence of the occupation ($p < 0.001$; chi^2 at 2 d.f. = 14.311).
98 It should be noted that this conclusion drawn from cross-sectional data at a point in time is subject to some error when used to discuss changes over time (though cf supporting data from Chapter 4). This is because neither the older children nor the father of some migrant families had ever been able to obtain other than labouring occupations. This effect is, however, to some extent counteracted by the probability that some men now in the labouring group (SEG VII) had earlier been in skilled factory occupations (cf Chapter 4 above).
99 When the proportion of sons of SEG IV fathers in SEG IV occupations is compared with the proportion of the sons of other SEG fathers in SEG IV occupations, the difference is significant $p < 0.05$ ($chi^2 = 3.193$) on a one tailed test.
100 Proposition 1.1 in Chapter 12.
101 Arnold (1864) 62.
102 PP1834 XXVIII 920A.
103 MCS 1 Jan 50 19; cf also on children leaving home in this way e.g. Watts (1866) 94; LDM (1859) 44; PHoC (1848) 73–4**; also refs in Sanderson (1966) 92. For its being blamed on high wages cf Hertz (1859) 35; Waugh (1881b) 71*; PP1834 XXXV 73g; MC 29 Oct 49; and, for a poignant case, MCS 6 Dec 49 5*.
104 PP1834 XX 21.
105 PP1833 XX D2 107; PP1834 XXXV 73g.
106 and cf also (on London) Bosanquet (1899) 106; MC 22 Jan 50 5.
107 Though early marriage may have been one way in which independence manifested itself. Figures dealing only with the unmarried must to some extent therefore be seen as minima. One would have suspected that migrants would have been more likely than the Preston born to break away, and that those children who did break away may have been more likely to migrate to other towns; their parents were in lower paid occupations so that the income differential between parents and children would be greater. A greater clash over expectations of family role performance might also be expected. The intensive survey data, however, did not confirm (though they did not deny) a proposition that migration, independently of occupation, might be important. These data, however, being based on a ten-year period, are rather inadequate for the purpose at hand.
108 Full-scale family reconstitution techniques might help here as elsewhere, but once again high rates of population turnover would raise serious problems.
109 In addition, a few would have left home to become apprentices or to take jobs elsewhere with parental consent. It is to be expected, however, that they would be rather few in number, and sufficiently randomly distributed over the population not to introduce any great bias into the figures.
110 Davies (1963) 31–4*.
111 MC 22 Jan 50; and cf PHoC (1845) 5; compare also e.g. PP1852 VII 182, 343, 428*; Nunns (1842) 12–13; MC 22 Jan 50 6*; and, on good treatment in the past as a condition of married children supporting their parents, Booth (1894) 137; Rathbone (1927) 37*. And contrast the attitude in Ireland discussed in Chapter 7 above.
112 PP1865 XX 92.
113 Gaskell (1897) 12; cf also *Hansard* vol 73 cols 1096–7*.
114 MCS 24 Dec 49 5.
115 PP1833 XX E 5.
116 and cf for modern data on this topic Slater and Woodside (1951) chaps 1 and 2.
117 Rowntree's 3*s* plus 10% for the higher cost of living (see Chapter 4 above).
118 See Chapters 4 and 5, pp. 202 and 47.
119 and cf also MC 29 Oct 49.
120 From PP1834 XX 21.
121 e.g. PP1863 XVIII 65–90; MCS 4 Jan 50 19; PP1833 XX D1 42.

122 PP1833 xx E 5.
123 PP1833 xx D2 17; cf PP1863 xxv 325.
124 and cf also MC 29 Oct 49. It should, however, be noted that some older children did, nevertheless, continue to give all their wages to their parents right into their twenties (PP1833 xx D1 37*, 39* and passim*; PP1849 xxii 32*, 59*; MCS 4 Jan 50 17*).
125 PP1852 vii 343; Nunns (1842) 12–13; Gaskell (1833) 93; Rowntree (1901) 30.
126 For the marriage rates assumed see note 53 to Chapter 5. The proportions of any age group who could be expected to have died in a ten year period were calculated from the local life table. The mortality and marriage rates were calculated on the basis of the quinquennial subgroups from which the data were derived, to allow as far as possible for differences in the age composition of the different groups.
127 PP1842 xvii 204.
128 PHoC (1851) App, Narr, 8; and cf also e.g. PP1842 xvii B26*; also the statement by a hand-loom weaver that children's disrespect for parental authority was directly due to their wages being up to twice their father's (PP1834 x 14).
129 Neale (1840) 47.
130 PP1816 iii 104.
131 PP1837–8 xix 272*.
132 This was particularly so where harsh treatment in the past meant that bargains were not biased in favour of parents by memories of past favours or by emotional bonds.
133 Some of the ideas in this section are obviously related to those of, for example, Hajnal (1965); Davies (1964); and Petersen (1965) 182–7; also cf Sussman (1953b).
134 cf also the generalised statements for the working classes at the end of the century in Bell (1907) 180–1; and Rowntree (1901) 140; also Goode (1963) 43; Zelditch (1964).
135 and cf PP1834 xxviii 920A; 1834 xx D1 161.
136 cf evidence cited by Redford (1926) 15–16; Jem's resolve in Gaskell (1897) 112*; PP1841 x 44; PP1834 xxviii 920A. It is worth noting that depressions, particularly if severe, led to a rapid fall in the marriage rate, presumably because the ability to provide oneself and family with an adequate level of income fell severely in these years (cf Arnold (1864) 613).
137 For contemporary views and evidence on the early marriage of cotton operatives, see LSP1819 cx 371; PP1844 xviii App, 47, 67, 77; PP1833 xx D2 49, 62. The evidence is discussed, (for reasons given below) in a not altogether satisfactory manner, in Hewitt (1953) 51ff.
138 Hewitt (1953) 51ff, by concentrating almost entirely on the age of marriage of women, misses this point.
139 and cf for a similar situation in rural Holland today Gadourek (1956) 174–5.
140 This has interesting implications for the study of the population rise in the eighteenth century. Then, the main economic changes seem to have been, on the one hand, in agriculture, from a small farm system to one based on hired day labourers, and, on the other, in industry, from a traditional and domestic economy to one dominated by factory industry. Further research on this topic is obviously necessary. For a preliminary attempt at extension of this analysis see Anderson (forthcoming b). cf for similar research in Holland, Petersen (1965) 166–92.
141 MC 29 Oct 49. Contrast the opposite pole, where individuals think of themselves at the phenomenal level, and are thought of by society, only as part of families (e.g. Thomas and Znaniecki (1958) 97).

10. CRITICAL LIFE SITUATIONS AS A FACTOR IN FAMILY COHESION

1 Some of the individual pieces of evidence which will be presented in this chapter are not as complete or as absolutely convincing as one would like. Taken *en masse*, however, I would argue that they are at least highly suggestive of the truth of the propositions outlined here.
2 In the terms of the formal analysis of Chapter 12, p_c has fallen markedly while $\bar{s}$ has risen markedly.
3 Litwak (1965) 290–303; cf Sussman (1965) 83–4; Rosser and Harris (1965) 280.
4 For a summary of the role of the family in the most important of these, sudden disasters, cf Quarantelli (1960); Young (1954); etc; and on the role of the family in other crisis situations e.g. Loudon (1961); Litwak (1965).
5 cf Rosser and Harris (1965) 297.
6 LDM (1860) 45.
7 Barlee (1863) 15; and cf 55.
8 Arnold (1864) 139; and cf 106; cf also Waugh (1881b) passim but esp 49.
9 Not that the Poor Law offered anything above an absolute subsistence minimum. Indeed, one may suggest that part of this reluctance on the part of the population to have anything to do with the

Poor Law resulted from the fact that their normal standard of living was high enough to enable most, by mutual assistance, to provide better for themselves even in adversity. At the structural level this would indeed possibly be the crucial factor.

10 PP1847–8 LIII.

11 cf PP1834 XXVIII 920A; data from a comparison of figures from PP1803–4 XIII with figures from the 1801 census (in PP1852–3 LXXXVI div VIII), with population age structure as of PP1852–3 LXXXVIIIa and b; and from Booth (1894).

12 cf esp PP1834 XXVIII 921A.

13 PP1842 XXXVb, 71; PP1846 XXXVIa and b; PP1859 Ses 2 VII 117–35; cf also PP1834 XXVII 89; Adshead (1842) 31; PP1847 XIb 180–1, 111–13; PP1860 XVII 256, 345.

14 The working of these organisations is described at length in PP1873 XXIII Pts I and II; PP1872 XXVI Pt II; see also Gosden (1961) and, more generally, PP1842 XXXVb 7, 77; PP1843 XIIb 57; PP1844 XVIII App, 48–9, 85; PP1836 XXXIV 27; PP1859 Ses 2 VII 149; PP1834 XIX D1 174.

15 The particular advantages of friendly society membership to the Lancashire population lay in the contractual basis in a mobile low trust society (proposition 9 in Chapter 12) in a situation where aid nets had to be large (proposition 13.0.3 in Chapter 12).

16 PP1873 XXIII Pt I App, 79.

17 There were about 725,000 men aged 20 and over in Lancashire at the 1871 census.

18 Gosden (1961) 75, 95; also e.g. PP1873 XXIII Pt II 92.

19 Stehouwer (1965) 145.

20 Reproduced in Anderson (forthcoming b).

21 Several cases are noted in the intensive study where married children moved back into the parental home when the mother or father was widowed (see also LDM (1860) 15*; PHoC (1848) Nar, 68*). And cf today e.g. Stehouwer (1965) 149, 151–2; and also the paper by Rosemayr and Kockeis there cited (154); Bell (1907) 110–11; Young and Willmott (1957) 20.

22 cf e.g. Shaw (1843) 28.

23 PP1845 XV 283.

24 I must thank David Thompson for referring me to this quotation. cf also LDM (1860)**; PP1834 XXVIII 910A; and on this factor during depressions, PP1863 XXV 311; and for a pair of widows PP1834 XXVIII 910A*.

25 Shaw (1843) 28; Kelly (1806) 7; PHoC (1845) 5*; and cf LePlay (1855) 206–9.

26 Unesco (1961) 219.

27 cf also Young and Willmott (1957) 16; Rosser and Harris (1965) 62–3, 249; Kahl (1959) 67; Stehouwer (1965) 149.

28 Foster (1967). For fuller details of Foster's findings see Chapter 11 below.

29 Barlee (1863) 29; Hewitt (1958) 131–2.

30 PP1863 XXV 339.

31 cf also on this point Rosser and Harris (1965) 191.

32 If the households with grandmothers in the house, and those with no suitable co-residing person are considered as two independent samples, the difference is significant $p < 0.01$ (chi^2 by the Smirnov test (one tailed) at 2 d.f. = 8.434).

33 It might be argued that wives worked in these families in order to support their mothers who were taken into the household for other reasons. This kind of data cannot reject such a proposition and, anyway, other feelings must have played a part. It does not, however, seem adequate as a total explanation both because most of the families where the wife worked were so poor that the wife would have wanted to work anyway (see Chapter 6 above), and in the light of the descriptive data to be presented shortly.

34 See Chapter 4 above, p. 31.

35 Waugh (1881b) 85.

36 PP1833 XX D2 3.

37 PP1835 XXXV 196 and cf e.g. MCS 1 Jan 50 16*.

38 PP1842 XXXVb 7; cf 77; cf also for modern industrial societies Geiger (1960) 449; and, more generally, Sussman (1965) 80; Rosser and Harris (1965) 191.

39 PP1836 XXXIV 69.

40 Sample and intensive study data; and cf PP1836 XXXIV 25; PP1859 Ses 2 VII 116; PP1837–8 XIX 309.

41 Booth (1894).

42 and cf PP1904 XXXII 338 cited by Hewitt (1958) 165–6.

43 PHoC (1851) App, 4*.
44 e.g. PP1834 XXVIII 921A*; and see Chapter 11 below p. 165.
45 cf also Davies (1963) 33*.
46 e.g. Barlee (1863) 138*; Waugh (1881b) 152–3*.
47 compared with 10% of married couples. This difference is not significant, though it is suggestive.
48 Crozier (1965) 19.
49 and cf Gaskell (1906c) 396*.
50 This difference is not significant, though it is possibly of some slight interest.
51 For the incidence to be expected see p. 34 above.
52 Cited PHoC (1851) App, 60; cf Taylor (1842) 82; PHoC (1848) 34n; PP1836 XXXIV passim; Parkinson (1841) 9–10; cf also Mrs Gaskell's novels passim; Nunns (1842) 29–30; Rowntree (1901) 43.
53 Rathbone (1927) 1–3*.
54 cf LDM (1860) 9*; also a very good case in London described in MC 21 Dec 49 5; and cf Gaskell (1897) 67*; Brierley (*c* 1886) 54*. Also a good village case PHoC (1855) 102.
55 Outside observers speaking of assistance from friends and neighbours may in fact have often been describing assistance from kin. Most outsiders would have no way of distinguishing kin from neighbours. Obviously data must be taken at face value. Nevertheless this seems to strengthen rather than weaken the case argued here.
56 PP1842 XXXVc 2–3.
57 and cf also e.g. Gaskell (1897) passim**.
58 Nunns (1842) 30.
59 cf Adshead (1842) 29*; Gaskell (1897) 55*.
60 *The Lion* 31 July 29 133; cf Gaskell (1897) 21*.
61 e.g. PP1833 XXI D3 12*; Dodd (1968) 78*, 170–1*; LSP1819 CX 126*; and cf Rowntree (1901) 38.
62 PP1836 XXXIV 23.
63 e.g. Ferriar (1795) 182.
64 Ferriar (1795) 195–6*; (1798) 78; Gaulter (1833) 175*; Soc for Poor (1802) App, 3, 21–3**.
65 Soc for Poor (1798) 106–7*, 108*; Gaulter (1833) 87*.
66 Parkinson (1841) 13n*.
67 e.g. Gaulter (1833) passim**; Gaskell (1897) 67–9*; Rushton (1909) 136*; MCS 4 Jan 50 17*; and cf PP1843 XIIb passim** for the national picture.
68 Gaulter (1833) passim**; Simmons (1849) 22*; PP1842 XXXVc 5*; Gaskell (1897) passim**. Also, many local friendly societies required members to attend funerals of other members (Gosden (1961) 121–2).
69 PP1849 XLVII 12–13, 32–3 gives figures. One might, however, expect that orphans would have had a high mortality rate in the early years of life, so fewer would have been left alive to be cared for.
70 PP1842 XXXVb 70–1; PP1834 XXXV 75g; LDM (1859) 41–2; Arnold (1864) 208–9*; LDM (1860) 46*; Rathbone (1927) passim**; cf Marshall (1926) 95–6.
71 Gaskell (1906e) 354.
72 Gaskell (1906f) 549.
73 PP1834 XXXV 73g, 77g.
74 LDM (1859) 41–2; Waugh (1881b) 59*; 119–20*; PP1833 XX D1 33*; Bamford (1893a) 97*; Livesey (*c* 1885) 4*; LDM (1860) 43*; PHoC (1851) App, 2*; PP1844 XVIII App, 48n*; PP1834 XXVIII 910A*; and cf Gaskell (1897) 73*; (1906f) 546–7*; (1906c) 357*.
75 p. 119 above – cf also the discussion there on trade recruitment of orphans more generally (p. 112).
76 Simmons (1849) 23; PHoC (1851) App, 28*; PHoC (1848) Nar, 63*; Bamford (1893a) 92–3*; PP1843 XV m27*; Hutton (1841) 6–8*; PP1852 VII 428*; Dodd (1842) 293*.
77 LDM (1860) 70*; MCS 4 Jan 50 20*; PP1843 XIV 66*; PP1843 XV m26*.
78 Davies (1963) 22*; and cases in intensive study suggesting this; also in rural areas e.g. PP1868–9 XIII 139.
79 Hull (1902) 361*; PP1834 XIX D1 126–7*. cf Crozier (1965) 18–19; and LePlay (1855) 206–9 who believed this fairly general in England.
80 and cf MC 22 Jan 50 6*; and (for Bilston) Leigh (1833) 26*.
81 Foster (1967).
82 and see Chapter 11 below, p. 165; and cf e.g. PP1834 XXVIII 910A*.
83 and cf PP1833 XX D1 34*; also on the ability even of orphan children to pay for their keep in the south of England, MCS 21 Dec 49 4.

84 and for supporting quantitative data on the distribution of kin by occupation of family head see Chapter 9 above.
85 PP1847 XIa 52; cf Cobden (1881) 193; also Waugh (1881b) 13; Engels (1958) 100, 140.
86 PHoC (1848) 38n; Waugh (1881b) 117; Taylor (1842) 145; note also a number of cases in the sample of servants and others 'out of place' being boarded by relatives; and cf in rural Cumberland PP1833 V 326.
87 PP1842 XXXVb 15; LSP1819 CX 210*. But note also the instrumental orientation sometimes brought to the surface by this kind of situation in the cases cited in Chapter 6 above, p. 70.
88 cf e.g. Taylor (1842) 145.
89 See e.g. PP1864 XXIIc 16–32, 92–4; PP1859 Ses 2 VII 145–7; Waugh (1881b) 14, 113; Bamford (1844) 65; Redford (1926) 104–5; PP1842 XXXVb 75.
90 PP1852–3 LXXXVI div VIII 57n; and see below p. 159. Some may have done this in order to claim poor relief there.
91 e.g. Taylor (1842) 216; PP1842 XXXVb 21, 84; PP1844 XVIII App, 80–1; LDM (1860) 38; Adshead (1842) 26, 32; Arnold (1864) 111, 615; etc.
92 Descriptions and cases may be found in e.g. Barlee (1863) 20, 30; PP1842 XXXVb App, 82, 104; PP1842 XXXVc 1; PP1863 XXV 311–12; Adshead (1842) 35; etc.
93 e.g. Taylor (1842) 171; Barlee (1863) 7–8; Adshead (1842) 18–23; Waugh (1881b) 46–8; etc.
94 Waugh (1881b) 23*; Derby (1881) 201; Barlee (1863) 15; etc.
95 Waugh (1881b) 17*; and cf Waugh (1881b) 3*, 15*, 68*; Barlee (1863) 137*; Ward (1953) for 10 Apr 64*.
96 See e.g. Watts (1866); Arnold (1864); PP1842 XXXVa and b; etc.
97 Formally, in terms of the analysis of Chapter 12, a situation had been reached where $c/\bar{s} > 1/p_c$; for the meaning of the symbols see note 6 to Chapter 12, p. 224 below.
98 PP1864 LII 1.
99 Gaulter (1833).
100 Gaskell (1897); (1906d); (1906e); passim.
101 Davies (1963) 35.
102 PP1834 X 382*.
103 PHoC 1848 Nar, 73*.
104 and cf also the data presented in Chapter 5 above.
105 Townsend (1965); see also Bell (1968) for a similar kind of analysis.
106 PP1863 XXV 316n.
107 Watts (1866) 158*; and cf other cases cited there. In this connection one may also note that out of 441 prostitutes admitted to the Magdalene Institutes in Glasgow and Edinburgh in 1859 and 1860, 90% had lost their mothers and almost one-half had lost both parents (Smout 1971).
108 Bamford (1893a) 72*.
109 Waugh (1881b) 151*; and cf 48*, 53–4*; also Bell (1907) 110; and for rural data PP1868–9 XIII App, 551.
110 Another table, not shown here, showed that there was no relationship by LCS when the data were controlled by this variable. When considering the effects of migration on kinship relationships discussion should be limited to certain classes of kin. There is no reason, in theory, why migration should *necessarily* alter the possibility of co-residence with directly *descending* kin (married children, grandchildren and so on), and if all persons born outside the town are taken together, some migrants will have come in as members of nuclear families, and will therefore be just as likely as the native population to have parents and siblings as household members. Here, therefore, only 'adult migrants' are considered (those with an eldest child born outside Preston, indicating migration after marriage) and only ascending kin, or those of the same generation and their descendants (siblings, nieces and nephews etc.) who must have come in outside the current nuclear family of the head, are counted as kin.
111 See below pp. 154–8.
112 e.g. Barlee (1863) 137*; PP1836 XXXIV 86; Waugh (1883) 170*; and cf Rowntree (1901) 112–13; also PP1835 XXXII passim on cash sent back by migrants to America.
113 See above p. 143 and p. 149; also cf e.g. (a Scottish witness on the Irish) PP1836 XXXIV 139–40.
114 Contrast the greater problems of migrants in present-day developing countries (Unesco (1957) 216–17; (1961) 186; (1965) esp 167).
115 cf Marshall (1961) 91.

116 PP1837–8 XIX 467.
117 Alexander (1861) 15–16*; cf Gaskell (1897) 31*, 90*; and the underlying assumption in Bamford (1893b) 272*.
118 PP1835 XXXV 199*; and cf 195–200**; PP1837–8 XIX 309, 469; and letters reproduced in PP1837 XVII 58–9**; cf also letters from emigrants from various parts of England reproduced in e.g. Letters (1837); and Knight (1818a and b) esp (1818b) 20–1.
119 PP1847 XIb 192; PP1833 V 181; PP1836 XXXIV 72; cf 33.
120 PP1836 XXXIV 68; PP1835 XXXV 23.
121 Waugh (1881a) 65*; Gaskell (1897) 309*; (1906i) 1–2*.
122 Bamford (1893a) 78*; Gaskell (1897) 30*, 68*.
123 cf Ward (1953) for 6 Apr 60, 7 Mar 61 etc.**; Gaulter (1833) 66–7*; Waugh (1883) 232*, 248–9*; Davies (1963) 15*; Engels (1958) 164n*; Bamford (1893b) 53*, 256, 337*. For this kind of lodging to have been possible, given the transitory nature of the population, it is clear once again that contact was being maintained so that addresses were kept up to date.
124 PP1836 XXXIV 60; cf 62, 64, 87, 139–40; also PP1837–8 XVIIIb 4.
125 PP1837 XVII 59*.
126 Davies (1963) 25*; and cf e.g. Barlee (1863) 137*; PP1834 XIX DI 126–7*; Taylor (1842) 145*; Bamford (1893a) 16*, 189*, 224*; (1893b) 47*; etc. cf elsewhere Humphreys (1966) 110; Gutkind (1965); Rundblad (1956); etc.
127 cf e.g. PP1836 XXXIV 20–1, 27, 65; MCS 4 Jan 50 17.
128 PP1846 XXXVIc 48.
129 PP1836 XXIX 412.
130 and cf for modern parallels Sussman (1965) 70; Talmon-Garber (1966) 96–101.
131 Waugh (1883) 170*.
132 Parkinson (1841) 13n*.
133 Ferriar (1795) 182*; also Aikin (1795) 194n*; PP1835 XXXV 194. See also Arnold (1864) 103 for the general problems of inmigrants in this connection.
134 Ferriar (1795) 202.
135 cf e.g. PP1859 Ses 2 VII 117; PP1854–5 XIII 246, 250.
136 and cf Goode (1963) 189–90; PP1837–8 XVIIIb 2; PP1837–8 XIX 472; Back (1965) 332–3; etc.
137 cf the discussion of occupational mobility in Chapter 4 above, pp. 25–9.
138 and cf Engels (1958) 107; Gaskell (1833) 187; PP1837–8 XIX 467, 472; PP1836 XXXIV 21–2, 66; PP1837 XVII 58; etc. cf also Lawton (1955) 104; Armstrong (1966) 6; I have explored this topic further in Anderson (1970a).
139 Moore (1889) 20*.
140 PP1836 XXXIV 5–6; cf PP1837 XVII 59*; Brierley (*c* 1886) 50–1*; Hall (1826) 9*; and the classic London description of this process in Booth (1892) 132–5.
141 PP1842 XXXVb 11; cf also MC 18 Jan 50 5.
142 and cf here for elsewhere Thomas and Znaniecki (1958) 103.
143 cf the discussion of generalised exchange nets in Chapter 12 below.
144 i.e. c was low and p_c was also low, while for most of those directly involved $\bar{s}$ was relatively high (and see Chapter 11 and Chapter 12, esp note 6, p. 224 below).
145 Booth (1892) 132–5. cf also for Lancashire Davies (1963).
146 and cf for assistance received by urban families from kin living in other towns, e.g. LDM (1860) 46 and, for present-day United States, Brown et al (1963).
147 Adshead (1842) 28*.
148 Rathbone (1927) 1–3*; cf Rushton (1909) 279*.
149 Hull (1902) 194*.
150 Bamford (1893a) 78–9; also, a rural case, the bringing home of a semi-orphan, Gaskell (1906j) 211*.
151 PP1859 Ses 2 VII 199–20; PP1860 XVII 271*; Neale (1840) 59*.
152 PP1835 VII 7; and cf Mayer (1961) 270; Comhaire (1956) 47.
153 e.g. PP1831–2 XV 318, 472–3**; Clegg (1877) 23*; Bamford (1893b) 45*; PP1837–8 XIX 292*, 354*; Howitt (1838b) 245–8; Davies (1963) 22*; Gaskell (1897) 164*, 90*, 31*, 287*; Ward (1953) on several bank holidays; etc.
154 LSP1819 CX 200*.
155 Kelly and Kelly (1957) 115–6; cf also Bamford (1893a) 160; Gaskell (1897) 125–6*; etc.; and PP1837 XVII esp 59*.

156 Ward (1953).
157 and cf elsewhere e.g. Brown et al (1963); Unesco (1961) 175–6, 213–4; Kahl (1959) 65; Beckett (1965) 9–16; Gutkind (1965).

11. POVERTY, AND THE TIME SPAN AND QUALITY OF RELATIONSHIPS

1 cf propositions 3.1 and 3.2 in Chapter 12 below.
2 Formally this, which was discussed in Chapter 8, follows propositions 3.2, 4.1, 4.3, 5.2 and 6 in Chapter 12 below.
3 Formally this follows proposition 4.2 in Chapter 12 below.
4 Waugh (1881b) 117*.
5 Barlee (1863) 137*; cf also ibid 135*.
6 PP1834 X 505; cf also PP1833 XX D2 7.
7 PP1842 XXXvb 70; cf also an aunt bargaining for relief if she was to support four orphans (PP1834 XXVIII 913A*); Chapter 10, p. 149 above; Waugh (1881b) 154*; PP1837–8 XIX 262; also the applications by agricultural families for assistance from the Poor Law as a condition of their helping kin (PP1834 XXVII esp 54).
8 See Chapter 6 above and cf also e.g. PP1833 XX D1 34*.
9 Data from PP1841 XI; 1842 XIX; 1843 XXI; 1844 XIX; 1845 XXVII; 1846 XIX; 1847 XXVIII; 1847–8 XXXIII.
10 Foster (1967) esp 108–10, and 161n.
11 See Chapter 10 above.
12 Northampton and South Shields.
13 From Foster (1967) 314.
14 It must be remembered also that there would be a substantial number of couples where the wife would have had no parents alive, or where, because her father had died, the family was anyway in poverty. These couples could only have gone to live with the husband's parents if they were to receive this kind of assistance.
15 See Chapter 10 above.
16 cf proposition 10 in Chapter 12 below.
17 PP1836 XXIX 412.
18 e.g. LDM (1860) 46*; PP1865 XXVI 485n*; Gaskell (1897) 90–1*; Adshead (1842) 29*; etc.; note also Leigh (1833) 8*.
19 cf e.g. Rathbone (1927) 35*.
20 Williams (1963) 109. And more generally for a theoretical analysis which in many ways parallels that outlined here cf Litwak and Szelenyi (1969); also cf the discussion in Back (1965) 337–8.
21 See Chapter 5, p. 206 above for references.
22 cf for a general theoretical statement Goode (1964) 46; also Sweetser (1968).

12. THE WIDER IMPLICATIONS

1 I have attempted a more general discussion of some of the problems involved in this kind of research in Anderson (1970b).
2 I refer readers to Anderson (forthcoming b) for a discussion of some of the techniques that may be useful in studies of this kind.
3 in particular the computerised record linkage techniques developed by Drake and Pearce.
4 At the present state of knowledge and theoretical sophistication in this field any attempt to specify propositions is fraught with dangers. Obviously these are no more than tentative ideas which summarise and seem to follow fairly clearly from the earlier analysis. They do, however, I hope, give some kind of overall perspective on the kinds of theories towards which I see this kind of analysis as ultimately leaning, and provide at the same time a set of notions into which the empirical elements of this study and of others can be integrated. This specification of the empirical elements of any situation is obviously a prime task for any research using these propositions.
5 These nets are not of the kind where A gives X to B and B reciprocates by giving Y to A. Rather, in situations 2.2.1 and 2.2.2 at t_1 $A+B+C$ give X to D; at t_2 $A+B+D$ give X to C; at t_3 $A+C+D$ give X to B and at t_4 $B+C+D$ give X to A. In situations 2.1.1 at t_1 $B+C+D$ give X to A; at t_2 $C+D+E$ give X to B; at t_3 $D+E+F$ give X to C etc.
6 Formally, where $2 \leqslant c/\bar{s} \leqslant 1/\bar{p}_c$ in the 2.2 case, and $2 \leqslant (c+\bar{s})/\bar{s} \leqslant 1/\bar{p}_c$ in the 2.1 case. The minimum net size is $c/\bar{s}$ in the 2.2 case and $(c+\bar{s})/\bar{s}$ in the 2.1 case. Where $c=$ the minimum cost of meeting a given crises; $\bar{s}$ is the mean surplus available to members of the potential net (N) in any

time period; $\bar{p}_c$ is the mean frequency with which events strike N in any time period. For purposes of analysis I have assumed that all these can be derived with precision. The fact that this is not the case, and that c and $\bar{s}$ are to some extent subject to voluntary modification only introduces imperfections into the analysis and does not affect the basic principles on which it is based.

Space considerations, and the comparatively marginal uses made of this analysis at later stages of the book have meant that I have not considered it necessary here to produce the proofs of the statements made. I hope, however, to elaborate this kind of analysis in a later paper.

7 In any one net, however large, in any one time period, there is always a risk, through random fluctuations in the incidence of events in a population (the pattern of incidence for any given net over time being formally considered as distributed according to the binomial expansion) as well as through fluctuations in p_c and individual s's, that the net (which can be seen as a sample of individuals from the total population) in that time period will not be able to meet its obligations. The same, of course applies to an insurance company, however actuarially sound its policies. Sampling theory shows that the larger the net the greater the probability that the net can meet its obligations with any given degree of certainty. However, the larger the population σp_c and σs the larger must the net be before any given probability is reached that the net will be able on any occasion to meet its obligations. Assuming s and p_c are normally distributed, the required N to handle one or other of these fluctuations could be obtained by recasting the formula by which one obtains the probability of sample means falling any given number of standard deviations from the mean. Thus if

$$Z = \frac{\bar{x} - \mu}{\sigma/\sqrt{N}} \qquad \text{then } N = \left(\frac{\sigma Z}{\bar{x} - \mu}\right)^2.$$

The introduction of binomial type fluctuations markedly increases the required net size, especially when p_c is relatively high.

In rough terms one may give the following indicators of the required sizes of aid nets at 98% certainty of meeting all needs:

14.1 Nets can be small (say under 10);

(*a*) where σs and σp_c are small, particularly if they are 10% or less of $\bar{s}$ and $\bar{p}_c$

if, (*b*) $c/\bar{s}$ is less than 10, since $c/\bar{s}$ sets an absolute minimum size to the net.

and if, (*c*) $1/p_c$ greatly exceeds $c/\bar{s}$

i.e. if crises are rather rare and the cost to any individual of meeting an individual crisis is not far in excess of what the individual could anyway afford.

14.2. Nets must be very large (say over 100), and are thus unlikely to arise except where obligations are contractual:

(*a*) where $c/\bar{s}$ approaches $1/p_c$, either because crisis events are frequent or are very expensive relative to individual surpluses.

(*b*) where σs and σp_c are high so that there is a good chance that on any one occasion $c/\bar{s}$ will approach $1/p_c$.

8 Formally, where (i) poverty is so great that $\bar{s}$ approaches zero.

(ii) $c/\bar{s}$ approaches $1/p_c$.

(iii) σs or σp_c become very large.

In each of these three conditions N obviously would have to be very large but if there exist subgroups within N where members taken together have even a slightly larger $\bar{s}$ or even a slightly higher $1/p_c$ then the effect of the binomial expansion is that subnets become viable for them at a very much smaller size, subject, of course to $c/\bar{s}$ being the minimum viable size.

9 Formally where N approaches $1/p_c$ but where $c/\bar{s}$ is much less than $1/p_c$.

10 Formally, where $c/\bar{s}$ approaches $1/p_c$.

11 Nimkoff and Middleton (1960); cf also Foster's interpretation of the nuclear family-based systems in the Latin-American village that he studied (Foster (1961)).

12 Simmons (1945) esp chap 3.

13 Similar relationships within societies (akin to those noted in Chapter 7 of this book) between size of property and the presence of kin in the household have been found in many places; e.g. in classical China and India (Nimkoff and Middleton (1960) 220), in fifteenth century Tuscany (Christiane Klapisch (personal communication), and in eighteenth century Corsica (Dupaquier (1969)). A similar underlying exchange mechanism can be posited. Compare also LePlay's analysis of the different effects of single and partible inheritance laws on parent–child relationships in nineteenth century England and France (LePlay (1855)).

14 Simmons (1945) chap 6.

15 Petersen (1965) 184.
16 Bicanic (1956) 81.
17 Gadourek (1956) 174–5.
18 Compare also the situation in Finland noted by Anderson (1960) 276–7.
19 Simmons (1945) esp 33.
20 Simmons found a correlation of +0.66 for men and +0.64 for women between constancy of food supply and the regular or occasional killing of the old. Put a different way this behaviour has been recorded in over three-quarters of the societies where food supply is very irregular, compared with only a quarter of the societies better endowed in this respect (from Simmons (1945) Tables VI and VII).
21 Sahlins (1965) 169.
22 Banfield (1958). My interpretation is obviously more akin to that of Pizzorno (1966). Compare also Foster's analysis of the normatively sanctioned calculative overtones in interpersonal behaviour in his Latin-American village (Foster (1961)).
23 e.g. Komarovsky (1940) 92–114; Bakke (1960).
24 There is obviously scope for further research into the parallels suggested by this kind of comparison.
25 cf e.g. Kahl (1959) 65–9; Goode (1963) 127–8, 171, 186, 207; Rosenfeld (1958). Even the somewhat exceptional Japanese case is not really so exceptional when viewed from this perspective, since traditionally low and family-paid wages and undeveloped social welfare provision seem to have been very important in impeding young men's independence from kin and thus holding the kin group together (Goode (1963) 325–54). Even in Japan, however, major changes have taken place.
26 e.g. Unesco (1961) 175–6; Kahl (1959) 59–65; Gutkind (1965); Goode (1963) 189–90; and cf Brown et al (1963); Firth (1956) 12.
27 I have attempted a similar analysis of changes in residence patterns in somewhat more detail in Anderson (forthcoming a).
28 esp Laslett (1969).
29 cf esp Laslett and Harrison (1963) 167; MacFarlane (1970) esp 129.
30 esp PP1834 XXVII 54**; cf also PP1836 XXXIV XXV.
31 cf PP1837–8 XVIIIb 21.
32 Hoggart (1957).
33 Young and Willmott (1957).
34 Rosser and Harris (1965) 4–18.
35 So too does the extent to which the picture we have of them is coloured by the rose coloured spectacles of time.
36 Booth (1894).
37 Thompson (1969) 17. The role of poverty here is obviously of great interest in view of the discussions in Chapter 11 above.
38 An interesting piece of supporting evidence here is the reactions of a ninety-year-old man to the introduction of the old age pension quoted in Avonson (1912) cited by Gilbert (1966). Instead of being a burden to his children he could now hand over his five shillings pension and that of his wife to his married son and 'it pays 'em to have us along with 'em'. Whereas before 'often 'ave we thought as 'ow it would be a-best for us to go; and sometimes a-most 'ave I prayed to be took; for we was only a burden to our children as kep' us; now we want to go on livin' for ever'. I am grateful to Alan Armstrong for drawing my attention to this observation.
39 At the same time various demographic changes have placed some strain on the system by reducing the extent to which needs of the two generations are synchronised. This has the effect of lessening the time span of reciprocation, and has possibly even introduced a greater calculative element into the married child–parent relationship. A good discussion of the demographic changes and their impact is in Rosser and Harris (1965) chap 5. On the calculative overtones see Townsend (1957) chap 5, and, in the middle class, Adams (1968b).
40 Ironically, just as the working class have become free enough from their problems to be able to escape from kin, so the young middle class couple, faced with a need to attain a middle class standard of living on an income which is still at the low point of its life-cycle pattern, is increasingly being forced to turn to kin for assistance if kin with suitable surplus resources are available (Bell (1970)). Thus it is rash to say that increased working class dependence on kin will never return. However, in the present context it seems improbable, given their life-cycle patterns of income, that working class kin will ever be able to render any great assistance in this particular critical life situation. Other problems, however, may well arise in time.

Index

Index

Index